ADVANCE PRAISE FOR

assault on KIDS

"So-called 'solutions' for improving public education interconnect in troubling ways—as is revealed insightfully and compellingly in this new and timely book. Ahlquist, Gorski, and Montaño have assembled an impressive collection of analyses that help us to unmask what are mere symptoms of broader movements to widen educational disparities, and to imagine alternatives and interventions with insight and conviction. *Assault on Kids* should cause us to pause, and reimagine, and should be read immediately."

> —*Kevin Kumashiro, Author of* The Seduction of Common Sense:
> How the Right has Framed the Debate on America's Schools;
> *President-Elect of the National Association for Multicultural Education*

"These are troubling times for classroom teachers and for public education. Alhquist, Gorski, and Montaño have collected a series of essays that add the provocative and vibrant voices of practitioners who face the everyday realities of 'hyper accountability' policies, programs and practices. These voices shed light on the dire consequences of high stakes tests, a narrow curriculum, and of the perilous 'reform' efforts currently eroding the very fabric of public education. I encourage all teachers, practicing and preservice, to read this book and to build a movement to keep the 'public' in public education."

> —*David Sánchez, current President of the California Teachers Association*

"The editors and authors of this volume dare to re-frame current 'debates' about the nature of U.S. public schooling. Dialogues about policy and practice have devolved into sound-byte chats about increasingly narrow curricular standards, ever more efficient—rather than effective—assessments of student learning, and endless means through which teachers' work is de-professionalized. In this context, we need the mindset offered by this volume in order to counter dangerous, de-humanizing trends. This text is a primer of our best thinking about how to make our public schools places where a public is made."

> —*Kristien Zenkov, Associate Professor, George Mason University*

assault on

KIDS

Studies in the Postmodern Theory of Education

Shirley R. Steinberg
General Editor

Vol. 402

PETER LANG
New York • Washington, D.C./Baltimore • Bern
Frankfurt • Berlin • Brussels • Vienna • Oxford

assault on
KIDS

How Hyper-Accountability, Corporatization, Deficit Ideologies, and Ruby Payne Are Destroying Our Schools

EDITED BY
ROBERTA AHLQUIST, PAUL GORSKI, THERESA MONTAÑO

PETER LANG
New York • Washington, D.C./Baltimore • Bern
Frankfurt • Berlin • Brussels • Vienna • Oxford

Library of Congress Cataloging-in-Publication Data

Assault on kids: how hyper-accountability, corporatization, deficit ideologies,
and Ruby Payne are destroying our schools / edited by Roberta Ahlquist,
Paul Gorski, Theresa Montaño.
p. cm. — (Counterpoints: studies in the postmodern theory of education; vol. 402)
Includes bibliographical references and index.
ISBN 978-1-4331-1229-4 (hardcover)
ISBN 978-1-4331-1228-7 (paperback)
ISSN 1058-1634

Bibliographic information published by **Die Deutsche Nationalbibliothek**.
Die Deutsche Nationalbibliothek lists this publication in the "Deutsche
Nationalbibliografie"; detailed bibliographic data is available
on the Internet at http://dnb.d-nb.de/.

The paper in this book meets the guidelines for permanence and durability
of the Committee on Production Guidelines for Book Longevity
of the Council of Library Resources.

CONTENTS

Foreword

The teaching profession is at risk. Public education is at risk. Students from working-class and poor backgrounds, and students from communities of color are being shortchanged. In *Assault on Kids*, Roberta Ahlquist, Paul Gorski, and Theresa Montaño have collected a timely series of essays on these conditions and the state of public schooling for classroom teachers, education activists, teacher educators, and critical scholars. The thirteen contributors explore the dire consequences of deleterious practices in American public education. They address the corporatization of and the effects of militarization on contemporary U.S. schools and the neoliberal ideologies that drive school boards and state and national governments to enact reductionist policies and place heightened emphasis on efficiency and school accountability. Taken together these essays present a portrait of the myriad of multifaceted, interrelated, and underlying practices and ideologies including standardized testing, Anglo-centrism, monolingualism, deficit ideology, and the culture of militarism that constitute an "Assault on Kids" at the beginning of the twenty-first century.

Assault on Kids encourages readers to examine how even the most well intentioned of us are complicit in the reproduction of stereotypes and racist and economically oppressive thinking. A rich history of scholarship and activism has exposed how deficit practices impact the ways that teachers treat some students. For example, young black girls are still seen by teachers as aggressive, loud, "unladylike," and, as a result, are assessed on their social skills rather than their academic behaviors (Fordham, 1996; Morris, 2005). Black and Latino boys' behaviors and dress may be the same as those of boys from other communities of color, but they are seen as "deviant" "bad boys" and are subject to more disciplinary actions (Brown, 2003; Hirschfield, 2008; Morris, 2005, Ferguson, 2000). Simply for being who they are, students are penalized, punished, and pushed out of school. The authors of *Assault on Kids* identify the ideological underpinnings of such practices and unravel their impact upon educational equity. Indeed, as Hannah Tavares (2010) argues:

> We have to understand how neoliberal governmentality and expert systems of knowledge constitute a space of management where "rubrics," "learning preferences" and "teaching styles" not only provide a grid of intelligible and, therefore, legitimate instruction but aim to curtail risk, uncertainty, and the limits of knowledge. (p. 216)

As the authors in this volume underscore, in an equitable education environment, educators legitimize students' languages and cultures. By contrast, educational workshop gurus like Ruby Payne, and others who blame students and their families for the achievement gap and advise repressive management techniques and advocate pedagogies that certainly do not facilitate teachers' understandings that the "gap" is rooted in economic, cultural, and racial inequality in both school and society. These "experts" peddle a constellation of discourses and practices consistent with an historical heteronormativity or other inequitable schooling conditions and an historical legacy of structural privilege and injustice. The authors in this volume tackle these ideologies and illustrate that educational and liberatory possibilities are endangered unless we engage in a radical restructuring of schools and society in order to abolish systemic inequities.

Assault on Kids illuminates the structural barriers to equitable education and proposes visions of more just and compassionate ways to reconstruct education. The authors desire transformation; new policies, bold new practices that give birth to equitable approaches for our youth. This volume is a call to teachers and teacher educators to understand the urgency of the present time, in which the Department of Education sustains and reproduces neoliberal practices of privatization, standardization, and accountability with initiatives such as Race to the Top. After all, what more evil Assault on Kids could be imagined than educational practices and policies that deny young people the education they deserve?

References

Brown, E. R. (2003). Freedom for some, discipline for "Others": The structure of inequity in education. In K. J. Saltman & D. A. Gabbard (Eds.), Education as enforcement: The militarization and corporatization of schools (pp. 127–152). New York: RoutledgeFalmer.

Ferguson, A. A. (2000). *Bad boys: Public school and the making of black masculinity.* Ann Arbor: University of Michigan Press.

Fordham, S. (1996) *Blacked out.* New York: Routledge.

Hirschfield, P. J. (2008). Preparing for prison? The criminalization of school discipline in the USA. *Theoretical Criminology* 12: 79–91.

Morris, E. (2005). Tuck in that shirt! Race, class and gender in an urban school. *Sociological Perspectives,* 48 (1), 25–48.

Tavares, H. (2010). Postcoloniality in education. In S. Tozer, B. Gallegos, and A. Henry, (Eds.) *Handbook of research in the social foundations of education.* (pp. 195–204). New York: Routledge.

Introduction

ROBERTA AHLQUIST, PAUL C. GORSKI & THERESA MONTAÑO

LIKE MANY BOOKS ABOUT THE CORPORATE MANIPULATION AND EROSION OF public education—of both the democratic notion of "public" and the public practice of schooling—this volume sprang from concern and indignation. The initial subject of our indignation was the growing influence on the U.S. education milieu of Ruby Payne, the baroness of teacher professional develop-ment. Her for-profit company, aha! Process, Inc., makes millions of dollars annually, and her book, *A Framework for Understanding Poverty*, is, perhaps, the single piece of literature most widely read by today's classroom teachers. Payne has made her millions and grown her empire by selling a theoretical framework, the "culture of poverty," which, for all intents and purposes, was dispelled, empirically and philosophically, as mythology by the early 1970s, a decade or so after it was introduced by anthropologist Oscar Lewis. In addition, Payne, despite the popularity of asset-based classroom rhetoric ("all children can learn"; "every student is gifted and talented") has continued to thrive as an unswerving broker of an ideology, often described as "deficit ideology," which locates societal problems as existing *within* rather than as pressing *upon* disen-franchised communities. Unfortunately, deficit ideology remains a fairly easy sell, supported, as it is, by notions of white supremacy and male privilege, English language superiority, hetero-normativity, capitalist hegemony, anti-immigrant nationalism, and Christian dominance. It is precisely these characteristics of Payne's work which have led to a rising tide of scholarship (books, magazine and journal articles, blog entries, conference presentations), discussion, and action responding to what, exactly, she's selling and the implications of her message to students, teachers, and the very notion of the "public good." We, along with several contributors to this book (whose chapters detail these phenomena in more detail than we have space to do in this introduction), have been and continue to be, in our roles as educators, activists, and scholars of educational equity and social justice, waves in that tide.

And yet, as we continued to engage in these analyses and actions we found ourselves, as critical educators tend to do, connecting Payne, the "culture of poverty" paradigm, and her employment of deficit ideology to larger educational, social, and political conditions. When we stepped back and considered her work in light of the growing neoliberal influence on U.S. schooling, as characterized by hyper-accountability, larger patterns of deficit ideology, and the privatization and corporatization of public schools, we came to see Payne not as the underlying problem but as a symptom, an illustration, a personification of something significantly bigger. In other words, the question wasn't simply, *How did Ruby Payne manage to assume such an inordinate amount of influence over how educators think about the education of poor and low-income students?* It was, as well, *What are the sociopolitical conditions in which somebody with Payne's ideas could gain this influence, how else are these conditions manifesting in schools and the larger society, and to whose benefit?*

When we began to ask these questions, assuming a broader view, we began to uncover the sorts of ideological interconnections that underlie a rash of socially and politically unjust conditions in the contemporary U.S. and the world. Yes, Payne is a deficit ideologue, but her popularity—the fact that district after district pay her tens of thousands of dollars or more to misinform them—demonstrates the way in which she's also a *product* of deficit ideology, a product of a society already conditioned to buy what she is selling. She's a peddler of hyper-accountability, having written and spoken passionately about why we must embrace No Child Left Behind and high-stakes testing despite living in Texas, where many of the Act's policy precursors, as instituted by then-Governor George W. Bush, proved devastating to the state's low-income families and families of color. But her reach is also a *product* of hyper-accountability and the desperation it breeds for a quick fix—for practical and immediate, even if misguided and fallacious, strategies for closing "achievement gaps." Payne, as well, is a facilitator of corporatization, selling her wares through a for-profit company, sometimes receiving hundreds of thousands of dollars from single school districts in exchange for helping them further institutionalize educational inequities. In fact, she even has found opportunities to flex her economic and corporate muscle, threatening lawsuits against individuals who have criticized her work. But she's also a *product* of corporatization, a star player in a capitalist and consumerist game which was tearing public education apart at its seams long before Payne arrived on the scene.

Certainly, in and of itself, Payne's influence can be understood quite clearly as an assault on kids—there is no lack of documentation of this. But in order to understand that assault in full, we need to understand it in context. We need not only to ask, *What is problematic about Payne?* but also, *What are the conditions in schools and the larger society that would facilitate the mass acceptance of such devastating ideas? How have we—teachers, school leaders, education and community activists—been conditioned to embrace oppressive ideas and practices, often in the name of "diversity," "multiculturalism," "equality," or "equity"? What explains the mass (although, of course, not universal) acceptance of Payne's ideas, not by those who mean to be oppressive, purposeful agents of hegemony, but by those who, as the rhetoric goes, want to see all kids succeed?*

And, as we found, even these questions are not quite sufficient, as understanding is only the first step toward change. So we came to ask, as well, *What can we do? How might we resist the corporatization of schools, deficit ideology, and hyper-accountability? How can we organize ourselves and build toward a different, more socially just, educational future?* The result—*An Assault on Kids*—is our attempt to hasten this discourse.

It is our attempt, as well, to create a space for cross-engagement around these concerns. The contributors to this volume include scholars, but they also include, and deliberately so, classroom teachers and educational activists as well as people who identify as combinations of these. Too often, in our experience, conversations about educational and social transformation happen in not-so-mixed-company: at academic conferences, for example, or in books or journals produced and read largely by a particular targeted audience. We acknowledge, of course, the importance of these different literatures, differently contoured urgencies, and varying pragmatics. But we chose, for the purpose of this volume, to cross-engage a broader array of perspectives and sight-lines from across the educational landscape—from those whose "data" are collected and analyzed in formal, controlled, ways; from those whose "data" comprise the informal and chaotic day-to-day implications of teaching or organizing under the weight of hyper-accountability and corporatocracy; and from those whose "data" fall somewhere on the continuum between the two. The resulting storylines of this volume, we believe, paint a fuller picture of the contemporary educational assault on kids than they might have if we had drawn on a more narrowly defined sample of voices.

That word—*assault*—and our decision to build this book's title around it, begs attention, as well. From the Tea Party to the Hoover Institution, Arne Duncan to President Obama, the rhetoric imploring our support for the imposition of the corporatocracy in supposedly public spheres, such as public education, floats to us, it seems, in a never-ending loop. The language itself is insidious, full of hegemonic ideas wrapped in language meant to draw upon people's deepest socializations as "American" champions of liberty, freedom, democracy, capitalism, and justice: "free market," "Race to the Top," "No Child Left Behind," "school choice," "merit pay." We, as educator-activists, are concerned particularly about the ways in which much of the discourse *among advocates for educational equity and social justice* has come to reflect this rhetoric; how the discourse about school reform has become mired more and more in decontextualized test scores, teacher "merit" and accountability, and achievement gaps.

In fact, there are few more poignant examples of deficit ideology's infestation of public education than this achievement gap discourse, which tends to locate the "problem" of, say, unequal educational outcomes as existing within low-income communities, communities of color, communities who speak languages other than English at home, and other disenfranchised communities. And it does so by drawing upon simplistic mental models, such as the "culture of poverty," which project stereotyped and, as Gorski details in his chapter on deficit ideology, *inaccurate* perceptions of their parenting, their attitudes about education, and their access to mentors while rendering systemic inequities, such as institutional racism and economic injustice, invisible. One function of this discourse—and, as contributors to this volume will attest, it is a purposeful function—is to train the collective scornful gaze *down* the power hierarchy so that efforts to reform public schooling focus squarely on "fixing" disenfranchised communities rather than the policies and practices which disenfranchise them. Meanwhile, these policies and practices, from closing or under-funding neighborhood schools to redistributing resources *out of* public schools and into semipublic charter schools, independent schools, and private enterprise, wreak havoc on disenfranchised communities even as unemployment rates continue to soar. But as much as this, they threaten the very existence of the public sphere. And this, we contend, is assault on a massive scale. It is an assault on thought; an assault on opportunity; an assault on the possibility of an equitable and just world. It is an assault on all of us, but it is an assault, most of all, on children who are compelled to participate in it simply by being students in our public schools.

One of the purposes of this book, of this conversation among a diversity of educators, activists, scholars, administrators, and parents, then, is to uncover and document this assault—to trace the educational roots of deficit ideology, hyper-accountability, corporatization, and the Ruby Payne empire, and to detail and counter their consequences. A second, and equally critical, purpose is to invite readers into a process of imagining a different future for public education; to consider ways of resisting the assault and constructing something more equitable and just. In this spirit, every contributor to this book has been asked not only to provide a critical analysis along one or more of these lines but also to imagine a just alternative and to recommend paths of resistance.

Certainly we do not claim that we have covered these complex topics and their many contours exhaustively. In fact, as we prepare this volume for print, we find that, as in any ardent attempt at inquiry, we often have uncovered more questions than answers. Thusly is laid the path toward real change. It is our hope that, with this book, we may nudge ourselves and our readers onto, or a step or two further along, that path.

Overview of the Book

Although we have organized *Assault on Kids* roughly around its four major themes—hyper-accountability, corporatization, deficit ideology, and Ruby Payne—these are inexact descriptors. Due to the interrelated nature of the topics covered in this book, several chapters address two or more of these themes or focus on points at which they intersect and overlap. For example, in Chapter 4, Brian Lack addresses the corporatizing, militarizing, and deficit implications of KIPP schools.

We begin with Roberta Ahlquist's "The 'Empire' Strikes Back via a Neoliberal Agenda," which provides a brief historical overview of the political forces acting on schools, especially neoliberalism, and sets the context for our four major themes and their relationship to neoliberal hegemony.

Ahlquist's chapter is followed by a section on hyper-accountability—high stakes tests and common standards—comprised of Chapters 2 and 3. In Chapter 2, "What We Don't Talk About When We Talk About the 'Achievement Gap,'" Sue Books examines how the domination of "achievement gap" rhetoric in educational reform discourses evolved. She details, as well, how obsession over the "achievement gap" has drained attention from the need for larger, more systemic, change.

In the second chapter in the Hyper-Accountability section, "Can Standardized Teacher Performance Assessment Identify Highly Qualified Teachers?" (Chapter 3), Ann Berlak, analyzes the implications of the Performance Assessment of California Teachers, an exit exam for teacher credential programs, the likes of which are endorsed enthusiastically by Secretary of Education Arne Duncan. Sounding a clear hyper-accountability warning bell for teacher credential programs around the country, Berlak explains the assessment's impact on teacher credential programs in California's state universities.

Brian Lack, in Chapter 4, initiates the section on Privatization and Corporatization of Public Schools with his critical analysis of charter schools run by the Knowledge Is Power Program (KIPP). He particularly hones in on the ways in which the KIPP philosophy embraces hegemonic notions of individual hard work and sacrifice while all but ignoring the systemic conditions which continue to deny students of color and low-income students equitable educational opportunity. His chapter is titled, "Anti-Democratic Militaristic Education: An Overview and Critical Analysis of KIPP Schools."

In Chapter 5, "Exposing the Myths of the Corporate City: Popular Education and Political Activism in Atlanta," Richard Lakes, Paul McLennan, Jennifer Sauer, and Mary Anne Smith examine the corporatization of Atlanta's public schools in light of a larger city-wide context of the privatization of public services. They share, as well, case studies of two local organizations that have played key roles in organizing resistance to these trends. They offer suggestions for teachers who are engaged in similar struggles.

"Ground Zero in A Corporate Classroom" (Chapter 6) is high school teacher Lisa Martin's personal account of how the educational "marketplace" withers and silences teacher voice, creativity, and power; endangers what ought to be the priorities of public education; and eases the accountability of the system even as teachers drown in accountability measures. She challenges us to consider a more robust, more just, conceptualization of what it means to be "accountable."

In the first chapter in the Deficit Ideology section of *An Assault on Kids*, "Why Aren't We More Enraged?" (Chapter 7), Virginia Lea traces the evolution of deficit discourses, beginning with the so-called "golden age" of U.S. public education, prior to World War II. Equipped with a deeper understanding of these discourses and how they shaped social policy, Lea guides readers, including teacher educators, on an exploration of ways to interrupt deficit ideology.

In Chapter 8, "Unlearning Deficit Ideology and the Scornful Gaze: Thoughts on Authenticating the Class Discourse in Education," Paul C. Gorski takes on the most current wave of class-based deficit ideology and how, in its insistence on locating the source of social problems in disenfranchised communities rather than in unjust social conditions, has functioned to misguide efforts to redress class inequities in U.S. education.

The final section contains three chapters, each of which offers unique insights into the many problems inherent in Ruby Payne's work. In the first of these, "A Framework for Maintaining White Privilege" (Chapter 9), Monique Redeaux offers a uniquely blended autobiographical and analytical examination of the fundamental underpinnings of Payne's framework. Her poignant connection between the "culture of poverty" myth and white privilege, both endemic in Payne's work, is supported by a systemic analysis of Payne's book, *A Framework for Understanding Poverty*.

Theresa Montaño and Rosalinda Quintanar-Sarellana in Chapter 10 ("Undoing Ruby Payne and Other Deficit Views of English Language Learners") offer what may be the first primarily language-identity analysis of *A Framework for Understanding Poverty*. Countering deficit language views and grounding their arguments in the work of California's bilingual education teachers and other advocates for English Language Learners, they seek both to uncover the linguicism in Payne's work and to honor the diversity of languages and voices of California's students, teachers, and teacher educators.

Finally, Chapter 11, Julie Keown-Bomar and Deborah Pattee's "What's Class Got to Do with It?: A Pedagogical Response to a Deficit Perspective," details the strategies by which two teacher educators in the Midwest U.S. have helped their students think more complexly and critically about class, poverty, and the deficit notions with which many of them enter teaching.

We hope that *Assault on Kids* will inform, engage, and stir you to thoughtful action. We hope that it will inform you about and engage you in deeper critical analyses of an educational crisis that is about more—about much more—than test scores and achievement gaps. This is not a how-to or prescriptive guide—there are no quick fixes here. Instead, it is our attempt to encourage a broader exchange of ideas about the present and future of public education and to consider how we can thoughtfully act on these policies and practices, individually and collectively, to ensure an equitable and just future in and out of public schools for *all* of our children.

· 1 ·

The 'Empire' Strikes Back via a Neoliberal Agenda

Confronting the Legacies of Colonialism

ROBERTA AHLQUIST

We cannot readily sort through and discard the colonially tainted understanding we carry, without devoting attention to how our view of the world has been shaped by imperialism's educational projects, which included fostering a science and geography of race; renaming a good part of the world in homage to its adventurers' homesick sense of place; and imposing languages and literature on the colonized in an effort to teach them why they were subservient to a born-to-rule civilization—John Willinsky (1998, pp. 3–4) *Learning to Divide the World: Education at Empire's End*

Schooling is political, and the socio-economic system defines the role and function of schooling in any society. This introductory chapter frames the present crisis of schooling within global colonizing capitalism. First, I clarify some underpinnings of neo-liberal policies that are relevant to public schooling in the U.S. at the present moment. These are (1) the uncontested acceptance of national and state high stakes testing as valid and reliable measures of teacher and student excellence. (2) the privatization and corporatization of public schooling; and (3) the resurgence of cultural deficit ideology. (4). The notion that the U.S. must continue to spend money on war in order to remain competitive in the world order. Each of these is a direct threat to a public, democratic, culturally diverse, and socially just schooling. Finally, I suggest ways that teachers can prepare students to challenge these anti-democratic assumptions in their workplace and communities in the interests of more democractic and socially just schools.

The U.S., Australia, Canada, and New Zealand are all white settler societies at late stage corporate imperialism that have imposed a colonizing Eurocentric ideology on most aspects of schooling. These white settler colonial powers are characterized by hegemonic cultural/ ethnic/racial/, gender, class, and language oppressions, and cultural imperialism—the unrestrained subjugation of a subordinate culture by a powerful, dominant culture. Post-colonial projects can confront and challenge the legacies of colonialism in the interests of the poor, the most dispossessed and oppressed and can affirm people at the bottom of the racial, class, gender, and language power hierarchies; their values, languages, histories, and knowledges.

Where do students learn about how democracy works in their schooling? Where do they learn about social justice and equity, fairness, affirming differences? Where do students learn about existing racial and class hierarchies, and how to affirm all people, including those on the 'downside of power'? Where do students learn to become responsible citizens, to question, challenge, and change undemocratic and corrupt practices in the political system and in their daily lives? Where do they learn how to critically analyze our major institutions, the media, the legal system? How can they understand how they are situated in the world when the corporate mainstream media give students such a narrow, U.S.-centric, pro-business, pro-government view of the world? Where do students learn the skills and practices to survive and thrive in a society that is quickly consolidating wealth and power, often at the expense of a large number of its citizens? Where do they learn about global politics and the implications of a world dominated by an international corporate elite? (Spring, 2004). Where do our students learn how to express themselves creatively, freely, and in their own 'voice'? (Robinson, 2009, 2007). These are some pressing questions that parents, teachers, administrators, and concerned citizens need to answer as children become increasingly disempowered from their right to a free, public, and democratic schooling (Ahlquist, 2011).

The neoliberal corporate elite has been engaged in reshaping schooling in its interests over the past 30 years or more. This is their agenda:

> In 1989 and again in 1995, the national Business Roundtable (CEOs of the largest 300 corporations in the U.S.) put its special brand on education reform, hammering home an agenda that defined reform thusly: state content and performance standards; a state-mandated test; rewards and sanctions based on test scores; school site councils composed of administrators, teachers, and parents; professional development focused on using test scores to drive instructional decisions; and phonics instruction in pre-kindergarten. (Emery & O'Hanian, 2004, p. 114)

The actions of neoliberal forces and 'shock doctrine' practices challenging public schooling, in the interests of 'reform,' nationally and internationally, should be of concern to all who care about equity, social justice and democracy (Klein, 2007). Neoliberals believe that unfetttered markets and meritocracy will benefit all who are deserving. However, school should provide an opportunity to challenge this ideology and to engage in dialogue about an array of issues related to local, national and global problems in relation to the public good. A critical, democratic schooling should include an examination of solutions that will lead towards progress in the interests of the public good.

Cultural Deficit Ideologies

Yet with few exceptions, historically the public school curriculum in the U.S. has promoted a deficit ideology about racial, social class, and language difference. Up until the Civil Rights Movement of the 1960s, the public school curriculum had been 'whitestream' and uncritical. Where people of color were concerned, life in general and schooling in particular was segregationist and openly racist. Today another form of deficit ideology—one that is combined with neoliberalism—reigns. Deficit ideologies serve to justify the existing racial and class hierarchies. If poor white people, and poor people of color are taught that they are 'less than' the dominant white culture, they more readily accept their 'place' in the existing hegemonic hierarchies. In the U.S. as governed by today's deficit model, the country continues to be segregationist along class, linguistic, and racial lines. It continues to be culturally, institutionally, and in many instances interpersonally racist, even with and/or as a consequence of the election of a Black president . Yet, the term "race" is absent from these practices. Indeed, the very mention of "race" is considered by many to be racist. This segregation of words facilitates the continued segregation of people since identifying racist oppression is now considered racist. The mainstream dominant culture media reinforce this segregation with the mantra that we live in a 'post racial' society and thus can now be colorblind.

'Color-blindness' is what Bonilla-Silva calls 'the new racism' (Bonilla-Silva, 2006). A Eurocentric, Western curriculum is pernicious for students in that it 'teaches no critical view of culture which would enable students to see that all cultures have strengths and weaknesses and that they operate within particular epistemologies' (Hickling-Hudson & Ahlquist, 2004). Since the 1960s there has been a systematic process of dismantling progressive educational reforms emanating from the Civil Rights era, and corporate and neo-liberal interests have imposed reductionist policies on public schools. Culturally diverse and social justice curricula have either been used by a small number of teachers in subversive ways, or these approaches to teaching have disappeared with the backlash against anything labeled 'multicultural,' or 'culturally and linguistically diverse.' Critical multicultural education, that promotes the equal worth of diverse ethnic cultures has always been contested by the 'powers that be,' hegemonic, Eurocentric patriarchy. Today students in white settler societies are increasingly diverse, yet Eurocentric curricula are pervasive. In Arizona a law has been passed outlawing the teaching of ethnic studies in high school. Yet as migration continues around the world our students are increasingly ethnically/racially, and linguistically diverse.

Neoliberalism

Several major shifts in U.S. and U.K. educational policy have occurred over the past thirty years, as globalization spreads across the world. To understand these shifts it is important to understand neoliberalism, a form of late-stage global corporate capitalism. In this section I briefly explain four dimensions of this economic period, promulgated over the past 30 years or so in the interests of the corporate business class. These conservative policies have reshaped schools, and other institutions and services as well, especially healthcare, jobs, salaries of city and state employees, and public services of any kind (Harvey, 2007).

First, under the guise of 'trickle down' economics, the goal of this economic stage of capitalism is to consolidate higher and higher rates of profit for the national and international corporate class, without concern for the general public. The lust for profit involves privatization of *all* that has been *publicly* owned and managed. Because, in the view of neoliberals, government is inefficient, key services such as schools, healthcare, even the water we drink, must be privately owned and run. (Harvey, 2010). This means that under these rules there would be no environmental pollution controls, no controls on food and water, nor any other regulations that serve to protect the public.

Therefore, to meet 'trickle down' capitalist goals, public expenditures must be cut for any and all social services, such as education, and healthcare, especially for the elderly and disabled; thus individual welfare is cut and transferred to corporate welfare. This form of deficit ideology is used to make people think that the U.S. is a meritocracy; i.e., it's your fault you're poor; you have only yourself to blame. This is a classic example of 'blaming the victim' strategies. 'Don't rely on the state for anything: even though we all pay taxes in some form, don't expect the government to pay.' 'If you don't have your basic needs met and you can't find work, it's your fault.' The message loud and clear is: 'You have some individual deficits so, overcome these, just work harder, and 'pull yourself up by those bootstraps.' Using deficit ideology as justification, money is being slashed from former governmental expenditures, such as public transportation, housing, and city-owned utilities. Services are being outsourced to private companies, such as private garbage collection. Safety-net services for the poor are gone. As a result, wealth is redistributed upwards, with obscene differences between the wealthy and the poor that are unprecedented.

This global economic system is impacting the public good in many countries. In England there is teacher resistance in the form of a national campaign. Susan O'Hanian (2010) reports:

> It is important to point out that the corporate elite who are against teachers are fighting the same educational wars in England with Duncan helping out. To counter this corporate-politico attack on local schools a group in England has formed the Local Schools Network, a national campaign group that aims to gather testimonies from parents, teachers and students about the strengths of their local school, and to promote debate about the issues that affect them daily. (www.susanohanian.org/show_atrocities .php?id=9524)

According to neoliberal doctrine, international investment and trade must be free from any restrictions or regulations; and there must be total 'freedom' by the business class to move goods, services, and capital. Over the past 30 years the U.S. business class has 'outsourced' most industrial and even non-industrial production to other countries where labor and resource costs are cheaper. We now produce little in the U.S. Furthermore, the business elite seek the consolidation of local and national governmental services in an effort to privatize these. As they push to maximize profits, the corporate class attempts to convince voters and leaders that unregulated markets are the best way to increase the growth of the economy

Neoliberalism requires deregulation of everything that might diminish corporate profits, whether it's health and safety concerns at the workplace, environmental protections, or public media regulations. The goal is no governmental intervention except in the service and welfare of the corporation. This means that there would be no environmental pollution controls, no controls on our health, safety food, and water, worker due process rights, nor any other regulations that serve to protect any aspects of the public. We now have industry regulating the government, rather than the government regulating industry.

Since the above process will only take place if the public consents to it, it is important for neo-liberals to eliminate the concept of the 'public good' or any idea of 'community' and replace it with individual, personal responsibility and further, to convince the public that they should identify with this ideology as Americans. This is another example of deficit ideology, blaming the poor: if you fail, it's because you are 'lazy.' These tenets of neo-liberalism are a much harsher form of globalizing imperialism, with significant consequences. It is 'dispossession by accumulation': it is the elimination of public schools—public services of any kind—in order for the business elite to accumulate and consolidate more of their profits (Harvey, 2010). An example of this was when Enron took over California utilities and then hijacked the state into paying spiraling costs by deliberately shutting off the power grid to the state. These policies are now being imposed, top-down, on the public school system in this country as well as in countries abroad. These restructuring moves are framed as the 'free market' system.

This global movement relies on all capitalist governments to follow suit in their agendas, such that the economic playing field supports increasing and consolidating corporate profits. This is done through groups such as the global G 20, the 20 most powerful countries in the world, aligning their common business interests and mandating policies for others to follow (Ahlquist, 2011). In education, this ideology is being used to rob youth of their right to free public schooling. It fundamentally intensifies the already authoritarian and undemocratic state of schooling: the goal in part is to make administrators, teachers, and students more accountable to conservative economist Milton Friedman's market-based economic agenda, including standardizing the curriculum, attacking teachers who don't raise standardized test scores, and privatizing schooling across the nation and the world. This is the new corporate agenda, but this time the stakes are far greater. The attack on schools is primarily an attack on the PUBLIC GOOD. Corporate forces have decided that PUBLIC is the problem because quality public schooling is getting too expensive for governments to finance. In spite of the argument that we need a highly skilled workforce, today the U.S. corporate economy doesn't need as many highly educated people for the jobs that remain. The majority of jobs are no-skill or semi-skilled service sector jobs. Therefore, to the minds of the corporate elite, public schooling must be commodified and tied to the marketplace to primarily serve at the call of the service sector of the corporate economy. This idea was formerly called 'reproduction theory' (Bowles & Gintis, 1976; Braverman, 1974), the idea that schools, as well as other institutions, mirror and reproduce capitalism, the hierarchical class, racial, and gender structure of corporate society. Capitalism doesn't really work on the basis of a meritocracy or reward people on the basis of their own individual merit. A critique of this claim recognizes that people of color, poor people, women, and others on the 'downside of power' are not treated on the basis of merit but as part of a hegemonic racial, gender, language and class hierarchy,. The system functions to reproduce the existing racist, sexist, and classist structure, not to change it. No one in patriarchal capitalist societies, not even white males, are treated solely on the basis of merit, although white males have automatic white and gender privilege. The entire meritocracy "myth" is just that. (Bowles & Gintis, 1976; Spring, 2004; McLaren, 2005; Wilkinson & Pickett, 2010).

Meritocracy is framed as a tenet of capitalist schooling. Students are taught the myth that if they work hard, learn the scripted, Eurocentric curriculum and get good grades and high scores on tests, they will be rewarded with a high paying job and achieve the 'American Dream—their own house, two kids, a good healthcare and retirement system'—the means to live the 'good life.' But, Brazilian educator Paulo Freire called capitalist schooling 'banking education' (Freire, 1995). 'Banking' means filling the 'empty bucket' of students' heads with assimilationist, carefully selected Eurocentric knowledge, defined and deemed important by the powers that be. Even if students fill their heads with the banked knowledge that is part of current schooling, there is no guarantee that students will achieve the goals of a 'good life.' There aren't enough jobs at the middle and upper levels of society for everyone. So, we might ask, what are the purposes of schooling? What should they be? Freire's alternative to banking education is called 'problem posing,' transformative, or liberatory education. This is schooling for critical consciousness, for critically engaging in and acting on the world in a responsible, creative, purposeful way, so that small and large problems can be solved to make the society a better, more democratic place for everyone to live (Freire, 1995). If we observe the condition of the world—increasing poverty, global warming, environmental disasters, wars, racism, nuclear proliferation, diminishing resources, exploitative sex trafficking, drug abuse, the gap between rich and poor increasing, etc.—we need problem-posing education more than ever before. Instead, with a neoliberal agenda moving across the globe, we face the creation of non-thinking, non-questioning, unethical, psychically disturbed, uncivil, warring, more egotistic, greedy and robotic consumers (McChesney & Foster, 2010; Lim, 2004; Chomsky, 2007).

The Role of Corporate Media—Shaping Our Views of Ourselves, 'Others' and 'Achievement'

In U.S. society, power means 'what we say goes' (Chomsky, 2007). Except for the few at the top, no others have access to the power and control of the class that rules. The corporate media provides a very narrow view of alternatives to their agenda. Noam Chomsky has observed: "Any dictator would admire the uniformity and obedience of the U.S. media." The ideology of corporate control is solidly entrenched in U.S. schools, even after the Civil Rights and affirmative action struggles of the 50s and 60s. Under the guise of bridging the 'achievement gap,' more accurately called the 'opportunity gap, or the educational debt' (Ladson-Billings, 2006), of high stakes test scores—separating poor from middle class students—public schooling has become so regimented and scrutinized that powerful forms of social control have been normalized, such as controlling all forms of student behavior, from clothing to speech, tracking poor kids into non-college preparatory programs or sorting them out of schooling entirely. (Lea & Ahlquist, 2010; Dale, 2010; also see Lea, this volume). Classroom management has become a major focus of teacher training, rather than teaching students how to develop a critical world-view and connecting it to the diverse needs of students. Our public schools are under surveillance; buildings look more like prisons than places for the exchange of diverse and critical ideas. Iron gates, locked doors, video cameras and metal detectors are just part of the apparatus of control. Some school workers, parents, and community activists are currently in a power struggle to keep the corporate powers that be from completely corporatizing, standardizing and privatizing schooling at all levels, starting with pre k-12 schooling. Higher education is also under siege. Teacher credential programs are imposing additional unfunded mandates in the form of standardized assessments on teachers (see Berlak, this volume). Tenure and academic freedom are on the chopping block. The United Kingdom has eliminated tenure in many universities.

This system is re-colonizing schooling, inculcating colonial assumptions and patterns of thought into the minds of our children, and seriously dumbing them down in the process. The majority of our children, as well as the last six or more generations, have been so socialized into the dominant culture that few were ever able to think outside of colonial patterns. If more of our generation had been socialized more critically we would have a stronger counter movement to critique and challenge the current sociopolitical system (Lea & Ahlquist

2010). Braverman's classic work, *Labor and Monopoly Capital*, (1974), and Bowles and Gintis' *Schooling in Capitalist America* (1976), deepen one's analysis of how capitalism works on institutions, including schooling. Emery and Ohanian's *Why Is Corporate America Bashing Our Public Schools?* (2004) provides current evidence of how the corporate class, especially the *Business Round Table*, has imposed their neoliberal agenda onto school districts throughout the U.S. There are three interrelated policies and practices that are moving this corporate agenda forward.

The Hyper-accountability Movement

Hyper-accountability, an essential tool of the neoliberal agenda, is a data-driven system for assessing teacher effectiveness or "metit," the "value" teachers add to student achievement and/or student achievement using high-stakes standardized tests. It is critically important to point out that these standardized tests do NOT measure critical reading or writing nor critical thinking skills. What these tests measure has come to be considered the 'basics.' Focusing on what can be assessed by standardized tests results in domesticating students and narrowing the curriculum. This form of accountability prepares students for the fastest growing job sector: low-skilled industry or service sector jobs rather than producing democratic and empowered citizens. This means filling the heads of students with the 'basics' of high-status academic disciplines: math, reading/writing, and to a lesser extent, science. This narrowed curriculum supposedly will make students more marketable for the economy they will serve. (See related stories countering challenges to academic freedom, standards, and test mandates for California teacher credential candidates in *Teacher Education Quarterly* [Ahlquist, 2003].) However, in the larger scheme of things, these test scores really don't matter. The test scores are really just a smokescreen that the corporate class wants to use to define "progress" in terms that suit their interests.

No one would deny that teachers and students need to be held accountable for what is taught and for what students learn. But the primary use of test scores from high stakes testing is with wresting control of the curriculum from teachers and local school boards of education, not promoting preparation for critical citizenship. Corporate use of test scores to mount a concentrated attack on public schooling, under the guise of reducing the so-called 'achievement gap' (more appropriately referred to as the poverty gap, the 'opportunity gap' or the educational debt) (Ladson-Billings, 2006), has resulted in dismantling local curriculum that served different populations, in different locations, and replacing it with 'common standards,' defined not by teachers nor the educational community but by corporate interests (Ahlquist, Berlak, & Lea, 2010). We are witnessing the replacement of a broad, albeit, assimilationist education with a narrow emphasis on basic math, reading, and writing. A limited focus on science remains, but physical education, ethnic studies, music, dance, the arts, drama, basic economics and finance, geography, histories of diverse groups in the U.S. and abroad, and global conflicts around the world, or anything else that doesn't serve the corporate agenda is gone or disappearing from most public high school curricular offerings. The target is for students to reach 9th grade math and reading levels, considered adequate for entry-level jobs in the service sector (Payne, 2005). Higher education for all of our children is just too expensive for the corporate class to support. In the view of the corporate class, we have too many college graduates these days for the low-paying service sector jobs that remain.

Globalization is exporting U.S. educational policies, practices, resources and tests around the world. Standardized tests are being used in nearly every capitalist country in the world. There is much criticism of these tests, and no evidence that they reflect either teacher effectiveness or student abilities, especially higher order thinking skills (Economic Policy Institute, 2010). Todd Farley, testing researcher and author *of Making the Grades: My Misadventures in the Standardized Testing Industry* (2009), a critic of standardized testing and its reliability and validity, ends his book with this statement:

> If I had to take any standardized test today that was important to my future and would be assessed by the scoring processes I have long been a part of, I promise you I would protest; I would fight; I would sue; I would go on a hunger strike or march on Washington. I might even punch someone in the nose, but I would never allow that massive and ridiculous business to have any say in my future without battling it to the bitter, bitter end. (Farley, 2009)

The corporate version of education that is available in public schools in the U.S. is being 'sold' to many parts of the world such as aid-funded Western-oriented textbooks published in the U.S. for Afghanistan, and Iraq. The norm is global television, shaped by dominant culture, replete with Eurocentric content via U.S. and U.K. programming. The government of Egypt has requested U.S. aid in developing a testing and standards-based curriculum, which will undoubtedly reflect U.S. interests. The U.S. has re-written texts for the schools in Iraq and in countries from South Africa to Australia who seek to mimic U.S. curriculum, materials, and tests.

Whenever there are 'bell curve' standards, we often teach to the lowest common denominator. By doing so we ignore how standards need to be flexible and varied to take into account students' special needs based on teacher judgment and professional experience. Certain standards may be suitable for a particular group of students but not for the special needs of other students. Tests are often too narrow, too Eurocentric, too out of context, and too basic. Yet standardized tests are driving the curriculum in the U.S. and in many other countries. In the U.K., a comprehensive bill that is supposed to improve the quality of children's lives is called Every Child Matters. This bill includes a rigid testing program that does anything but meet the needs of every child. South Africa and Australia have Outcomes Based Education, and the European standardized assessment for the European Union is called the Program for International Student Assessment (PISA). This latter test claims to also assess problem solving as well as basic facts. Finland scores at the top in most categories on PISA while U.S. comparable scores are quite low. But what do these scores really mean? Furthermore, what is the achievement gap? What does this term really mean? We should call it the standardized test-score gap, not the achievement gap. We have no evidence that low-income students cannot achieve in critical and creative endeavors because of lower test scores on Eurocentric standardized tests.

In the U.S. standardized tests fall under the deceptive program titled, No Child Left Behind, (NCLB), Bush's 2001 federal mandate originating from business and corporate leadership, and Obama's more recent *Race to the Top* (RTTT), like NCLB, is driven by the Business Round Table (BRT) agenda (Emery & Ohanian, 2004). The BRT is comprised of the 300 CEOs of the largest corporations in the U.S. The BRT has spun off an educational policy group called the Business Coalition for Student Achievement (BCSA) and has given its public stamp of approval to Duncan and Obama for implementing the first phase of its program Race to the Top. This program, created under the American Recovery and Reinvestment Act of 2009, consists of $4.35 billion in funding. States, districts and teachers are being pitted against each other in a competition for monies to keep our public schools functioning. Because of budget cuts across the entire nation, school districts are scrambling to write grants to seek out this additional funding, even if they are against the competitive,' drill and skill' teaching and testing which teachers resort to in order to increase test scores. Improved student test scores are interpreted as 'achievement.' The stated goal is to close the 'achievement gap' and to increase college enrollment rates even though funding sources have dried up. Scholarships are no longer as available, and tuition costs are skyrocketing. In California alone, tuition has increased over 300% from 2001–2010, not to speak of the shrinking available spots for incoming freshmen at universities, as classes are eliminated and professors are laid off and not replaced.

The *Elementary and Secondary Education Act* (ESEA) passed in1965, replaced the 1958 *National Defense Education Act* (NDEA), which primarily targeted federal monies for science and education. ESEA authorized federal monies for public schools for disadvantaged youth as well as teacher education programs formerly funded by state and local expenditures. In turn, No Child Left Behind legislation, signed into law by G.W. Bush (2001) increased the involvement of the federal government in education, in policy and economic terms. This participation has been based on the tenuous assumption that standardizing Pre-K-12 curriculum and establishing 'high stakes' measurable goals would improve individual student outcomes in education, thus closing the 'opportunity gap.' These premises ignore abundant evidence that students from higher income families score higher on standardized tests because of the culturally and economically biased nature of the tests. While it is questionable whether all students should be expected to adopt white middle class corporate American cultural and economic assumptions about the world, it is without question that kids don't begin schooling on the same level playing field because of classism, sexism, racism and other forms of oppression. Indeed, education has traditionally meant teaching poor kids of color and poor white kids to be like their white middle class brothers and sisters. The assumptions of American Indian mission schools have been generalized to the masses (Spring, 2004). Those who have access to books, healthcare, nutritious food, well-educated parents, English as a first language, travel experiences, computers, electronic tools, and educational resources in general, have far greater opportunities to achieve the norm, otherwise known as doing well in school. This does not mean that much of the content of Pre-12 schooling is not valuable, if presented critically, in a culturally and socially relevant, problem-posing manner.

Now we face a so-called 'crisis' in education. We are told that the U.S. is no longer the educational leader in the world and that we are losing our competitive edge. These crises-driven 'shock doctrine' tactics have been with us for years (Klein, 2007). Typically, these tactics follow a predictable pattern: Find a natural crisis, or make one up, and use it as a way to impose an agenda that serves corporate class interests. For example, if we look back to the origins of the Stanford Binet IQ Tests, this 1920s IQ testing movement coincided with the Eugenics Movement and was designed to restrict the access of Jews and southern Europeans to U.S. colleges. In the late 1960s in the U.S., the corporate and business world challenged teachers with an accountability movement called the 'back-to- basics' movement. The desire of the corporate class to have more control over all aspects of public education has been longstanding. Yet this time the stakes are much higher. Students will either pass these standardized tests, including a high school exit exam, and graduate, or they will drop out or be pushed out. Many more poor minority and poor white students will end up on the streets, in the court system, in jail or prison, or the military service.

These standardized tests are called 'high stakes' tests, not only because the cost to students is high if one fails to pass them, since students drop out or are forced out of the system, but also because the stakes are high for teachers, schools, and districts. Aggregate school scores that fall below performance goals set by arcane formulas threaten to undermine federal and state funding. Other punitive measures include shutting schools down entirely and replacing the teaching and administrative staffs, which are occurring in New Orleans, Chicago, New York City, and Oakland, to name just a few. The consequences of these policies are that poor students will have even less access to a college education as tuition increases, scholarships are cut, and unemployment rises. National 'common core' standards, in addition to state standards, are being imposed upon everyone, not by teachers, nor administrators, but by the corporate elite, who have set this draconian agenda in motion. Yet too many teachers and administrators have become complicit. By the silence of the many, the few control the agenda. Under the ruse that more teacher/student accountability is needed, a scripted, dumbed-down, boring and assimilationist curriculum has been devised to frame the content of public school students' lives.

Privatization and Corporatization of Schooling: Charter Schools

The restructuring agenda for the U.S. is clearly stated by one of the masterminds of this privatization agenda, Milton Friedman of the 'Chicago boys,' a conservative group of economists from the University of Chicago. It was first implemented in the Chilean school system, with disastrous repercussions.

> The only way to make a major improvement in our educational system is through privatization to the point at which a substantial fraction of all educational service is rendered to individuals by private enterprises. Nothing else will destroy or even greatly

weaken the power of the educational establishment—a necessary pre-condition for radical improvement in our educational system. . . .[In addition,] the privatization of schooling would produce a new, highly active and profitable industry. (Milton Friedman 1995)

The pressures for more 'accountability,' actually for more control over the content and methodology of teachers, have resulted in not only common national content standards and high stakes tests (as a sorting process to filter out those who cannot attain the levels needed, defined by business interests) but also in efforts to privatize and corporatize public schools. After the failure of efforts to introduce a voucher system, which would have given parents a set amount of money to use at a private or public school of their choice, privatization is currently taking the form of charter schools. These schools are most often privately run and publicly financed and are replacing public schools that fail to meet the new testing mandates.

A prime example of how charter schools are replacing public schools is seen if we look at what happened after the Katrina disaster in New Orleans. New Orleans has become a city with an overwhelming number of charter schools as a result of the 'shock-doctrine' crisis of Katrina (Klein, 2007). In an opportunistic move to get rid of New Orleans' public schools, private corporations were brought in to tear down dilapidated public schools and replace them with corporate-developed and privately run charter schools. Chicago schools have quickly followed in line. Rather than attempting to impose the discredited neoconservative voucher scheme again, which would have given parents a set amount of money to use at a private or public school of their choice, corporate interests have concluded that charter schools can serve the same function. These schools are organized, funded, and controlled in great part by private companies, with private managers, who often know little about teaching or pedagogy. The scheme is one of sanctions and rewards. Companies are given federal monies to be used as incentives to raise test scores. Teachers are rewarded or punished accordingly. Such schools serve primarily working class communities, usually offer small class sizes, and have a 'drill-and-kill' regime that deskills and thus abuses teachers, as they are driven to narrowly focus all instruction on increasingly standardized test scores. In many schools teachers have been given a scripted curriculum that doesn't reflect student learning levels but rather is a mechanistic programmed set of instructions and content that views the teacher as technician rather than educator. When scores go up, these schools are acclaimed as models for others to emulate. Most teachers in these schools work 12-hour days, and then work a good part of the weekend, especially

English teachers, who have scores of papers to read on a regular basis. Public school teachers do this too but are not compensated for it. In their zeal to prove the superiority of charter schools, administrators reward teachers for exemplary efforts such as picking students up from home, driving them back, and staying late after school to work with students on tutoring projects. Because these schools often are designated as models, they frequently have access to discretionary funding that allows them to pay teachers roughly $10,000 to $15,000 more starting salary than public schools do. This pay factor, and smaller class sizes, pits public school teachers against charter school teachers. All teachers need higher pay and smaller class sizes.

Some of the better-known corporate backers of corporatized charter schools are people such as Bill Gates, Sam Walton of Wal-Mart, and Eli Broad. Broad has even set up an institute to prepare 'administrators,' trained in business management techniques but with few teaching skills or experience, to run such schools. Often *Teach for America* (TFA) teachers—young, enthusiastic but with little real experience teaching and limited pedagogy—are hired by charter schools. There is a symbiotic relationship between TFA and The Knowledge Is Power Program (KIPP) schools. KIPP is a for-profit, private charter school conglomerate that hires many Teach for America graduates. These schools are often highly authoritarian, basic-skills oriented, and militaristic (See Lack, this volume). 'Race to the Top' monies are used as an incentive to get public schools to buy into a one-time stimulus package that would enable corporate interests to manage and control more charter schools. If public schools that receive these federal monies are not able to raise test scores within a certain period of time, these schools are in danger of being closed and replaced with charter schools. Because many public schools will not be able to raise test scores to the level required by NCLB mandates in 2014, the way will be paved for the wholesale replacement of many public schools with charters. Finally, few or no allowances are made for the overwhelming inequalities between inner city urban schools, attended mainly by working class kids of color, and English language learners and suburban schools of white middle class students. This charter school program is a major threat to public schools as it encourages public schools to move into the private sphere as local and state monies disappear. Most urban charter school students are from poor and working class backgrounds. The few charters that cater to middle and upper class students are often designated as specialty schools, such as science magnets, or boutique art schools. (Also, charter schools are not required to take special needs children and can reject those students with behavior problems, truancy problems and learning problems that public schools take on as a matter of course.) These boutique charters resemble voucher schools, in that parents must apply and students must be admitted. One high school teacher said of these magnet schools:

> Most of these cooperative ventures with businesses fizzle out fairly quickly when they don't show the desired results or they reveal that the commitment in time and resources is greater than the business interests anticipated. Businesses generally think teaching is much easier than it actually is. The more lock step they get, the lower the results become. Even though teachers may be compliant, students are the ultimate stumbling block and passively resist regimented learning no matter how hard business tries to disguise their interventions as innovative. (A northern California high school teacher, requesting anonymity)

The Resurgence of Deficit Ideologies and Ruby Payne

Deficit ideology is a regressive ideology that has been around for a long, long time (see Valencia, 1997). It is an ideology that renders any differences—such as skin color, phenotypes, and/or accent—from the white, Euro-American hegemonic norm as 'less than' or inferior. It is a form of cultural/racial and genetic 'othering,' a way of dividing humankind on the markers of phenotype, language, accent, culture, name, and class. Deficit ideology alone doesn't account for the complex hegemonic, institutional and structural inequities produced within capitalism, but it IS a major force in the society at large and in schooling in particular. It is an outcome of capitalism—the dividing of subgroups of workers from one another and providing a justification for the school and societal failure of poor children and children of color. Thus, kids of color, and many poor students in general, stereotyped as 'less intelligent' because they don't often have the same advantages or opportunities coming into public schooling as white, middle and upper middle class students, are tracked into lower level classes, viewed as 'below average,' lacking in requisite knowledge, skills, and ability, and often categorized as limited, unmotivated, or 'slow.' This is most often because they don't have the cultural, economic, or social capital that provides them with the knowledge and skills to compete on an equal footing with middle class students in a process set up to favor these students. They are viewed as 'problems,' or 'difficult students,' rather than placing blame where it needs to be placed—on an unequal, unjust social system rife with structural inequalities within corporate society.

Deficit ideology fits well into the ideology of capitalist relations, for it places blame on the individual rather than taking into account the complex institutional and structural inequities reproduced in a capitalist society which labels entire marginalized communities as "other" or "less than." Deficit ideology must be challenged because under the guise of reform for children in poverty, it is in reality, another spin on genetic determinism. Deficit theorists such as Ruby Payne fail to address and document the systemic ways in which the structural arrangements and cultural realities of society: class, race, cultural, linguistic, and gender identities, within which most humans are immersed from birth, impact, shape, and socialize all of us. (Ryan, 1971). We cannot escape this ideology; it is built into the entire framework of the corporate system. Deficit ideology justifies harsh discipline and serious consequences for those students who rebel against the regimented curriculum, pedagogy, and official rules and school policies.

Deficit ideology is a prime example of how schooling colonizes poor children's minds, dislocates their identities, and often infantilizes them, and their efforts at schooling. Deficit ideology focuses on the failures of individuals as a result of their culture, and how teachers can "fix" students rather than on structural causes of school failure and poverty, which require long-range solutions that involve a challenge to the fundamental values of society. A deficit analysis of the sources of school failure permits a cheaper and easier 'quick fix.' Historically, U.S. public educational policies promulgate deficit ideology in many ways, one of which is that government solutions have been bereft of long-term solutions to poverty. Instead, *individual* superficial 'quick fixes' have been made to provide the illusion of serious action to address solutions for generationally poor children.

Deficit ideology pathologizes poor children. Ruby Payne is a deficit theorist. She is a native Texan, a millionaire, and an educator. She has developed her own for-profit company, *Aha! Process, Inc.*, and she has run a traveling road show for the past nine years, giving probably over 40 workshops yearly, mostly two-day events, at $295+ per person per session. It is common for school districts to pay $600,000 for her weekend trainings for teachers. Deficit ideology supports superficial quick fixes such as Payne's simplistic individual prescriptions like "Behavior related to poverty: Little procedural memory used in poverty, Sequence not used or valued. Intervention: Write steps on the board. Have them write at the top of the page the steps needed to finish the task. Have them practice procedural self-talk" (Payne, 2005), rather than developing long-term governmental policy solutions for poor children in particular, and people living in poverty in general, Payne was married for ten years to a working-class Cherokee and white American, and this marriage experience is the anecdotal 'research' she uses about poverty (Payne, *Crossing the Tracks for Love*, 2005). She self-published a book, *A Framework for Understanding Poverty* (2005), which has sold all over the world. This ideology serves the current neo-colonial global corporate program for schooling, with shameful outcomes of segregating and dividing poor children, children of color, those with non-whitestream languages or characteristics, from access to equitable schooling within our society.

Furthermore, Ruby Payne supported G.W. Bush's No Child Left Behind program. She contributed to Bush's election campaign. If Ruby Payne isn't a part of the National Business Roundtable, she certainly should be considered an honorary member. Her actions reflect their long-term agenda. When a group of teacher educator colleagues asked her at one of her workshops why she didn't mention 'race' at all in her book, she said, 'I don't know anything about race, I'm white.' This is a telling comment about her views about race and racism.

In our research on Ruby Payne, we discovered that at least one state teacher-credential program in the U.S., in Montana, has mandated that all prospective teachers be taught the value of Payne's simplistic generalizations as they go through their teacher-credentialing program. Perhaps they will reconsider this policy after reading about the implications of such classist and racist pedagogy. This volume includes several chapters that provide detailed critiques of her theories and knowledge base (see chapter by Redeaux among others).

When profit, rather than a humane, culturally and socially relevant curriculum drives a system, where do students learn about their place in the nation and in the world? Where do they learn about their origins and potentialities in schools? Because of the drill-and-skill, teach-to-the-standardized tests, these important concepts are not being addressed in the public school curriculum. Where in schools do students get to see and practice democracy, fair decision-making or how to become socially responsible citizens? Instead, students are offered the "carrot" of individualistic competition for scores, grades, and extrinsic rewards. Teachers are finding that competition for funding, high stakes standardized testing, tracking by class and zip code, and corporatization of the curriculum are having devastating effects on equality and social justice outcomes for everyone: students, teachers and administrators, and there are serious negative consequences for the quality of public schooling in general. Public discourse about this regressive accountability movement is framed in terms of the so-called deficiencies of students and teachers, and these critiques have deterred many social justice teachers from engaging in teaching and practices that challenge students to think more critically. Teachers who question these attempts to deprive students of equitable, high-quality education are threatened with increased student loads, more basic level classes and even job loss. Further, we argue that students are being dumbed down, shaped into compliant test takers, rather than learning about becoming more productive, thoughtful, and politically responsible contributing citizens of this society.

The Elephant in the Room: Militarism and the Decline of Public Education

The last area of major concern regarding public schooling is the increasing militarism and neo-liberal empire-building of the U.S., which have global implications. We are spending more money on wars and weaponry than at any other time in history. Far too many people have come to believe that perpetual, unending war is inevitable. The military industrial complex has subsumed much of the private sector economy. Yet military dominance does not translate into concrete benefits to our society. War is not beneficial to any society. The U.S. is the most powerful military nation in the world at this time. Our national security need not require us to be militaristic, to invade and occupy Iraq or Afghanistan or any other country. Why are we invading and occupying countries around the world? The simple answer is to provide corporate class dominance over resources deemed necessary for continued profitability and control. The grand deception is to get U.S. taxpayers to foot the bill. The military industrial complex is a hugely profitable business (Chomsky, 2007; Gibson, 2003). Our military budget currently is over $700 billion a year. Monies for schooling and healthcare here are being diverted to wars for oil and control over the dwindling resources around the globe. We must make alternative sustainble energy affordable.

The military industrial complex and the prison industrial complex are fast growing sectors of a fractured U.S. economy that provides fewer and fewer jobs for all people, let alone for those who do not receive a high school diploma. Low-skill and lower-paying service sector jobs are now not available for those who drop out. What kind of future do these young people face? Currently, with an official unemployment rate of around 12–25% in some parts of the economy, jobs are few and far between even for college grads. Nonetheless, the educational testing and textbook companies are booming, as they prepare standardized tests and revised textbooks for millions of school age students. One outcome of this imposed testing mania is that corporate test developers such as the Educational Testing Service, and textbook companies, many based in

Texas, are reaping huge profits. Developing and publishing these high stakes tests and the textbooks to accompany them is a flourishing and profitable industry, much like the military industrial complex.

There are no simple, clear-cut solutions to the old and new problems we face in the schools, yet imagine what we could do with the money spent on the military for schools, healthcare, jobs, and housing for our society. We are now a seriously debt-ridden and oil-poor nation, and if these irrational invasions of other countries continue, we will have even fewer resources for schooling. We now have fewer resources for healthcare, adequate housing, and other social services—basic survival needs of society. It is critical to see that diverting huge expenditures into militarism means that money is then diverted away from schooling and other social service issues.

Our Fight for Democratic Public Schools: Striking Back at the Empire

Increasingly, adults and young people exhibit excessive concern with 'self,' a form of inexhaustible individualism. The ideology of capitalist society promotes competitive individualism—concern with our own lives, our own families, friends, our own city, state, and country, not with our neighbors, our global communities, and especially not people on the 'downside of power,' the poor, the disenfranchised, 'new immigrants,' and promotes indifference to problems in Africa, Asia, Latin and South America and the Middle East. Five global corporations own and control most of the media in the world. The corporate media and public school textbooks shield students from information that does not support the ideology of capitalism and the superiority of the U.S.

White supremacy, consumerism and imperialism are supported by neoliberal policies and practices. However, we are all intricately interrelated, part of a planet that is under siege by greed. Research shows that more material possessions don't make us happier (Wilkinson & Pickett, 2010). The cult of individualism that pervades the U.S. serves to perpetuate a form of isolation, a lack of concern, or responsibility for and commitment to others, and a lack of concern for a sustainable global society (Putnam, 2001). Research also tells us, however, that greater equality makes societies stronger and people happier. (Wilkinson & Pickett, 2010). If we want to 'grow' children who have a commitment to a humane, socially just world, we need to turn the neoliberal agenda around. Our past history of the treatment of 'others' has been unjust, unequal and genocidal. We only need to look historically at how we have treated the indigenous peoples of our society (Spring, 2004; Loewen, 2007)

There are many wonderful, hard-working teachers who are doing their best to teach against the grain, as these testing and other neoliberal dictates come down from the business and corporate elite. Teachers need to be supported and affirmed. Much of the union movement is challenging neoliberal policies as it fights for its own survival. Teachers need to actively support union efforts, support each other, and engage parents in supporting them as well. What can teachers do in pockets of resistance, to keep the PUBLIC in schooling? There are no easy solutions, no 'quick fixes.' Too many teachers and parents are so overworked that they haven't much time to become better informed and assess what they might do to turn things around. This syndrome of work-induced fatigue serves the system well. However, becoming better informed is the first step. Sharing what you learn with parents and interested others is also important. Teachers need to carve out time to discuss their views and have more of a voice in these important changes in their professional work lives. Long term, we must fundamentally reform the funding for public schooling and fight to keep schooling public. We must develop a funding program that serves schools more equitably. We also need to stop giving tax cuts to the rich while at the same time cutting monies for the needs of the poor. We need to 'imagine an economy that puts people first' (Greider, 2009). We need to discuss these conservative attacks on public schools with parents and community members. Too many people are uninformed about what is happening in schools and know little about this neoliberal movement. Finally, in ongoing exchanges with interested parents and teachers, we need to imagine a new system, one that serves all of our children, with dignity, equity, and social justice.

> Imagine an education system that does not restrict access to schooling; a system that does not discriminate, stratify or exclude groups on the basis of class, ethnicity, gender, sexuality, disability or location; a system that does not tolerate anachronistic curricular and pedagogical traditions or management strategies, a post-national system that reaches beyond the boundaries and identities of nation-states. Imagine an education system that disrupts preconceptions about knowledges and power relations, and about its own ability to establish final and forever appropriate structures and solutions. (Hickling-Hudson & Ahlquist, 2004)

We need to realize that this vision of schooling will face determined opposition from the market-driven constraints of the current economic system. In the meantime we need to engage in courageous conversations about this power-grab over public schooling ,and thoughtful actions to support all students. We must strengthen alliances with supportive administrators, teachers' unions, parents, and community activists. We need to value, and affirm teachers, trust them, give them flexibility, pay them well, and treat them with respect. We can also learn from countries where things are going much better for students and teachers, and deeper, more meaningful learning is a part of the curriculum. We can learn much from countries like Finland, even though it is a small and homogenous country (Gamerman, 2008; Quinn, 2010). In Finland teachers' views and practices are valued and respected, they are paid well, the curriculum is wide, deep, critical and creative, and most students are engaged in learning. Long term, we must educate everyone about the nature of capitalist schooling and the contradictions within capitalism that undermine equity and social justice. Finally, we must stress that radical change is necessary if public schooling is to survive. It will be up to committed teachers, parents, administrators, community activists, teacher educators, and others interested in social justice issues to thoughtfully ACT in the interests of ALL of our children.

References

Ahlquist, R. (Forthcoming). Whose schools are these anyway—American dream or nightmare? Countering the corporate takeover of schools in California. In Carr, P. R. & Porfilio, B. (Eds.). *The phenomenon of Obama and the agenda for education*. Charlotte, NC: Information Age.

Ahlquist, R., Berlak, A. & Lea, V. (2010). The unbearable persistence of the achievement gap: Can multiculturally responsive teachers make a difference? National Association for Multicultural Education (NAME). November , Las Vegas, Nevada.

Ahlquist, R. (2003). Challenges to academic freedom: California teacher educators mobilize to resist state-mandated control of the curriculum. In *Teacher Education Quarterly*, Volume 30, Number 1.

Apple, M. (2006). Understanding and interrupting neoliberalism and neoconservatism in education. *Pedagogies, 1*(1), 21–26.

Apple, M. (2010a). *World Congress of Comparative Education Societies (WCCES)*. June. Istanbul, Turkey.

Apple, M. (2010b). *Educating the "Right" way: Markets, standards, God, and inequality*. New York & London: Routledge Falmer.

Bonilla-Silva, E. (2006). *Racism without racists: Color-blind racism and the persistence of racial inequality in the United States*. Lanham, MD: Rowman & Littlefield.

Bowles, S., & Gintis, H. (1976, 2001). *Schooling in capitalist America*. New York: Routledge.

Brayboy, B. M. J. (2005, December). Toward a tribal critical race theory in education. *The Urban Review, 37*(3), 201–219.

Braverman, H. (1974). *Labor and monopoly capitalism: The degradation of work in the 20th century.* New York & London: Monthly Review Press.

Chomsky, N. (2007).*What we say goes: Conversations on U.S. power in a changing world.* New York: Metropolitan.

Dale, R. (2010, June). Knowledge, "new" world order & "new" education-panel. World Congress of Comparative Education Societies. Istanbul, Turkey.

Duncan speeches, Hispanic Chamber of Commerce. (2009, March; 2010, July). Teachers College, Columbia University.

Economic Policy Institute Report. (2010, August 29). Retrieved from newsletter@epi.org online report on tests.

Emery, K., & Ohanian, S. (2004). *Why is corporate America bashing our public schools?* Portsmouth, NH: Heinemann.

Farley, T. (2009). *Making the grades: My misadventures in the standardized testing industry.* Sausalito, CA: PoliPoint.

Friedman, M. (1995), Public schools, make them private. Cato Institute June 23. Reprint from the *Washington Post,* 2/19/95. www.cato.org/pubs/briefs/bp-023

Freire, P. (1995). *Pedagogy of the oppressed.* London: Continuum.

Gamerman, E. (2008, February 29). What makes Finnish kids so smart? *Wall Street Journal.* Retrieved from *www.WSJ.com*

Gibson, R. (2003). Can communities of resistance and transformation be born from the social context of school? *Teacher Education Quarterly,* Winter. *www.teqjournal.org/back-vols/2003/30_1/gibson.pdf*

Grieder, W. (2009). The future of the American dream: Imagining an economy that puts people first. *The Nation,* May 25.

Harvey, D. (2010). Interview on economy. 8/4/10. 'Against the Grain.' Pacifica Radio.

Harvey, D. (2007). *A brief history of neoliberalism.* Oxford, UK: Oxford University Press.

Hickling-Hudson, A. & Ahlquist, R. (2004). Whose culture? The miseducation of aboriginal children in community schools: Implications for anti-racist teacher education in Australia. *The Journal of Postcolonial Education.* 3(1), 67–88. Victoria, AU: James Nicholas.

In response to increasing state and national control over the teacher education profession. (Winter 2003). *Teacher Education Quarterly* 30(2). California Council on Teacher Education., San Francisco: Caddo Gap.

Klein, N. (2007). *The shock doctrine: The rise of disaster capitalism.* New York: Picador.

Ladson-Billings, G. (2006 July). From the achievement gap to the education debt: Understanding achievement in U.S. schools. *Educational Researcher,* 35(7), 2–13.

Lea, V., & Ahlquist, R. (2010). Obama's neoliberal educational agenda: Global implications. World Congress of Comparative Education Societies. June 2010. Istanbul, Turkey.

Lea, V. (2010). Informal discussion about the status of critical thinking in U.S. students. June, Istanbul, Turkey.

Lim, S. (2004). *Consuming kids: The hostile takeover of childhood.* Chicago: Dearborn Trade.

Loewen, J. (2007). *Lies my teachers told me.* New York: Simon & Schuster.

McChesney, R. (2008) *The political economy of media.* New York: Monthly Review Press.

McChesney, R., & Foster, J. B. (2010, June). Capitalism, the absurd system: A view from the United States. *Monthly Review,* 62(2), 1–16.

McLaren, P. (2005). *Capitalists & conquerors: A critical pedagogy against empire*. Lanham, MD: Rowman & Littlefield.

Ohanian, S. (2010, November12) Retrieved from Outrages, Benn, Melissa, A Covert War on Schools, *The Guardian*, www.susanohanian.org/show_atrocities.php?id=9524

Payne, R. (2005). *A framework for understanding poverty*. Highlands, TX: Aha! Process, Inc.

Putnam, R. (2001). *Bowling alone: The collapse and revival of American community*. New York: Simon & Schuster.

Quinn, T. (2010). Wise, wiser, teacher: What I learned in Finnish schools. *Rethinking Schools*. 24(4), 36–37.

Robinson, Sir K. (2007). *Do schools kill creativity?* Retrieved from www.youtube.com

Robinson, Sir K. (2009). *Ken Robinson says schools kill creativity*. Retrieved from *www.ted.com*

Ryan, W. (1971). *Blaming the victim*. New York: Random House.

Saltman, K. J. (2007). *Capitalizing on disaster: Taking and breaking public schools*. Boulder, CO: Paradigm.

Saltman, K. J., & Gabbard, D. A. (Eds.). (2003). *Education as enforcement: The militarization and corporatization of schools*. New York: Routledge.

Spring, J. (1998). *Education and the rise of the global economy*. Mahwah, NJ: Lawrence Erlbaum.

Spring, J. (2004). *How educational ideologies are shaping global society*. Mahwah, NJ: Lawrence Erlbaum.

Spring, J. (2010, June 17). *Globalization of education*. Panel. World Congress of Comparative Education Societies. Istanbul, Turkey.

Valencia, R. R. (Ed.). (1997). Introduction. *The evolution of deficit thinking* (pp. ix–xvii). London: Falmer.

Wilkinson, R., & Pickett, K. (2010). *The spirit level: Why greater equality makes societies stronger*. New York: Bloomsbury.

Willinsky, J. (1998). *Learning to divide the world: Education at Empire's end*. Minneapolis, MN: University of Minnesota Press.

SECTION I
Hyper-accountability

· 2 ·

What We Don't Talk About
When We Talk About the
"Achievement Gap"

SUE BOOKS

MORE SO THAN AT ANY TIME I CAN REMEMBER, EDUCATIONAL REFORMERS SEEM to be agreeing, if not on a solution, at least on a major problem in public schooling: the racial achievement gap. A cornerstone of the Bush and now the Obama Administration's educational reform agenda, the achievement gap has attracted the attention of scholars with a range of political commitments. Many books that purport to explain the gap and point the way forward have been published recently—ranging, to mention just a few, from the very conservative Abigail and Stephan Thernstrom's *No Excuses: Closing the Racial Gap in Learning* (2003) and Rod Paige's and Elaine Witty's *The Black-White Achievement Gap: Why Closing It Is the Greatest Civil Rights Issue of Our Time* (2010) to Richard Rothstein's *Class and Schools: Using Social, Economic, and Educational Reform to Close the Black-White Achievement Gap* (2004), Pedro Portes' *Dismantling Educational Inequality: A Cultural-Historical Approach to Closing the Achievement Gap* (2005), and Pedro Noguera and Jean Yonemura Wing's edited book, *Unfinished Business: Closing the Racial Achievement Gap in Our Schools* (2006).[1]

The numbers warrant the alarm. Scores on the National Assessment of Educational Progress (NAEP), a Congressionally mandated test administered periodically to a national sample of students, show that the reading and math skills of Black and Latino high school students are about on par with the skills of white middle-school students, and that the reading and math proficiency of eighth-grade Black and Latino students is closer to that of white fourth graders than to that of white eighth graders. Reading and math achievement among Black and Latino students climbed substantially during the 1970s and 1980s and the achievement gap relative to white students narrowed. Progress essentially stopped in the 1990s. The Black-White gap in reading scores among 17-year-olds was greater in 2008 than it was in 1990 (Rampey, Dion, and Donahue, 2009). Although NCES charts long-term trends in achievement gaps for only the three largest racial/ethnic social groups (classified as white, Black, and Hispanic), a similar gap persists for Native American students as well (Chudowsky, Chudowsky, and Kober, 2009).

Poliakoff (2006) uncovered an even-more distressing picture in her review of the 2005 NAEP scores. Results are categorized as below basic, basic, proficient, or advanced, with "basic" denoting partial mastery of knowledge and skills. Among white fourth graders, 24% scored below basic on the reading assessment. However, among black fourth graders, 58% scored in this category, and among Latino fourth graders, 54%. Barton and Coley (2008) looked at the other end of the spectrum: the percentage of students scoring in the "proficient" range in reading. In 2007, whereas 43% of white fourth graders scored in this range, only 14% of black fourth graders and 17% of Latino fourth graders attained "proficiency." The eight-grade assessment in both reading and math showed the same pattern.

As alarming as the numbers are, these statistics are not really news. Indeed, the achievement gap has existed for almost a century—at least since the U.S. Army began using large-scale "intelligence" testing to assess recruits (Paige and Witty, 2010). The focus in this chapter instead is on talk about the achievement gap. As Ladson-Billings (2006) has noted, the phrase "the achievement gap" has become "a crossover hit . . . invoked by people on both ends of the political spectrum," with little argument about its meaning (p. 3). What, therefore, are we really talking about when we talk about "the achievement gap"? One way to explore this might be to consider what closing the achievement gap would and would not accomplish, and what the discourse on "the achievement gap" does and does not address.

Familiar Scapegoats

Let me start with two observations about talk about the achievement gap. First, as Poliakoff (2006) notes, "not a week passes without a news story or book

review relating the tale of a school that has turned the tide." These stories generally follow a formulaic approach: "first, identify schools that succeed in making headway against the achievement gap and, second, discover the recipe for
their success." A case in point is a *Washington Post* profile of North Glen
Elementary in Arundel, Maryland, a racially diverse suburban school where
two-thirds of the students qualify for the federally subsidized lunch program and
where black third graders' scores on the Maryland School Assessment rose dramatically over a two-year period. The *Washington Post* reporter, true to form,
attempted to pinpoint the elements responsible for the jump—"a new county
superintendent . . . a new statewide test . . . five new teachers, and a new principal, Maurine Larkin, a giddy educator who occasionally allowed herself to be
wheeled around the campus on a dolly"—and concluded that North Glen
"illustrates how a public school can go a very long way in a very short time with
the help of a charismatic principal, an enthusiastic staff and supportive parents"
(De Vise, 2005, p. B6).

Unfortunately, this popular search for an isolated "secret of success" serves
as a distraction from any substantive analysis of the problem. The Thernstroms
(2003) take this invitation and run with it. Their book *No Excuses: Closing the
Racial Gap in Learning* is filled with anecdotal stories about schools that "work"
as well as sweeping stereotypes that stand in for analysis. The Thernstroms
(2003) praise Asian Americans who, they argue,

> typically care more about academic success, and are more deeply engaged in their
> schoolwork than their non-Asian classmates. They take Advanced Placement cours-
> es at triple the white rate. They have embraced the American work ethic with life-or-
> death fervor. Their parents expect nothing less. (p. 98)

On the other hand, they assert,

> Something about the lives of [African American] children is limiting their intellec-
> tual development. Some risk factors have been identified by scholars: low-birth weight,
> single-parent households, and birth to a very young mother. There seem to be racial
> and ethnic differences in parenting practices as well, and the relatively small number
> of books in black households and the extraordinary amount of time spent watching TV
> appear related to those parenting practices. . . . [B]lack students have disciplinary prob-
> lems throughout their school careers at much higher rates than members of any other
> ethnic group. Although some believe that racism explains this pattern, there is no con-
> vincing evidence for that charge. (Thernstrom & Thernstrom, 2003, p. 147)

Although many scholars, of course, have found very "convincing evidence" that
racism shapes black students' school experience significantly (e.g., Ferguson,

2000, and Tutwiler, 2006), the Thernstroms (2003) reject what they characterize as the conventional wisdom about the causes of the achievement gap—namely, "inadequate funding, racial segregation, and too few teachers with professionally sanctioned credentials" (p. 152). Instead, they construe the fundamental problem as the absence of an "academic culture" in too many schools. They blame teachers' unions as well as the alleged values, beliefs, and parenting practices of many African Americans, and favor school choice as the best way to cut through the roadblock of "a culture hostile to reform" (p. 267). Note here how easily concern with the achievement gap leads to the all-too-familiar scapegoating of schools and families, without tackling the "600 pound gorilla that most affects American education today"—namely, poverty (Berliner, 2005) and the well-documented and disproportionate toll it takes on children, families, and communities of color;[2] widespread practices of "apartheid schooling" (Kozol, 2006); or persistent inequities in school funding (Arroyo, 2008).

Let me be more explicit. The racial achievement gap reflects a national failure to address historical injustices or to live up to our most basic democratic ideals, including the provision of equal educational opportunity. Consequently, both children and the democracy suffer. Much of the talk about closing this gap trivializes its significance by failing to make the link between test scores and broader social failings. Instead, closing the achievement gap is construed as basically a standalone problem—that is, a school-based technical challenge, a problem beyond the reach of schools (because rooted in the alleged values and beliefs of families and communities of color), or, most commonly, an odd combination of both. Given this definition of the problem, what would solving it mean? What could we hope for? What if, based on common prescriptions, schools and/or families and communities could somehow be "fixed" in a way that would result in a closer alignment between the test scores of Black and Latino students and their white peers?

An Educational Attainment Gap

Eliminating the racial achievement gap in NAEP scores seemingly would increase the chances that young people of color would be accepted more proportionally into "good" colleges or universities and also would make the competition for a shrinking number of good jobs fairer. *For these reasons, closing or at least narrowing the racial achievement gap is a vitally important social project.* However, closing the racial, K-12 achievement gap would not necessarily close the educational attainment gap between students from rich and poor families.

Although low-income students in the U.S. are disproportionately non-white, race and class cannot be conflated. Low-income students of all races and ethnicities increasingly find they have not been prepared to go on or have been priced out of college.

In a study based on the Michigan Panel Survey of Income Dynamics, Haveman and Wilson (2007) found that less than 7% of all college graduates come from the 25% of families with the least income and greatest financial need. Looking at this pattern from a different angle, Haycock (2006) notes that whereas 75% of students from affluent families (those in the top income quartile) graduate from college by age 24, only 9% of students from poor families (those in the lowest income quartile) do so. Poorer students are also significantly less likely than their wealthier classmates to transfer from community colleges to institutions granting baccalaureate degrees (Dougherty and Kienzl, 2006). In their analysis of two national representative data sets Dougherty and Kienzl (2006) found that even after controlling for "differences between more or less well-off students in precollege academic preparation and educational aspirations . . . most of the impact of socioeconomic background on transfer is still left unexplained" (p. 15).

Even if low-income students were not hurt by a very large college-preparation gap (Burris and Welner, 2005), "a quarter century of tuitions rising much faster than family incomes, family incomes becoming more unequal, huge disparities of wealth and savings by class and race, and a dramatic shrinkage in the proportion of college costs funded by need-based student aid" has put higher education beyond many students' reach (Orfield, 2004, p. xi). Unpreparedness is systematically produced in high-poverty schools, then "discovered" in the competition for college aid, increasingly based more on test-based assessments of merit than on financial need.

The student-loan provisions of the health care overhaul of 2010 will expand the federal Pell Grant program and make these student loans easier to repay (Baker and Herszenhorn, 2010). However, this pushback runs against a strong counter-tide. Whereas need-based financial aid increased 110% between 1994 and 2004, merit-based aid increased 508% during the same period (Redd, cited in Kahlenberg, 2006). Many colleges have been shifting back to more need-based aid but then defining "need" so liberally that the "upper, upper middle class" benefits from this shift much more than the poor who face stiffer and stiffer competition for initial admission (Grynbaum, 2008). Another trend has been to reduce the sticker tuition but then also to cut back sharply on aid to compensate for the loss of revenue. Consequently, "students who can afford to pay full freight get a discount right off the bat, while poor students no longer get institutional need-based aid and must meet higher academic standards to qualify for merit aid" (Grynbaum, 2008). Taking out a private loan has also become more difficult. As part of the fallout of the credit crisis of 2008 and subsequent recession, "some of the nation's biggest banks have closed their doors to students at community colleges, for-profit universities and other less competitive institutions" (Glater, 2008, p. A1)—that is, to prospective borrowers at institutions that traditionally have served low-income students.

Wage and Income Gaps

Admission to more selective colleges and universities is so competitive in part because young people (and their parents) know graduates will face even stiffer competition in the job market. Contrary to popular belief, most of the job growth in the U.S. is in lower-skill positions, not jobs that lead to intellectually stimulating careers or provide much financial security. Of the 10 occupations projected to have the largest numerical growth between 2008 and 2018, only two require at least a bachelor's degree: college professor (which generally requires a doctoral degree) and accountants/auditors. Six of the 10 occupations in which the chances of finding a job are the greatest require only on-the-job training: home health aides, customer service representatives, food preparation and service workers, personal and home care aides, retail salespeople, office clerks, and nursing aides. The other two occupations with the largest projected growth are registered nurses and nursing aides, both of which require some postsecondary training but not a bachelor's degree (U.S. Department of Labor, 2009).

Closing the racial achievement gap would not change this bleak picture. Nor would it necessarily change practices of wage discrimination. "The pay gap between men and women with college degrees hasn't budged over the last 15 years. Full-time female workers with a bachelor's degree made 75% as much as their male counterparts in 1992—and 75% as much in 2007" (Leonhardt, 2008). The Center for American Progress Action Fund calculated the "career wage gap" for women with varying degrees of education and found "an egregious (gap of) $713,000 on average over 40 years" among women with at a least a bachelor's degree (Arons, 2008, p. 4).

Among women, "after narrowing for decades, between 1980 and 2002 the black-white wage gap...more than doubled, increasing from 7% to 17%"

(Dozier, 2007). Even within higher-wage professional, managerial, and sales positions, black women earned 13%, 10%, 28% less, respectively, than white women in 2002. "We are starting to see that the income gap is largely an education gap," a White House spokesperson said in response to a report documenting the astonishing concentration of wealth among the wealthiest Americans (Johnston, 2006). Such an assertion squares with only the most simplistic view of the facts.

In a study of economic mobility, Isaacs (2007) found that a black-white gap in median family income has persisted for decades, virtually unchanged. In 2004, the median family income of blacks ages 30–39 was only 58% that of white families in the same age group. Also, unlike children of white middle-income parents, who tend to exceed their parents in income, a majority of black children of middle-income parents tend to fall below their parents. Perhaps most startlingly,

> Almost half (45%) of black children whose parents were solidly middle class end up falling to the bottom [quintile] of the income distribution, compared to only 16% of white children. *Achieving middle-income status does not appear to protect black children from future economic adversity the same way it protects white children* (italics added). (Isaacs, 2007, p. 2)

In short, there is little evidence that closing the racial academic achievement gap would alter the broader opportunity structure.

Perspective Gaps

Finally, closing the black-white achievement gap would not undercut the propensity, especially evident in the legal arena, to focus on a single aspect of educational inequality in a way that obscures its complexity. For decades, too many educational reformers have focused on segregation without considering disparities in funding or achievement or on funding without considering segregation or achievement. Consider, for example,

- the landmark *Brown v. Board of Education* case (1954) in which the U.S. Supreme Court overturned the doctrine of separate but equal (affirmed in *Plessy v. Ferguson* 1896) but failed to address disparities in funding;
- the Rochester schools case (*Paynter v. State of New York*, 2003) in

which New York's highest court found that, given what it regarded as adequate funding, the state bore no responsibility for the racial segregation and admittedly appallingly low levels of achievement in the Rochester city schools;

- the Massachusetts case (*Hancock v. Driscoll*, 2005) in which the commonwealth's Supreme Judicial Court found that, given "a general improvement over time" in test scores in four property-poor focal districts, the state's system of school funding was constitutional, even though very large majorities of the special education students, English-language learners, low-income students, and racial and ethnic minorities in these districts were still failing; and

- the Seattle, Washington, case (*Parents Involved in Community Schools v. Seattle School District*, 2007) in which a divided U.S. Supreme Court declared that public schools cannot seek to achieve or maintain integration through measures that take a student's race explicitly into account.

Although the central issue in the Seattle case was the constitutionality of factoring race into admissions decisions, funding disparities were part of the larger emotional and political context (Judge, 2007).[3]

Given our history of looking selectively at funding, segregation, and achievement, I fear that the widespread focus on the achievement gap, as welcome as it is in so many ways, is providing a rationale for ignoring persistent disparities in funding, widespread practices of "apartheid education" (Kozol, 2006), and a history of shortchanging that has created an enormous "education debt" with respect to the schooling of African Americans, American Indians, Latinos, and immigrant students (Ladson-Billings, 2006). Decades of litigation over school funding attest to the widespread recognition that money matters tremendously in schooling, and the U.S. Supreme Court's declaration in *Brown v. Board of Education* more than 50 years ago still stands: "Segregation of white and colored children in public schools has a detrimental effect upon the colored children" in part because "separate educational facilities are inherently unequal."

Nevertheless, funding disparities persist along with segregated schooling. Among states, among districts within states, and among schools within districts, significant funding gaps continue to constrain educational opportunity (The Southern Education Foundation, 2009; Roza and Hill, 2004). In 2006, students in Alaska (which spent $15,827 per pupil), New York (which spent $14,292 per pupil), and New Jersey (which spent $13,165) had funding that was rough-ly double that of their peers in Utah ($6,321 per pupil), Tennessee ($6,457 per pupil), and Mississippi ($7,274 per pupil). In a second layer of disparity, fund-ing discrepancies within states in 2006 ranged from a low of 25% in West Virginia (where the highest-funded district received 25% more per pupil than the lowest-funded district) to an astonishing discrepancy of 276% between the highest- and lowest-funded districts in Montana (Southern Education Foundation, 2009). What does this mean for a school or for a student's high school experience?

> In New York, the state's funding gap means that a high school with an average of 900 students in the lowest-revenue district has $12.4 million less per year to spend on edu-cating its students than a similar high school in the highest-revenue district. Over four years of high school, the difference in revenues between these schools amounts to an astronomical $49.6 million. (The Southern Education Foundation, 2009, p. 14)

Carol Kellerman, president of the Citizens Budget Commission, noted in a *New York Times* op-ed article that "during the 2007–2008 school year, the richest 10% of New York School districts were spending $28,754 per pupil (on top of local revenues), almost three times the national average," and wondered, "Why did the state provide $3,809 per pupil to support such lavish spending in those districts?" (Kellerman, 2010, p. 12). Good question.

Black and Latino students on the whole not only receive less state and local funding than their white peers (Arroyo, 2008) but also attend increasingly seg-regated public schools. Contrary to the popular belief that schools have steadi-ly desegregated since the *Brown* decision, in fact, after 10 years of virtually no progress followed by a period of significant desegregation, the number of black students attending predominantly minority schools rose dramatically across the nation in the 1990s. This reversal was largely the result of a series of U.S. Supreme Court decisions that essentially provided a how-to program for districts seeking to shed desegregation orders. "Resegregation is now occurring in all sec-tions of the country and is accelerating most rapidly [where] the most was achieved for black students, in the South" (Orfield and Lee, 2007, p. 14). In a recent Civil Rights Project report, Orfield (2009) notes:

> The percentage of students in intensely segregated schools, where the population is 90% to 100% nonwhite, is, of course, very low for whites—less than one student in a hundred. . . . The most serious segregation affects Latinos and African Americans—in both of these populations about two of every five students attend intensely segre-gated schools, up from less than a third in 1988. (p. 12).

This stark segregation matters so much, in part, because it goes almost hand in hand with concentrated poverty, which decades of research has shown almost always overwhelms schools (Books, 2004). Whereas in 2006 the average white child attended a school in which 32% of the students qualified for the federally subsidized lunch program (a common proxy for poverty), 59% of all Black students and 58% of all Latino students attended such schools. These schools tend to have weaker teaching staffs, students with more health and nutrition problems, families with less residential stability and income, and communities exposed to more crime and gangs, and all of this affects achievement significantly. Not surprisingly, therefore, these are also the schools that in disproportionate numbers are "failing" under the No Child Left Behind criteria (Orfield, 2009).

Politics of the Discourse

As Ladson-Billings (2006) has argued, an historical "education" debt cries out for redress. African Americans were punished brutally during times of slavery for even trying to learn to read and thereafter were subjected to schooling designed to maintain servitude. The "education" of American Indians in boarding schools similarly was used as a means of forced assimilation and subjugation. Latinos have been subjected to gross inequities in resources and to politicized battles over language that continue today. Given the prevailing disparities and practices of segregation (in actuality, if not specifically by law), compounded by a history of oppression, an achievement gap is virtually guaranteed and should not be surprising to anyone. Why, then, is there so much focus on the gap itself rather than on all that has created it?

Scholars and policymakers with very different ideas about its causes are all weighing in on "the achievement gap." The Thernstroms (2003), for example, look at the NAEP scores and other statistics and see a deficit in cultural values among specific social groups. Former Secretary of Education Rod Paige and Elaine Witty (2010) see a lack of leadership from within the African American community. The Association for Supervision and Curriculum Development (Poliakoff, 2006) sees a problem with roots both inside and "beyond the school doors." Rothstein (2004) and Berliner (2005) look at the numbers and see a "600 pound gorilla" (poverty) that is being systematically ignored. Gelberg (2008) similarly argues that "it is not possible to decouple children's educational well-being from their overall well being." Kozol (2006) condemns a society that condones a school system so segregated that it amounts to "apartheid education," and Holcomb-McCoy (2007) notes that "the achievement gap seems to be most prevalent in those schools that are not attending to issues of social justice; that is, to issues of equity, equality, and possibility for all students" (p. 6). These authors all support "closing the achievement gap" but do not agree at all on what this means. Consequently, their analyses and commentaries point to a range of disparate solutions—from school choice, to staff development, to devoting considerable social energies to eradicating child poverty, to changing public policies and attitudes that support segregation and ghettoization of communities of color, to a "call to service" to African American leaders.

Because it means so many different things to so many different people, talk about closing the achievement gap actually means very little—and, I suggest, has been so broadly embraced partly for this reason. Somewhat like declaring a war on terrorism with no agreement about what constitutes terrorism and little understanding of its root causes, tackling the achievement gap does not necessarily require either sophisticated analysis or significant social change. At its worst, a commitment to closing the gap requires nothing more than pointing fingers at African American parents and undercutting the power of teachers' unions through support of school choice. This free-floating rhetoric is available to be used as almost anyone sees fit, including as a way to assure that some questions are raised while others are not.

What's Needed

As Poliakoff (2006) notes, "The achievement gap is a signal, a warning that something has gone gravely wrong with the education of young people. It is not a diagnosis of what has gone wrong." Singham (2005) makes a similar argument in *The Achievement Gap in U.S. Education: Canaries in the Mine.* Canaries have been used, of course, to gain insight into conditions in a mine, not into the makeup of canaries or their habitats. Regarding the achievement gap as a warning that something is awry with respect to the foundations or conditions of schooling in the U.S. is a far more useful approach than either zeroing in on a single school to discover the "secret" of its apparent success or construing a whole group of parents as being simply not up to the job.

David Grissmer and his colleagues' (1998) article is exemplary in this regard. In "Why Did the Black-White Score Gap Narrow in the 1970s and 1980s?" they explored the question from an historical perspective and noted that black students' reading and math scores improved significantly between

1971 and 1996 while white students' improved only moderately. This caused the achievement gap to narrow before it subsequently reopened. In trying to figure out why, Grissmer, Flanagan, and Williamson (1998) noted that family environments improved between 1970 and 1996. Parents, especially black parents, had considerably more education as well as fewer children in 1990 than in 1970. Anti-poverty programs initiated in the late 1960s and early 1970s helped black families more than white families. Also, some school districts made strides in desegregation. Such efforts were especially significant between 1968 and 1972 in the South, where black test score gains were largest. At the same time, there was a push in many schools to offer more demanding courses and smaller classes. Paige and Witty (2010) recall the 1970s and 1980s as a time when "the African American community was still glowing from the high hopes emanating from the *Brown v. Board of Education* decision....The power of education rang from the pulpits of the black churches; it was discussed in black social settings and work sites" (p. 5). Looking at the achievement gap over time and in its broader social and public-policy context promises to provide much more insight about the conditions under which we can expect the gap to narrow than a tunnel-vision inspection of a single "star" school.

I am not trying to delineate a methodology of study, however, but rather to raise questions about the *discourse* of the achievement gap. The good news is that we seemingly have a common language and a point of agreement. No one regards the achievement gap as unimportant; no one is "against" closing it. The challenge will be to keep the conversation open and to use it to ask questions that amount to more than either "a cascade of blame-shifting" (Kahlenberg, 2006) onto parents and families or a narrow search for one's school's "secret." What does the achievement gap tell us not about children of color and their families but rather about the broader society that condones high levels of child poverty, which children of color bear disproportionately, and about the resegregation of the public schools? Keeping this question front and center will not close the achievement gap in and of itself but will, I believe, enable us to see through more clearly to what has been obscured and therefore to engage in a more open and honest inquiry about the histories of injustice the "achievement gap" reflects.

Arguments like the one laid out in this chapter cry out, if not for a "solution," at least for a suggestion of how to move forward. As I have tried to emphasize, the racial as well as socioeconomic achievement gaps must be closed. Given the prominent role we have given standardized test scores in the allocation of social opportunity, anything less than a sustained, concerted effort to significantly reduce these gaps is a betrayal not only of some of our most meaningful political ideals but, more importantly, of the moral responsibility of one generation to care for the next. Opportunity must be actively shared, in part by actively dismantling barriers, and that work must be guided by a deep understanding of the reality of the task in all its complexity. Sound bites and political slogans will not do; the stakes are too high.

There is a central role and responsibility for educators and education scholars in this work. Our business is teaching and learning, and we traffic in communication. Educating perhaps first ourselves and then our colleagues, teacher-education students, and the broader public about the causes and complexities of the achievement gap would be a significant contribution to the broader social project of creating and sustaining opportunity for all. Let me conclude therefore with a story I often share with my students although I do not know its origins:

> Three friends were walking along a river one day when they spotted some turbulence in the water. Two people waded in and, alarmed, discovered a drowning child. They pulled the little boy up on the bank but then saw more turbulence. This time it was a little girl flailing and fighting for her life. They pulled her out too—then realized their buddy was missing. They called out and eventually he walked back.
>
> "Where were you?" one man said, exasperated. "We needed your help and you wandered away!"
>
> "I know," the friend responded, "but somebody needed to find out who was throwing the children in the river to start with."

I tell this story not, of course, to argue against rescuing drowning children, but rather to underscore the need both for attending to immediate needs *and* to ferreting out causes that may originate far up river. The discourse on the achievement gap, to my mind, has seriously shortchanged the latter.

Notes

1. This chapter is a revised and updated version of Books, S. (2007). What Are We Talking about When We Talk about "Closing the Achievement Gap?" *Journal of International Learning* (14), 2.

2. Thernstrom and Thernstrom (2003) acknowledge that poverty affects educational achievement but insist that the effect is "less than one might expect—or than many assume" (129). Considerable scholarship challenges this assertion (see Anyon, 1997; 2005; Books, 2004; and Rothstein, 2004).

3. Ballard High School, which was 62% white and the focus of much of the contestation, received considerably more private funding than, for example, Franklin High School, of comparable size and in the same district but with 90% students of color. The Ballard Athletic Booster Club gave Ballard High $171,000 during the 2005–2006 school year alone, and the Ballard High School Foundation raised more the $250,000 for the construction of a greenhouse the year before. The Franklin Alumni Association, by contrast, donated just over $170,000 to Franklin High for extracurricular activities *over the previous ten years* (Judge, 2007).

References

Anyon, J. (1997). *Ghetto schooling: A political economy of urban educational reform.* New York: Teachers College.

Anyon, J. (2005). *Radical possibilities: Public policy, urban education, and a new social movement.* New York: Routledge.

Arons, J. (2008). Lifetime losses: The career wage gap. Center for American Progress Action Fund. Retrieved from http://www.americanprogressaction.org/issues/2008/pdf/equal_pay.pdf

Arroyo, C. G. (2008). The funding gap. Washington, DC: The Education Trust. Retrieved from www.edtrust.org

Baker, P., & Herszenhorn, D. M. (2010, March 30). Obama signs bill on student loans and health care. *The New York Times.* Retrieved from www.nytimes.com

Barton, P. E., & Coley, R. J. (2008). Windows on achievement and inequality. Educational Testing Service Policy Information Center. Princeton, NJ: ETS. Retrieved from www.ets.org/research/pic

Berliner, D. (2005, August 2). Our impoverished view of educational reform. *Teachers College Record.* Retrieved from www.tcrecord.org

Books, S. (2004). *Poverty and schooling in the U.S.: Contexts and consequences.* Mahwah, NJ: Lawrence Erlbaum.

Books, S. (2007). What are we talking about when we talk about "closing the achievement gap"? *Journal of International Learning* (14), 2.

Burris, C. C., & Welner, K. G. (2005, April). Closing the achievement gap by detracking. *Phi Delta Kappan*, 86(8), 594–598. Retrieved from www.pdkintl.org/kappan/k_v86/k0504bur.htm

Chudowsky, N., Chudowsky, V., & Kober, N. (2009). Are achievement gaps closing and is achievement rising for all? Center on Education Policy. Retrieved from http://www.cep-dc.org/document/docWindow.cfm?fuseaction=document.viewDocument&documentid=292&documentFormatId=4388

De Vise, D. (2005, October 31). Arundel school closes achievement gap. *The Washington Post,* p. B6.

Dougherty, K. J., & Kienzl, G. S. (2006). It's not enough to get through the open door: Inequality by social background in transfer from community colleges to four-year colleges. *Teachers College Record.* Retrieved from www.tcrecord.com

Dozier, R. (2007). Accumulating disadvantage: The growth in the black-white wage gap among women. Paper presentation. American Sociological Association Annual Meeting, New York City.

Ferguson, A. A. (2000). *Bad boys: Public schools in the making of black masculinity.* Ann Arbor, MI: University of Michigan Press.

Gelberg, D. (2008, April 10). Closing the achievement gap: Schools alone cannot succeed. *Teachers College Record.* Retrieved from http://www.tcrecord.org on October 12, 2010.

Glater, J. (2008, June 2). Student loans start to bypass 2-year colleges. *The New York Times.* Retrieved from www.nytimes.com

Grissmer, D., Flanagan, A., & Williamson, S. (1998). Why did the black-white score gap narrow in the 1970s and 1980s? In C. Jencks & M. Phillips (Eds.), *The black-white test score gap* (pp. 182–226). Washington, DC: Brookings Institution.

Grynbaum, M. M. (2008, April 20). Keeping the lid on. *The New York Times.* Retrieved from www.nytimes.com

Haveman, R., & Wilson, K. (2007). Economic inequality in college access, matriculation, and graduation. In S. Dickert-Conlin & R. Rubenstein (Eds.), *Economic inequality and higher education: Access, persistence, and success.* New York: Russell Sage Foundation.

Haycock, K. (2006, August). Promise abandoned: How policy choices and institutional practices restrict college opportunities. Washington, DC: The Education Trust. Retrieved from www.edtrust.org

Holcomb-McCoy, C. (2007). *School counselling to close the achievement gap: A social justice framework for success.* Thousand Oaks, CA: Corwin.

Isaacs, J. B. (2007, November). Economic mobility of black and white families. The Brookings Institution. Retrieved from www.brookings.edu/topics/economic-mobility.aspx

Johnston, D. C. (2006, January 29). Corporate wealth share rises for top-income Americans. *The New York Times.* Retrieved from www.nytimes.com

Judge, D. (2007, January). Housing, race and schooling in Seattle: Context for the Supreme Court decision. *Journal of Educational Controversy,* 2(1). Retrieved from http://www.wce.wwu.edu/Resources/CEP/eJournal/v002n001/Index.shtml

Kahlenberg, R. D. (2006, March 10). Ways and means. School & College. *The Chronicle of Higher Education,* pp. B51–B52.

Kellerman, C. (2010, March 28). No more aid for the affluent. *The New York Times,* p. WK 12.

Kozol, J. (2006). *The shame of the nation: The restoration of apartheid schooling in America.* New York: Crown.

Ladson-Billings, G. (2006). From the achievement gap to the education debt: Understanding achievement in U.S. schools. *Educational Researcher,* 35(7), 3–12.

Leonhardt, D. (2008, May 21). A diploma's worth? Ask her. *The New York Times.* Retrieved from www.nytimes.com

Noguera, P., & Wing, J. Y. (Eds.). (2006). *Unfinished business: Closing the racial achievement gap in our schools.* San Francisco, CA: Jossey-Bass.

Orfield, G. (2004).*Dropouts in America: Confronting the graduation rate crisis.*Cambridge, MA: Harvard Education Press.

Orfield, G. (2009). *Reviving the goal of an integrated society: A 21st century challenge.* Los Angeles, CA: The Civil Rights Project/Proyecto Derechos Civiles at UCLA.

Orfield, G., & Lee, C. (2004). *Brown at 50: King's Dream or Plessey's nightmare?* Cambridge, MA:

The Civil Rights Project, Harvard University.

Orfield, G., & Lee, C. (2007). *Historic reversals, accelerating resegregation, and the need for new integration strategies.* Los Angeles, CA: The Civil Rights Project/Proyecto Derechos Civiles at UCLA.

Paige, R., & Witty, E. (2010). *The Black-White achievement gap: Why closing it is the greatest civil rights issue of our time.* AMACOM.

Poliakoff, A. R. (2006, January). Closing the gap: An overview. Info brief. Association for Supervision and Curriculum Development. Retrieved from www.ascd.org/portal/site/ascd/menuitem.203b9955edb150a98d7ea23161a001ca/

Portes, P. R. (2005). *Dismantling educational inequality: A cultural-historical approach to closing the achievement gap.* New York: Peter Lang.

Rampey, B. D., Dion, G. S., & Donahue, P. L. (2009). The nation's report card: Trends in academic progress in reading and mathematics 2008. National Center for Education Statistics. Retrieved from http://nces.ed.gov/nationsreportcard/pubs/main2008/2009479.asp

Rothstein, R. (2004). *Class and schools: Using social, economic, and educational reform to close the black-white achievement gap.* Washington, DC: Economic Policy Institute.

Roza, M., & Hill, P. (2004). How within-district spending inequities help some schools to fail. *Brookings Papers on Education Policy.* Brookings Institution. Retrieved from http://muse.jhu.edu/login?uri=/journals/brookings_papers_on_education_policy/v2004/2004.1roza.html

Singham, M. (2005). *The achievement gap in U.S. education: Canaries in the mine.* Lanham, MD: Rowman & Littlefield.

Southern Education Foundation. (2009). *No time to lose: Why America needs an education amendment to the U.S. constitution to improve public education.* Atlanta, GA: The Southern Education Foundation.

Thernstrom, A., & Thernstrom, S. (2003). *No excuses: Closing the racial gap in learning.* New York: Simon & Schuster.

Tutwiler, S. W. (2006). How schools fail African American boys. In S. Books (Ed.), *Invisible children in the society and its schools* (3rd ed.). Mahwah, NJ: Lawrence Erlbaum.

U.S. Department of Labor, Bureau of Labor Statistics. (2009, December 11). Employment projections: 2008–2018 summary. Economic news release. Retrieved from http://www.bls.gov/news.release/ecopro.t06.htm

· 3 ·

Can Standardized Teacher Performance Assessment Identify Highly Qualified Teachers?

ANN BERLAK

MOST TEACHERS AND TEACHER EDUCATORS ARE UNITED AGAINST THE NOTION, deeply embedded in Obama/Duncan's Race to the Top policy, that teacher quality should be assessed in terms of students' scores on standardized tests. If educators reject this value added policy, which has been thoroughly discredited in a devastating critique by The Educational Policy Institute (EPI, 2010), what is the alternative? One proposed alternative, endorsed by Duncan himself, already well entrenched in teacher credential programs in California and spreading rapidly across the US, is Teacher Performance Assessment. This chapter will examine whether teacher performance assessment is a better way.

In an October 22, 2009 speech to teacher educators at Teachers College, Columbia University, Secretary of Education Arne Duncan proclaimed that revolutionary change in the education of teachers is essential if we are to solve the problems facing US society and its schools. Punctuating his speech with military and corporate metaphors, Duncan declared that the supreme purpose of public schooling is to keep America competitive and that the decline in our standing in the world order can be attributed to the fact that the institutions that prepare teachers "are doing a mediocre job." Duncan's conclusion: "Teacher preparation programs need revolutionary change, not evolutionary tinkering." Toward the end of his speech he declared that a standardized performance-based system for assessing teachers was key to bringing about this change.

According to Duncan the "core mission" of teacher education programs is to bring about "substantial increases in student achievement." He proposes to accomplish this by requiring credential candidates to pass a "performance-based" standardized exit exam that will measure both their competence to teach and the quality of their credential program, just as pupils' scores on standardized tests are believed to measure their abilities and the quality of their teachers and schools. Teacher credential programs whose candidates score well on the exam would be rewarded while those who do not would be subject to punitive sanctions. Part of the $4.3 billion in Race to the Top funds would provide resources and incentives to construct and promote these assessments. These plans to reform teacher education take as a given the need for corporate-dominated, top-down management, a view Duncan shares with virtually every major corporate think tank, the Heritage Foundation, the Business Roundtable, and the Broad, Gates, and Walton family foundations. They also take as a given that the primary purpose of schooling is to preserve and promote the US corporate order.

Near the end of his Teachers College speech Duncan named the particular exam he had in mind for assessing the competency of credential candidates and programs: PACT, the Performance Assessment of California Teachers. Few listening to Duncan's speech that day had heard of PACT, but it has been a fixture in California for a number of years, and many teacher educators and credential candidates in California are already quite familiar with it. In this chapter I examine the ways in which PACT has affected the elementary education programs in several state universities in California and what teacher educators might expect if they become subject to its requirements.

How PACT Works

In 1998 the California Legislature passed a law requiring teacher credential candidates to pass a state-approved exit exam in order to receive their credentials. Many credential programs in California, including the state university where I teach in the elementary credential program, chose PACT, devised by selected members of the education faculties at Stanford University, Mills, all the universities of California, and two state universities. The alternative to PACT was CalTPA, an assessment system designed by the state in consultation with the Educational Testing Service. Our College of Education elected to use PACT because it purported to be qualitative, not quantitative, and to assess "authentic" teaching performance in "real world" contexts.

PACT's creators and chief advocates expected PACT to provide the cru-cial link in the chain of evidence connecting the classroom performance of indi-viduals at the end of their credential programs to achievement of their pupils in their first year of teaching, as measured by standardized tests (Pecheone and Chung, 2006). In academic lingo this is called predictive validity. The assump-tion, then, was that PACT would identify how well various credential programs promoted teaching practices and learning outcomes valued by federal and state authorities.

Like all the other states, California already had a complex and comprehen-sive accountability system for teacher education, including an elaborate set of state-mandated entrance and exit assessments. These included the C-BEST (a test of basic literacy, i.e., reading comprehension, writing, and mathematics), C-SET (a standardized test of content knowledge), RICA (a test of knowledge about teaching reading), student teaching supervision, and GPA requirements. Our programs were also assessed by an increasingly prescriptive National Council for the Accreditation of Teacher Education (NCATE), the national accrediting body that imposes an entirely separate and largely redundant assess-ment system. PACT added another layer to these systems of assessment. It is well known that each additional test introduces yet another hurdle that dispro-portionately affects people of color and those for whom English is not their first language. Although one of the models for PACT, National Board Certification, has a lower pass rate for people of color (Wayne et al., 2004), correlations of PACT pass-rates with race and ethnicity of credential candidates are yet to be investigated.

PACT assesses two types of performance: the Teaching Event (TE) and the embedded signature assignment. Each signature assignment is a single, usual-ly culminating, course assignment which faculty are required to implement and score according to PACT-designated and state-approved criteria—a clear intru-sion into the institutions' and faculty members' prerogative to set their own cri-teria for assessing students. I will focus on the TE, a three-lesson learning segment in a single subject, and a 15-minute video that is a *segment* from one of the lessons, selected and taught by the candidate during the final semester of student teaching. The lesson is accompanied by a portfolio of approximate-ly 50 pages of teaching plans, teaching artifacts, student work samples, written reflections, and commentaries related to the TE. The guidelines and the more than 50 prompts specifying the elements of the portfolio are laid out in detail in a student handbook. Students submit the TE data (including the video recording) via a computer program. To say that the preparation for the Teaching

Event consumes an inordinate amount of time and psychic energy is a serious understatement. The specifications for the Teaching Event are available on line (pacttpa.org); readers should access them to appreciate what completing the TE involves.

Scorers, trained by official state PACT trainers in two day-long sessions and then "calibrated" annually to assure scorer consistency, assess the TE video and accompanying documentation using a series of standardized rubrics. After the rubric scores for the signature assignments and the TE are submitted, a computer program transforms them into numbers that purport to represent the effectiveness of individual credential candidates, and these are forwarded to the state. Thus, in the end, this is a quantitative, not a qualitative assessment. If the submitted numbers are at or above the cut score, the candidates will have fulfilled the PACT criteria for earning a credential.

The scorers are anonymous and must not know the candidates they are scoring. Although the scorers may be faculty members, there is no requirement that they have any background in teaching or expertise in the area they assess. For example, a social studies specialist may score a teaching event where math is being taught. Since remuneration is a central motive for engaging in the tedious, highly regulated scoring task and scorers are paid per head, they have an incentive to score as rapidly as possible.

Faculty members are not considered qualified to do PACT assessments unless they have been approved by PACT trainers. One professor at a state university in Southern California who is recognized as a national and international expert in second language acquisition was appalled by the notion that after two days of training, a calibrated scorer's judgments about candidates' competency to teach English language learners was considered more valid than hers. She told me she resented being calibrated, with her 30 years of teaching and research in this discipline, to rate candidates on questionable rubrics alongside scorers who may have no knowledge or experience teaching English language learners. In her view, PACT is a death knell for the longstanding respect for academic scholarship and expertise.

A faculty member at another California State University wrote:

> Our faculty do not want to be involved in scoring the PACT teaching events, as it is very time consuming and tedious. We may be moving to a process that is almost exclusively scored by persons who know little about and who do not teach in our program. This is very troubling. I see institutions "farming out" the assessment of PACT to regional centers to cut costs and to score the huge numbers of events that will need to be scored. In short, PACT seems to violate everything we know about designing assessment. What kind of assessment have we created that faculty who teach in the program do not want to score?

Does PACT Assess Good Teaching?

The PACT brochure proclaims: "A candidate who passes this assessment has shown he or she is a better prepared teacher who can help (k-12) students succeed." What do the PACT authors mean by "succeed" and by "better prepared"? Better prepared than whom and for what?

In his Teachers College address Duncan proposed to "reward states that publicly report and link student achievement data to the institutions and programs where teachers and principals were credentialed" and advocates "longitudinal data systems that enable states to track and compare the impact of new teachers from teacher preparation programs on student achievement over a period of years." Since the quantity of student achievement data and longitudinal data systems Duncan refers to are inconceivable in terms other than students' standardized test scores, good teachers apparently are those whose students score well on standardized tests.

The rubrics or criteria used to assign PACT scores are based on state standards and are supposed to identify elements of teaching that scientific research has shown enable students to reach these standards. Teaching patterns valued by PACT are primarily aspects of explicit, systematic, direct instruction that will instill in students knowledge specified by the state-mandated standards and measured by standardized tests. (At present the state legislature seems to be deciding that 85 percent of the state standards must be isomorphic with national standards. The folly of attempting to establish such percentages has, evidently, not been considered.) PACT cannot and does not aspire to assess teachers' perseverance, readiness and ability to think on their feet, hear and respond to feedback, learn from experience, listen to students, or promote student self-confidence and critical thinking, qualities that are, among others, essential if teachers are to prepare students for democratic participation.

Each rubric is intended to represent one aspect of a concise checklist designed to assess a component of teaching (e.g., instruction, planning, or assessment). To achieve test-scoring consistency PACT assessors are trained (calibrated) to make similar if not identical inferences from their observations as the basis for assigning scores on each of the rubrics. Thus, those who construct the rubrics and train the calibrators hold considerable power over how good teaching is defined and identified. Do the training and calibration actually achieve reliable or consistent scoring? A close analysis of reliability data suggests that inter-rater agreement is only 57 percent.[2] The authors of PACT claim failing candidates' TE's are double scored. Nevertheless, even one known example of a case where initially almost a quarter of candidates in a program were told after they had graduated, that they had failed PACT raises questions about how reliable (and valid) even double scoring is. All of the failed candidates had successfully passed their courses and received at least passing evaluations by their student teaching supervisors. When they showed their TEs to calibrated scorers who had not scored these particular students' TE's, some of these scorers disagreed with the original scorers' assessments and one calibrated scorer suggested resubmitting the TE without making any changes.

I want to be very clear: many of the attributes assessed by the rubrics are important components of good teaching. However, if we know anything for certain about the effects of standardized testing, it's that what's not tested is unlikely to be taught. So what is not assessed by PACT? PACT does not assess most of the qualities that Duncan himself in his Teachers College speech lists as attributes of great teachers—teachers who "(C)an literally change the course of a student's life . . . light a lifelong curiosity, (promote) a desire to participate in a democracy, instill a thirst for knowledge, reduce inequality and fight daily for social justice."

What's more, no one who has been specifically prohibited from interacting with a candidate personally can, on the basis of observing a videoed 15-minute teaching segment and reading supporting evidence, identify with any certainty many of the teaching attributes and dispositions most of us value most highly. Nor can assessors acknowledge teaching attributes and actions they might deem as valuable but have been "calibrated" to ignore.

There's also the obvious question of whether the videotape of a small segment of instruction can actually capture authentic teaching. ("Not to mention," a teacher educator writes, "that the quality of the videos is often poor unless we spend hours training students' video skills.") Many credential candidates themselves argue that the video-recorded Teaching Event is artificial and contrived and does not represent their real teaching. Several reported that during the TE they were preoccupied with keeping in mind all the rubrics the assessor would be bringing to bear on the 15-minute performance and whether the camera was picking up their students' voices. Such concerns militate against a holistic reflective teaching performance. Many students elected to plan the simplest and most technically unchallenging lessons they could think of. One credential candidate reported to a faculty member that he was encouraged to teach his PACT lesson for practice the day before the videotaping.

Because of PACT timeline logistics, students usually complete lesson plans for the TE weeks before they teach it, thus discouraging contingent and learner-centered instruction. One student told me:

I spent about 15 hours writing about the lesson I was going to videotape, citing resources, spouting theory, explaining my best practices, and then the first stormy day of the year threw everything off track. It started hailing, the kids ran to the windows as branches came crashing down and garbage whipped the windows. I had never planned so hard for a lesson in all my life, and I had never had one go that badly. It went badly because no matter how much you plan, a lot of teaching happens in the moment. A huge part of teaching, especially for beginning teachers, is finding that feeling in your gut that says "step in now!" or "sudden change of plans!"

PACT's Effect on Teacher Education

Because PACT is an unfunded mandate, credentialing institutions have to pay for the video equipment and the costs of administering and scoring the assessments. Some institutions did so, in part, by reducing student teacher supervision. When supervision is reduced and students receive no feedback from PACT assessments unless they do not pass, the PACT regimen can severely limit candidates' opportunities to engage in the reflective dialogue with experienced practitioners about their teaching and dialogue is central to learning to teach.

Most of the credential candidates' responses to PACT cited on the official PACT website are positive. However, almost all of the students at my institution and at least four other California State Universities found PACT to be a serious and significant distraction from their course work and student teaching, creating unnecessary anxiety and exhaustion as they tried to satisfy the requirements of what they perceived as repetitive, bureaucratized tasks. A systematic interview study of responses of credential candidates at the University of California-Davis indicated that the vast majority of credential candidates had overwhelmingly negative feelings about PACT, citing excessive writing demands, the stress of assembling portfolios at the same time as student teaching, and the toll it took on their health and personal relationships. They found PACT minimally helpful regarding classroom management and instructional strategies (Okhremtchouk et al., 2009).

In the department where I teach, the first half of student teaching in the final semester came to focus on preparing for the Teaching Event to the consternation of many student teaching supervisors, master teachers, and the candidates themselves. Some students were absent from student teaching in order to complete the PACT documentation. One student told me, "I wasn't really able to take student teaching seriously until I'd completed the Teaching Event." Preparing for the TE has become the focus of student teaching seminars that had formerly been devoted to examining the interface of theory and practice. Lisa, who graduated in December, reported:

> We sacrificed 90% of our third semester practicum class working on PACT, when we could have been discussing how to handle situations we were facing in student teaching. We sacrificed a lot to prove to the legislators in California, and everyone they answer to, that we were ready to teach. And of course PACT didn't prove that at all.

Like the frog in slowly heating water that offers no resistance and eventually is boiled, it wasn't until our department had been subjected to PACT for several years that many of the faculty began to recognize the effect it was having on our program and morale. We were more stressed and were working harder than ever before, not out of internal motivation, but because of the requirements PACT thrust upon us. In exchange, PACT added no information that helped us improve our credential programs (and provided no feedback to credential candidates unless they failed their TE) but instead diverted time and resources from programmatic commitments to prepare teachers to educate the "whole" student, promote democratic citizenship, and reduce the opportunity gap. It resulted in curriculum changes that had no justification beyond adapting to the exigencies of PACT. This was as demoralizing and disempowering to many faculty members as standardized testing has been to K-12 teachers.

Technical and logistical issues regarding PACT came to dominate our faculty meetings, and substantive discussions, such as how we as a faculty should respond to the increasing focus on high-stakes testing in the schools, virtually disappeared. One author of PACT was quoted on the official PACT website as follows: "[PACT provides a great] opportunity to talk with other faculty about expectations for candidates and what we value. A real treat to engage with faculty over substance." Perhaps prior to PACT there had been no such discussions in this woman's department. But before PACT our faculty did have discussions about issues of substance on a regular basis.

In sum, PACT promoted mindless teaching—just the opposite of its declared intention but perhaps consistent with the hierarchical corporate orientation from which it had sprung. Many students engaged in what has been called "bureaucratic ventriloquism: an inauthentic response so markedly detached from the individual's own beliefs, that the utterances themselves appear to be projected from elsewhere." (Rennert-Ariev, 2008, p. 111) One talented candidate declared, "The teaching for PACT wasn't coming from me."

A student who graduated in December wrote,

> I tried not to let myself question PACT's usefulness while going through it because it would just make me angry and no matter what, I would still have to do it. It was eas-

ier to just put the question of PACT's usefulness out of my mind and write, and write, and write, all of what would have been 50 hard-copy pages had I printed it out. . . . To me PACT was just another hoop I had to jump through in order to get my teaching credential. Viewed in the most positive light: jumping through hoops is a useful life skill, especially if I plan on working for the state for the next 35 years.

Evidently Duncan's ideal is that every certification program in the nation conclude with a PACT-like assessment. Approximately a year after Duncan's speech *Education Week* reported that education programs across 19 states are piloting a performance-based assessment for teacher-candidates that potentially could serve as a common pre-licensing measure for new teachers. Five of the states taking part in the work—Massachusetts, Minnesota, Ohio, Tennessee, and Washington—have committed in legislation to use a performance-based licensing test, and officials have signed memoranda of understanding, agreeing to adopt the assessment if it proves to be technically valid and reliable (Sawchuck, 2010). The particular performance instrument *Education Week* is referring to is PACT. Evidently, in the months to come there will be many certification programs that have to make accommodations similar to the ones thirty credential programs in California have already made.

The quality of teacher education programs certainly varies, and most teacher educators are well aware of the need for continuing improvement. However, imposing PACT, an invalid and unreliable system with no record of success, will surely have the same withering effects upon teacher education that high stakes standardized testing has had on K-12 teaching At the same time, it will provide the missing link in the circle of control over schooling that is central to the hegemony of the audit culture.

What is to be done? The audit culture has infiltrated—to varying degrees—the hearts and minds of every teacher educator who did not take early retirement when they saw the handwriting on the wall. Most faculty reluctantly went along with PACT from the beginning. There were, of course, some who fully embraced this form of assessment from the start. Some of us who continued to prepare teachers for US schools in the face of the growing surveillance PACT embodied spoke out against it—for a time. However, when we realized that the state was not going to revoke the unfunded standardized exit exams, our vocal resistance abated.

At the end of an in-depth account of the neo-liberal audit context in which we are now living, Taubman wrote, "Faced with the inexorability of the transformation I have mapped, what alternatives do we have? What can we do given the current state of education?" (Taubman, 2009, p. 197). Over the past decade, as I, from a vantage point of almost forty years as a teacher-educator, began writing about what I saw happening, I came to realize that if Duncan has his way there soon will be no "old timers" who can remember when many teachers and teacher educators were, at least to some degree, respected as competent professionals whose role is to promote curricula and pedagogies that are relevant to time and place and to contribute to the construction of a more just and joyful world.

As I have become more deeply aware that the exit exams imposed by the state are essential elements of the audit culture, I have become increasingly unwilling to offer simplistic solutions to problems that are near-totalizing. I don't want to participate in what Duncan-Andrade refers to as "hokey hope" (Duncan-Andrade, 2009). At one point in the evolution of my understanding I had written,

> A cornerstone of Duncan's plan for improving K-12 schooling is the institution of a high stakes standardized regime of exit exams for teacher credential programs. Since it is widely agreed among educators that K-12 standardized testing is a failed policy, *mandating an additional system of high stakes testing in pursuit of improving K-12 schooling is, in fact, quite stunning.*

Now that I have looked more closely at the context in which teacher educators have been and are presently working and have come to more fully recognize the dimensions of the transformations generated by the discourses and practices of standards and accountability, I have begun to understand that teacher performance assessment may at this point be simply too hegemonic to resist (Taubman, 2009, p. 197). Though class sizes and university fees and tuition are rising and education and other human service budgets are being slashed, there seems to be no stopping the expensive and useless state and federally mandated teacher performance assessments that likely will become naturalized, normalized aspects of teacher education soon.

There are enormous pressures, both from within and outside our universities, to comply with PACT. What we can do at this point in time is make sure our students understand the grave concerns about the values and worldview implicit in PACT while at the same time providing them with the knowledge and skills required to pass it. I have chosen to write about what I have seen to clarify for myself and others the significance of this rapid transformation unfolding before our eyes. Fathoming its impact and significance is prerequisite to action.

Perhaps as the consequences of the "accountability movement" in teacher education become even more onerous, this critique and others will contribute to loosening the hold upon teacher educators of the discourses that support the audit culture. Perhaps teacher educators will begin to reject the fears of worthlessness that Duncan's blame of them has stimulated and reinforced. Perhaps they will become outraged and join with one another to resist. Teacher educators cannot, however, go it alone. Parents, K-12 teachers, and university teachers across the disciplines also must challenge the anti-democratic rhetoric of blame and fear that is central to the survival of the audit culture of "standards" and "accountability."

Notes

1. The distinguished authors of Economic Policy Institute's *Problems with the Use of Student Test Scores to Evaluate Teachers*, include four former presidents of the American Educational Research Association; two former presidents of the National Council on Measurement in Education; the current and two former chairs of the Board of Testing and Assessment of the National Research Council of the National Academy of Sciences; the president-elect of the Association for Public Policy Analysis and Management; the former director of the Educational Testing Service's Policy Information Center and a former associate director of the National Assessment of Educational Progress; a former assistant U.S. Secretary of Education; a former and current member of the National Assessment Governing Board; and the current vice-president, a former president, and three other members of the National Academy of Education.

2. PACT, March, 2007. See Table 11 titled "Campus Scores—Audit Scores Consensus Estimate" (2003–04 Pilot Year). The authors make the claim, based on the pilot, that they were able to obtain 91% agreement between scorers on the TE. In order to get this 91% agreement they had to say that agreement exists when the score is the same or within PLUS OR MINUS 1 point. ("Table 11 indicates that there was about a 91% level of exact agreement *or agreement within one point*. p. 36") If you have only 4 possible scores you must have an exact match in order for there to be agreement, not within 1 point. In essence, the authors are saying that if someone gives a score of 1 and someone else scores it a 2, then they agreed or if someone scored it a 2 and someone else scored it a 3, then they agreed. Overall, the authors used bad statistics to prove the validity of the PACT. If you take out the PLUS OR MINUS 1, then the inter-rater agreement falls to 56%, which isn't much better than flipping a coin. At a minimum, these rubrics should have been taken back and redesigned for a better level of granularity in order to improve the scorer agreement.

References

Arne Duncan policy address at Teacher's College, Columbia University. Oct.22, 2009.http://www.tc.columbia.edu/news/article.htm?id=7195

Duncan-Andrade, J. (2009). Note to educators: Hope required when growing roses in concrete. *Harvard Educational Review, 79*(2), 181–194

Economic Policy Institute. (2010). *Problems with the use of student test scores to evaluate teachers.*

Okhremtchouk, I., Seiki, S., Gilliland, B., Ateh, C., Wallace, M., & Kato, A. (2009). Voices of preservice teachers: Perspectives on the performance assessment for California teachers (PACT). *Issues in Teacher Education, 18*(1), 39–62.

PACT Brochure: Teaching performance Assessment in California http://www.pacttpa.org/ _files/Main/CalTPAPromo-Teacher.pdf

PACT Technical Report. (March, 2007). Technical report of the performance assessment for California teachers (PACT): Summary of validity and reliability studies for the 2003–04. Pilot Year. Retrieved from http://www.pacttpa.org/_files/ Publications_and_Presentations/ PACT_Technical_Report_March07.pdf

Pecheone, R. L., & Chung, R. R. (2006). Evidence in teacher education. The performance assessment for California teachers (PACT). *Journal of Teacher Education. 57*(1 January/February), 22–36

Rennert-Ariev, P. (2008). The hidden curriculum of performance-based teacher education. *Teachers College Record, 110*(1), 105–138.

Sawchuck, S. (2010, August 30). State group piloting teacher prelicensing exam. *Education Week.* Retrieved from http://www.edweek.org/ew/articles/2010/09/01/021icense.h30.html?tkn =XXUF7/FBMWrH4vSr1NbtldI18sWORFzHK1el

Taubman, P. (2009).*Teaching by numbers.* New York: Routledge.

Wayne, A., Chang-Ross, C., Daniels, M., Knowles, K., Mitchell, K., & Price, T. (2004). *Exploring differences in minority and majority teachers' decisions about and preparation for NBPTS certification.* Arlington, VA: SRI International.

SECTION II

The Privatization and Corporatization of Public Schools

· 4 ·

Anti-Democratic Militaristic Education

An Overview and Critical Analysis of KIPP Schools

BRIAN LACK

Romanticizing School Reform

SEVERAL YEARS AGO, AS I WAS WATCHING TELEVISION ONE DAY, MY CURIOSITY WAS piqued by the sound of Anderson Cooper and Oprah Winfrey extolling "a radical new type of schooling" that had dramatically "turned students' lives around." This innovative approach, Cooper and Winfrey inferred, might finally provide the silver bullet that would forever fix a perennially miserable public school system. Was this, as Tyack and Cuban (1995) put it, just another shooting star reform destined to burn out in due time? Or were Cooper and Winfrey really on to something? What they revealed was certainly nothing new: a video clip of two highly-educated white men, claiming they had discovered the new fix for urban schools; a group of downtrodden, poor kids of color in school uniforms reciting their times tables aloud in chorus; and an extended school day and year buttressed by claims of extra homework assignments. In fact, the schools—Knowledge Is Power Program (best known as KIPP schools)—looked more like a military school than anything that remotely resembled a progressive pedagogical approach to teaching and learning. The TV segment went on to describe how KIPP schools differed from the typical public school, which I will attempt to summarize in the following sections.

An Overview of KIPP

As of 2009, a total of 82 KIPP schools (mostly middle schools, along with a few elementary and secondary schools) exist across 16 states and Washington D.C., reaching more than 21,000 students (KIPP Foundation, 2010a). "Beating the odds" has been the linchpin of KIPP schools' success thus far and is likely the primary reason for its widespread popularity in the U.S. Despite serving a high-poverty, high-minority student body, KIPP schools are apparently outperforming many public schools with similar student body characteristics. The KIPP Foundation claims that its schools cater to a more challenging student body than the typical urban public middle school, although this assertion has not been supported by empirical evidence. KIPP officials buttress this claim by pointing to demographic data. For instance, while African American and Hispanic students make up 70% of the student enrollment in urban public schools, KIPP serves a student population that is over 90% African-American and Hispanic. Sixty-three percent of students at the typical urban school receive free or reduced lunch; at KIPP schools nationwide, over 80% of the students have their lunches subsidized (Educational Policy Institute [EPI], 2005; KIPP Foundation, 2010b).

KIPP was conceived in 1994 by two Ivy League grads and former *Teach for America* protégés, David Levin and Michael Feinberg. While working in the Houston public school system, they grew flustered with "variables" that they felt stymied their pedagogical creativity and severely limited their ability to close the racial achievement gap. As subordinate-ranked classroom teachers, they felt their only viable option was entrepreneurship; so they worked hard to produce an educational concept that would alleviate the tensions of what they perceived to be the result of an over-centralized bureaucracy. Consequently, they came up with the blueprint for KIPP (Headden, 2006). While still wanting to deliver services exclusively to urban youths, Feinberg and Levin sought to redefine some of the basic programmatic regularities (Sarason, 1971) featured in most public schools by extending the instructional day in addition to holding classes on Saturdays and for three weeks during the summer—all without the traditional degree of oversight from the district central office. Based on the personal conviction that all children could achieve high academic success, they adopted a slogan that was consistent with this assumption: *No Excuses*. KIPP schools would operate on the ideology that "there are no shortcuts to success" (KIPP Foundation, 2010c). Given this mantra, KIPP would attempt to eliminate the variables that Levin and Feinberg perceived to be the major contributors to the academic failure of urban students—namely, lack of time, low expectations, compulsion, and bureaucracy.

Bureaucracy is often used as a pejorative term by school choice advocates who believe that hierarchical systems of governance are inherently inefficient (see Chubb & Moe, 1990). KIPP schools are governed by an open-enrollment organizational framework, meaning that KIPP schools are not accountable to teacher unions and the local school district in the same way that traditional public schools are. Principals have the flexibility to appropriate public funds the best way they see fit, choose from a wider range of curricular and instructional approaches, lengthen the school day and year, and hire and fire teachers with greater ease. As Michael Feinberg (2005) notes, this allows KIPP schools to stay lean on administrative staff and instead funnel more resources directly into classrooms.

Debate over the amount of time spent in school both daily and annually and its relationship with student achievement has abounded in recent decades. While students at a nearby regular public middle school begin classes at 9:20 A.M. and are out by 4 o'clock, at most KIPP schools, the instructional day begins at 7:30 A.M. and lasts until 5:00 P.M. Attendance is also compulsory on every other Saturday from 8:00 A.M. to 12:30 P.M., in addition to three weeks of full-day instruction in the summer. Altogether, KIPP students gain 62% more instructional time than their public school counterparts (KIPP Foundation, 2010c): Regular public school students (i.e., middle school students) spend approximately 1,200 hours in school each year; KIPP students are in school about 1,944 hours per year. Feinberg (2005) has likened the KIPP experience to students receiving 5 years worth of education in only 3 years. Also, teachers are "on-call" 24 hours a day, 7 days a week, and are provided with cell phones for students to contact them at will with questions about homework (Feinberg, 2000; Thernstrom & Thernstrom, 2003). Feinberg (2000) claims that it is not unusual for some students and teachers to stay at school until 9 o'clock at night.

Students and parents actively choose to enroll in KIPP schools rather than being assigned to a particular school by ZIP code, as done in conventional public schools. Admission is not extremely rigorous, at least in the academic sense. Students are accepted purely on the contractual agreement that they will embrace KIPP's *Five Pillars* of success (a point I will return to specifically in a later section), with the caveat that teachers can be fired and students can be disenrolled for failing to uphold the *Commitment to Excellence* contract (see Appendix for sample copy).

Teacher expectations about students' abilities have the potential to become self-fulfilling prophecies in student achievement outcomes (see Rosenthal & Jacobson, 1968). Students are held to "high expectations for academic achievement and conduct that make no excuses based on the students' backgrounds" (KIPP Foundation, 2010c). Moreover, "students, parents, teachers, and staff create and reinforce a culture of achievement and support through a range of formal and informal rewards and consequences for academic performance and behavior" (KIPP Foundation, 2010c). KIPP students are given 2 to 3 hours of homework each night, and can earn KIPP currency for working diligently. A unique characteristic of KIPP schools is that they openly subscribe to the mission of placing all students in post-secondary institutions of education. Classrooms are named after the college that the residing teacher attended. Graduating eighth graders are encouraged to join the *KIPP to College* alumni program, which provides ongoing support "to continue to use the scholarly habits, knowledge, and qualities of character learned at KIPP" (KIPP Foundation, 2010d).

For more specific information on KIPP Schools, visit their official website at http://www.kipp.org.[1]

Research on KIPP Achievement Results

Critics of KIPP are hard to find. Popular press accounts have dubbed KIPP the savior of a failing public education system. Since its inception, KIPP has received face-time on television shows like *60 Minutes, Oprah Winfrey,* and *PBS's Making Schools Work* in addition to garnering attention in high-profile media outlets like *U.S. News, People, Newsweek, Forbes,* and even *The New York Times* and *The Washington Post.* Students from KIPP Academy in Houston even made a national TV appearance at the 2000 GOP Convention (Hendrie, 2002). Since that same year, Doris and Donald Fisher of GAP, Inc. have donated more than $40 million, which helped to establish the KIPP Foundation, a non-profit organization whose purpose is to help train KIPP school leaders and replicate the schools nationwide (Duxbury, 2006). Although much criticism has been published about charter schools in general—the Edison Schools, in particular (see Saltman, 2005)—hardly any criticism of KIPP is available in extant literature (Saltman, personal communication, June 22, 2007), and very little peer-reviewed research on KIPP has been published over the 16 years since KIPP was founded (Henig, 2008; Macey, Decker, and Eckes, 2009).

Although only a handful of empirical studies on program effects have been published as of 2010, most have been generally favorable in terms of student achievement gains. The first study, commissioned by New American Schools (NAS)[2], surveyed 5th graders across three KIPP schools to determine their academic gains over one school year and compared them with annual gains of 5th graders enrolled in surrounding local public schools. Despite the authors' claim that "each school increased levels of academic achievement performance for students, regardless of background or label" (Doran & Drury, 2002, p. 27), KIPP students did not fare all that spectacularly across the board. For instance, 5th graders at 3D Academy in Houston scored only just as well as other similar students in the Houston Independent School District (HSID). One might reasonably presume that 62% more time in school would provide at least a slight advantage, but in this case it did not. The draw in achievement comparisons between KIPP and regular public schools isn't too disappointing until one considers that KIPP students spent nearly 750 more hours in school than their counterparts! Had they spent the same amount of time in school, would it not be safe to presume that the KIPP students would have been easily outperformed? Furthermore, claims that students from the KIPP DC/KEY Academy in Washington D.C. made greater achievement gains in math than any other middle or junior high school in the D.C. area were tempered by the use of a fall administration of the test to serve as a proxy for end-of-the-4th-grade-year achievement benchmarks. In other words, given the well-known tendency for student achievement to dip over the summer months while most kids are not in school, the KIPP students' Fall- 5th-grade test scores were most likely lower than their Spring-4th-grade test scores, which would predictably yield a higher difference in comparisons. In my review of the original study conducted by researchers from NAS (Doran & Drury, 2002), it was not evident that either the control or experimental group scores were statistically adjusted for this threat to validity. The point is that although KIPP students appear to do better in some cases, the jury is still out on its wholesale efficacy with respect to higher test scores.

Two additional studies offered more of the same results but with a significant degree of cautious optimism. Ross, McDonald, Alberg, Gallagher, and Calloway (2005) conducted a year-long mixed methods study on school climate and achievement outcomes at a KIPP school in Memphis and found that KIPP students demonstrated "significantly higher achievement" (p. 24) than control students on four out of six 5th grade tests. Again, these results are hardly laudable since KIPP students had much more time-on-task than the students in the control group. (I will expound on the issue of extended time in a later section of this paper.) In similar fashion, but with a much larger study sample, researchers from Educational Policy Institute (2005) found statistically significant gains across twenty-four 5th grade KIPP cohorts. Although KIPP students showed a "dramatic increase well above normal growth rates in reading, language, and mathematics" (p. 12), the study design had several limitations, including a lack of a control or matched comparison group and the use of aggregated school-level data.

An exhaustive study recently published by the Stanford Research Institute (SRI) raved of significant gains on standardized math and language arts tests made by 5th graders at a San Francisco Bay Area KIPP school (Woodworth, David, Guha, Wang, and Lopez-Torkos, 2008). The researchers used a rigorous design to compare performance on standardized tests between public-school 5th graders and KIPP 5th graders by matching KIPP and non-KIPP students based on demographic data, where they lived, and their 4th grade test scores. What the report fails to underscore is the likelihood that KIPP students may have differed significantly from their non-KIPP counterparts in ways that statistical analysis could not control for or capture. For instance, perhaps the parents of the KIPP students were more involved in supporting their children's education, or maybe the KIPP students were more motivated to adhere to school policies and expectations.

One of the prominent writers about KIPP is educational columnist Jay Mathews of *The Washington Post*. He has followed the development of KIPP schools for the last half-decade and seems to be unequivocally supportive of the movement. Despite his general affinity for KIPP, he has exposed some of the program's failures—not because he wishes to cast it in a negative light but rather, because of his attraction to the type of cut-throat accountability that KIPP espouses. In a recent article on KIPP, he highlights some of the less-than-stellar outcomes (which are conspicuously missing from the collection of press reports on the KIPP website):

> Most of the schools are showing healthy gains in nearly all grades, but some are not. KIPP LA Prep in Los Angeles reported a drop in reading from the 40th to the 39 [sic] percentile for sixth-graders in spring 2005. Sixth-graders that same year at the KIPP South Fulton Academy in Atlanta dropped from the 44th to the 38th percentile in reading, and sixth-graders at the KIPP Ascend Charter School in Chicago dropped from the 35th to the 34th percentile in reading. The KIPP Ujima Village Academy in Baltimore was significantly above the average scores for that city in reading, but its seventh-graders showed a drop from the 38th to the 33rd percentile on the Stanford 9 reading test in spring 2005. The KIPP Reach College Preparatory school looked

impressive when compared to the average for other public schools in Oklahoma City, but its seventh-grade's reading score dropped from the 63rd to the 43rd percentile in spring 2005 compared to what those same students did the previous spring....Two schools, the KIPP Chicago Youth Village Academy and Atlanta's KIPP Achieve Preparatory Academy, have had the right to use the KIPP name revoked effective at the end of this school year....there were many efforts to help them, but the Chicago school still "struggled with low enrollment and low reading scores relative to the district average" and the Atlanta school "struggled with financial reporting and viability and did not properly administer voluntary tests that would demonstrate growth over time." (Mathews, 2006, 24–28)

A Critical Analysis of KIPP

Radically Different? A Closer Look Inside KIPP Schools

David Tyack and Larry Cuban (1995) suggest that in spite of the incessant claims of radical change in education, reformers tend instead to merely tinker with the routines and regularities that have long stood the test of time. Public appeal of such regularities (e.g., teacher-centered instruction, testing, etc.) has as much to do with this constancy than most school reform critics are willing to concede (Cuban, 1993). Put another way, as Sarason (1971) prefers, "the more things change, the more they remain the same" (p. 58). Although Anderson Cooper's conception of the term *radical* is likely different than my own, as Jeffrey Mirel (2001) has observed, "break the mold" reform designs— in the vein of A.S. Neill's Summerhill School—are simply not congruent with hegemonic extramural forces (e.g., push toward national standards, prevalence of standardized testing, consumer demands, etc.). These compelling forces severely limit the degree of radical change reformers can embody in their approaches while retaining a substantial degree of appeal to potential consumers. Therefore, policy talk about radical change is often heavy on rhetoric but tenuous on actual promise.

Despite being celebrated as something starkly different from the norm, KIPP schools still have egg-crate classrooms bounded by walls, within which an adult teacher leads a group of younger students in daily lessons about reading, writing, and arithmetic. In my review of the literature on KIPP, I found only 3 studies that addressed the specific quality of instruction. The results across these sources were unanimous in describing teaching at KIPP as quite traditional. For instance, findings of an ethnographic study conducted by Ross et al.

(2005) of a KIPP school in Memphis revealed that the dominant instructional strategy was teacher centered, and that "team teaching, multi-age grouping, systematic individualized instruction, individual tutoring, parent/community involvement (in the classroom), sustained reading, independent inquiry, use of computers for instructional delivery, performance assessment, and student self-assessment were very rarely or never observed" (p. 21).

A two-year study conducted by Macey et al. (2009) sought to examine the strategies that KIPP schools utilize to promote academic achievement. After spending an undisclosed number of hours observing teachers across 3 separate KIPP sites, the researchers share only a limited narrative account of the quality of classroom instruction:

> Whether a KIPP student is in a morning reading classroom or in an afternoon math classroom, the lesson plans follow a similar structure. For instance, as soon as the students enter the class in KIPP Urban, they read "PDN," which stands for "please do now" and begin working on a task the teacher has organized to start the lesson. Also, the day's agenda, objectives, and homework assignment are typically visually available to the class. Every classroom we observed used a very similar approach. Furthermore, most lessons appear to be teacher-directed. The teacher asks questions of the students and the students respond briefly. (p. 234)

Likewise, Thompson, McDonald, and Sterbinsky (2005) discovered that KIPP teachers predominantly implemented direct instruction, lecture, and independent seatwork. There was minimal observation of student-centered strategies such as cooperative learning and student discussion, and the use of instructional technology by teachers and students was rarely observed. As a caveat, Thompson et al. state that the use of traditional teacher-centered forms of instruction was more prevalent among teachers who had "not fully bought into the KIPP program" (p. 28), suggesting that KIPP espouses modern, student-centered instructional approaches at least in theory. As a researcher with nearly 10 years of classroom teaching experience, I have encountered many teachers who advocate child-centered instructional practices in rhetoric but invariably engage in traditional methods of teaching behind closed classroom doors. The point to be taken away here is that very little empirical evidence exists that portrays KIPP teachers as innovative, child-centered practitioners, and in fact, the existing empirical evidence supports the conclusion that the content of KIPP schooling is no more innovative than what goes on in successful public schools (Macey et al., 2009). In short, KIPP may appear to be a radical approach on the surface because of its extended school day or its juxtaposition of school uniforms and poor neighborhoods, but in reality, it is bounded by rather conservative, traditional practices.

In spite of the shortage of KIPP's critics and the media's early tendency to sanctify its mission and romanticize its efficacy, the most troubling aspects of the movement have little to do with improved test scores. Thus far, the attention that KIPP has received in academia and the press has focused on achievement gains while ignoring the more dire sociopolitical concerns. According to Saltman (2005), however, this is not at all unusual. The tendency is for education experts to focus on flaws in research design or methodology at the expense of the more critical social implications. The widespread popularity of a "whatever works" mentality lures many scholars toward debates about efficacy in quantifiable terms (e.g., effect sizes, standard deviations, standard error) and away from the dangerous utilitarian assumption that schools exist to prepare workers for the economy. Put another way, placing value on achievement outcomes has become a reflexive tendency; thinking about underlying social and political ramifications has not. What little criticism of KIPP exists is generally representative of arguments proffered by typical charter school opponents. Primarily, KIPP schools have been criticized for only accepting the brightest and most motivated students (Mathews, 2005; Rothstein, 2004). Rothstein's (2004) accusation was based on the fact that of all the 5th grade students at a KIPP school in the Bronx, 41% entered at or above grade level in reading and 48% entered at or above grade level in math (which is not much different than the 50% one might expect, given a normal distribution). Because students choose to enroll in KIPP schools, Rothstein argues, they are a more motivated subsample than the general urban student population, hence the higher test scores.

Recently, KIPP schools have come under fire for alarming student attrition rates. Robelen (2007) reported that fewer than 50% of 5th graders who entered three San Francisco KIPP schools in 2003 were still enrolled in 2006–07. Even more drastic, a nearby KIPP school in Oakland only managed to retain about one-fourth of students from its 5th grade class of 2003. An analysis of the students who left these Bay Area campuses over this time period suggests that a majority were among the lowest-performing group of students, which would obviously provide a significant boost in longitudinal test-score comparisons (Woodworth et al., 2008). The researchers noted that about half of the exiting students in these schools left because of irreconcilable differences with KIPP policies, such as the extended school day, the strict disciplinary code, and KIPP's firm stance on conditions required for academic promotion. Others cited special needs that KIPP could not meet, such as learning disabilities or emotional/behavior disorders. Alex Molnar says it best: "To some advocates, KIPP is the savior of public education....If a large number [of students] don't stay, how can we say this is a model for public education?" (Robelen, 2007, p. 6).

Other critics bemoan a form of social Darwinism inextricably linked to the charter school ideology (see Wells, Lopez, Scott, & Holme, 1999). That is, only the academically advantaged or motivated students survive, while others are inevitably pushed out. In fact, KIPP's Commitment to Excellence contract is rather blunt about this in warning students that "failure to adhere to . . . [the contract] can cause me to lose various KIPP privileges and can lead to returning to my home school" (KIPP Foundation, 2010a). Critics often use such arguments in countering claims that charter schools offer a panacea to failing public schools and in suggesting that charter schools can never be taken to scale across the nation.

Examining the Goals of KIPP Schools

Neoliberal critiques of public education, in general, focus on the clash between market ideology and democracy. The fundamental question about education when applying a neoliberal analytical lens is simply put: can and should schools operate like corporations? Because the goals of education in the U.S. over the last 100 years have largely been driven by interests of *social mobility* (i.e., gaining educational credentials leads to social advantages) and *social efficiency* (i.e., training productive workers for bolstering the economy)—as opposed to *democratic equality* (i.e., producing good, critically conscious citizens)—an education like the one KIPP claims to offer can almost be characterized mostly as a private good (Labaree, 2000), that is to say, one that exists to: train workers for the economy, sort students based on compatibility with a set of dominant cultural values and perceived level of human capital, and emphasize the accumulation of educational credentials (e.g., diplomas, academic honors, college prep classes) over quality of learning. Because of this, the goals of education that public schools were essentially founded upon—namely, democratic equality—have taken a backseat.

> Much of what is most familiar and enduring in the American system of education can be traced to this goal: the neighborhood elementary school . . . populated by students from the entire community; whole-class instruction and social promotion; the stress on general over specialized education; and the emphasis on inclusion over separation of students (Labaree, 2000, p. 32).

The goal of democratic equality is certainly not at the forefront of KIPP's mission, especially given the fact that KIPP administrators hold the authority to jettison students from the school at will. Teaching all students regardless of background, behavior, or ability is not within the scope of the KIPP educational framework; that is solely for the public schools to address.

Based on narratives included in the current literature on KIPP schools, it's clear that KIPP is driven by social mobility and social efficiency goals as the remainder of this chapter will point out. The tension between democratic politics and capitalist markets that Labaree (2000) speaks of has been pronounced in the recent decades of education reform, and KIPP schools are certainly not insulated from this tension, as their mission is clearly driven by market ideals. KIPP's Pillars to Success are inherently undemocratic and smack of an individualistic orientation that ultimately rewards and punishes students to the extent that they themselves are willing and able to work hard to overcome the conditions of poverty. Moreover, the social climate at KIPP schools is imbued by a distinctly capitalistic and militaristic ideology. In short, KIPP's approach does little to address the plight of low-income students or alter the status quo.

The Five Pillars

KIPP schools are ideologically undergirded by five pillars, according to the KIPP Foundation (2010a): (1) *high expectations*, (2) *choice and commitment*, (3) *more time*, (4) *power to lead*, and (5) *focus on results*. The premise behind the pillars is that each component can and will offset the variables that lead to failure among poor minority students. Of these pillars, *focus on results* has been the focal point of debate about the effectiveness of the KIPP model, and as I have pointed out, the few studies that have examined this domain to date have generally portrayed KIPP schools favorably but have also been abated by empirical design flaws. It is also important to reiterate (especially to readers who are skeptical of using such measures as the sole arbiter of educational quality and performance) that *focus on results* is unabashedly defined by KIPP officials to mean the results of annual standardized test scores. The pillar I will turn attention to in the remainder of this chapter is "more time."

The Fallacy of "More Time"

One factor that most educators agree contributes to educational achievement (high and low) is the constrained resource of time (Lortie, 2002). Unsurprisingly, however, what no one can seem to form consensus on is exactly how much time is needed and how time should be spent. KIPP advocates clearly assume that the amount of time spent on instruction is highly correlated with higher standardized test scores. Some even claim that time spent working in general is a reflection of ethic and individual dedication, and the simplest way to assert one's position in the American social hierarchy. Joel Spring (2003) argues that virtue and moral character in a consumerist society such as the U.S. can be traced back to the principles of the 19th century Puritan work ethic. Unquestioned within this popular individualistic assumption is the idea that hard work is a reflection of moral excellence and invariably leads to social success. Thus, the easiest and most sensible way to explain poverty is to link it to poor work ethic or downright laziness. Ultra-conservative political critic Neal Boortz (1998) captures this ideology in claiming that the standard 40-hour work week is for "losers. . . . You don't see highly successful people clocking out of the office every afternoon at five. Losers drive home in traffic. Winners drive home in the dark." (p. 49). (*I wonder if it has ever occurred to Boortz that, first and foremost, highly successful people do not clock in or out.*) KIPP's co-founders clearly believe in this dictum. In a PBS interview with Hedrick Smith, Mike Feinberg's words on the rationale behind an extended school day hold an eerie resemblance to those of Boortz:

> Every single school in this country has a teacher car in the parking lot at seven o'clock in the morning and that car is still there at five, six o'clock in the evening. What's different at KIPP is that all the cars are there at seven in the morning and all the cars are there at five o'clock in the afternoon (Feinberg, 2005, ¶72–73).

The question that appeals to most, however, is not a political one but a question of science. In short, does more time equal higher test scores? The concept of more time equating to more learning is a dangerous assumption that perhaps John Goodlad (2004) summed best:

> If our interest is in quality educational experiences, we must not stop with providing only time. I would always choose fewer hours well used over more hours of engagement with sterile activities. Increasing . . . [time] will in fact be counterproductive unless there is, simultaneously, marked improvement in how this time is used. (p. 283)

Using Goodlad's reasoning, I would argue that more time spent in a school that promotes undemocratic practices such as militaristic discipline, pro-consumerism, and authoritarian modes of instruction (all of which I address in subsequent sections) is actually worse for students, especially with regard to the democratic goals of education.

Another time-related concern is the caution of teacher burnout associated with extended work hours, which is also related to the practical question, Who will be willing to teach in such schools? One of the most consistent findings about why people choose education as a profession is because of the teacher's work schedule (i.e., summers and weekends off, early daily release time) and its conduciveness to raising children and spending time at home with family (Lortie, 2002). In fact, according to Feinberg (2005), the average KIPP teacher has only 3 to 6 years of teaching experience and has no children at home. Most KIPP teachers are in their 20s or 30s and are single (Macey et al., 2009). Moreover, given the grim numbers on teacher attrition in the traditional public school settings where teachers are only required to work about 7 to 8 hours a day, (see Darling-Hammond, 2003), one can only wonder how long the average KIPP teacher stays in teaching. Can not the same logic that Feinberg applies to students getting 5 academic years of education in only 3 years be applied to teachers feeling as if they've put in 5 years of work in only 3 years' time? Moreover, although KIPP teachers are compensated an extra 15 to 20% in annual salary (keeping in mind that KIPP schools operate 62% longer each year than traditional public schools), how fair is it that they only amass up to 3.6 years worth of salary over 5 years of working time?

Lost on all the policy discussion of whether more time-on-task is a practical solution to the achievement gap are the voices of the KIPP students who spend almost two-thirds more time in school than traditional students. The tendency for press accounts and research studies to totally whitewash the students' feelings about the protracted time in school is disturbing: Ross et al. (2005) merely dedicate two sentences to students' perspectives in their 43-page report on school climate outcomes:

> When asked if it was easy or hard to adjust to the differences between KIPP and their previous school, several students mentioned getting out of school at 5:00 P.M. as a difficult adjustment . . . most students appeared to view the extended hours as a standard part of KIPP. . . (p. 15)

While it is hard to argue that students should spend less time studying than they typically do (see Steinberg, 1996), asking poor students of color to put in 62% more time in a school like KIPP is simply more vexing upon closer inspection of the social climate that permeates KIPP's walls.

Militaristic Discipline

The parlance of war is not new to education. Most visible to this day is the neoliberal treatment of the manufactured school crisis in *A Nation at Risk* (1983), which unabashedly adopted militaristic phrases like "educational disarmament," "unfriendly foreign power," and "act of war." According to Finley (2003), militarism further penetrates the academic structure of schools, as evident by the current push for standardization, tracking, rote and prescriptive learning, tougher academic requirements, additional courses and longer school days and years. Militaristic discipline has essentially become entrenched in the mainstream practices of behavior management. Immediately coming to mind is the image of Arnold Schwarzenegger in *Kindergarten Cop*, who portrays a cop-turned-substitute-teacher who finds out rather quickly that the easiest way to manage a class of twenty unruly 5-year olds is to assume the role of a didactic drill sergeant. Even though they cater mostly to middle-school students, KIPP schools espouse a strikingly similar approach.

At a KIPP school I visited in 2005, it was not unusual to see students lined up against the walls of the hallway like soldiers while being lambasted by an angry teacher. Students who violate behavioral expectations, as referred to in the Commitment to Excellence contract, are stripped of the right to wear their KIPP shirts. (Other KIPP schools have sanctioned students by forcing them to wear their KIPP shirts inside-out all day long [Thernstrom & Thernstrom, 2003].) Miscreants are routinely sent to a time-out area better known as "the bench" or "the dugout" (Ross et al., 2005). Even though such practices have been thoroughly shunned by developmental psychologists such as William Glasser (1998) and Becky Bailey (2000), KIPP proponents utilize a "whatever works" mentality to the ends of compliance and academic achievement. Interesting and somewhat ironic, however, is the tendency for KIPP supporters to evade the negative connotation that comes with the militaristic characterization of KIPP schools. No one euphemizes KIPP's harsh tactics better than co-founder Mike Feinberg (2000), who was confronted on this very topic during a radio interview by *The Connection's* Christopher Lydon. Particularly interesting are Lydon's use of the term "militaristic" in describing the social climate in KIPP schools and Feinberg's knee-jerk reaction to temper the negative connotation of that term:

> Lydon: KIPP sounds more like a military school than the typical public or private school. Their idea is a highly structured curriculum, conduct codes, a long school day— nine and a half hours—and rigorous disciplinary standards: students caught misbehav-

ing have to wear their KIPP T-shirts inside out; girls can't wear makeup; boys can't wear hats; KIPPsters rap their multiplication tables and they chant slogans on the playground...

Feinberg: It's interesting that you use the word 'military' because, we don't, you know, it paints a picture that I don't think is quite accurate. If you go to KIPP right now, you walk around and see 323 children all with big smiles on their faces. . . .I would say that the school mirrors what happens in most families' homes and what happens out there in life. And that is that there are expectations that are put forth to the children: When they do the right thing, good things happen; when they do the wrong thing, there are consequences. . .in public education, we could easily create a bubble where everything is fair, where kids artificially are pumped up with self-esteem. . .where everything is on an equal level, but that is not what happens as we know out there when it is time to apply to college or time to get a job out there in the real world. . .we're trying to prepare our kids to be able to be contributing members in our society.

In one of the few qualitative studies conducted thus far, Ross et al. (2005) found that students rated the harsh disciplinary features as the worst thing about KIPP. Another qualitative study conducted by Thompson et al. (2005) describes students' dissatisfaction with the extended instructional day, especially when "they knew that other children were out playing" (p. 30) while they were still in school. The authors also provide a narrative account of a student who transferred to KIPP from a local public school and subsequently "found KIPP policies rather restrictive as she did not have as many opportunities to make choices" (p. 30). It is important to point out that "choice" is certainly a hallmark of democracy, but KIPP schools primarily boast choice only in a market-driven sense (i.e., choosing private over public, not a student choosing what or how she wants to learn). Moreover, by consenting to the notion that the school should mirror the existing power relations of the larger society, Feinberg candidly condones the existing social inequalities and the maintenance of the status quo.

Although shrouded by claims that all KIPPsters will attend post-secondary education, it seems as though preparation for subordinate jobs may be the real mission behind KIPP. Saltman (2003) distinguishes between the two forms of militarized schooling in American: the more explicit *military education* and the more institutional *education as enforcement*. According to Saltman, education as enforcement is the result of corporate globalization, which is driven by neoliberal pursuit of market values through practices such as scripting, standardizing, accountability, and testing (all of which are only enforceable through compliance). KIPP officials openly embrace these values and, like most schools in general, are clearly dedicated to a brand of efficiency that reduces basic human processes like learning and decision-making to tightly controlled and highly regulated activities. Any pretense of freedom is effectively surrendered for the sake of docility and social control. But, again, Feinberg is impeccable when it comes to rationalizing and sugar-coating KIPP's harsh disciplinary approach: As he once stated in an interview, "I suppose some people think that KIPP is like the Army; that's their perspective. But I think as you spend some time here at our schools, you sense a whole lot of joy beyond the structure and discipline."

Although KIPP schools may masquerade as democratic institutions or schools of "choice," by reinforcing student obedience and conformity, its rigid disciplinary practices are clearly a means of preparing students for "participation in social, bureaucratic, and industrial organizations" (Cuban, 1993, p. 250). And because KIPP serves a predominantly low-income, minority population, claims of racism and classism are not far-fetched. To help bolster this point, Brown (2003) argues that while a culture of privilege and freedom pervades the schools of the wealthy, a culture of discipline and militarism suffuses the schools of color and the poor. Put differently, what would middle-class white suburbanites think about their children being placed on the bench during field trips or having to wear their shirts inside out all day long for not completing homework assignments? This is not to treat the disparate cultures of suburban and urban families monolithically but simply to underscore the implicit inequity of describing coercion and humiliation as "what works" for one group but as outlandishly inappropriate for another. What works may be just another form of institutional racism and systematic stratification: "The ascendant culture of militarism in poor schools of color hearkens back to the legal and extralegal forms of coercion used by the early advocates and opponents of public education, imbued with the warning, 'Stay in your place'" (Brown, 2003, p. 138).

Capitalism and Consumerism at KIPP

A key aspect of indoctrinating and controlling students is also teaching them how to be good consumers, and KIPP officials make no attempt to hide the fact that they intend to run schools like mini-consumerist societies:

> There are weekly paychecks in KIPP dollars that reflect such qualities as attendance, promptness, organization, and neatness, hard work, behavior outside of class, and the

respect given to other "teammates." Checks. . .can be used to purchase school supplies and other items in the KIPP store. Those whose paychecks maintain a certain average are eligible for trips to places like Utah, California, and Washington, D.C. (Thernstrom & Thernstrom, 2003, p. 72).

As Molnar (2005) argues, this conveys to children unequivocally that the good life is only possible through consumption and that working hard to purchase more is a sure-fire route to goodness and happiness. The implicit danger of this ideology is intensified when extended to low-income groups, simply because they have less of what it takes to consume (money and power). Sadly, in such cases, as Joel Spring (2003) argues, equality of opportunity to succeed and be happy has become conflated with equality of opportunity to consume. Simply put, the principles that undergird a militaristic approach are at the foundation of anti-democratic forms of education.

No Excuses (for Institutional Classism and Racism)

At first glance, KIPP's vehement defense of a zero-tolerance, no-excuses-approach to academic success may seem unassailable on moral grounds. After all, like the majority of schools in the U.S., KIPP embraces meritocratic ideals and thus aims to inculcate students with abilities, values and beliefs that will potentially position them for success in a market-based capitalist social and economic system. KIPP teachers and administrators are certainly not unique in the fact that they expect all students to maximize their educational production in spite of any impeding external factors such as the general lack of support from parents at home or students' own lack of motivation to participate in classroom activities or complete assignments. Schools claim to give all students equal opportunity to be educated and to demonstrate mastery of educational goals—should some fail to do so, it's merely a function of lack of will, either on the part of students alone or students and parents together. In the end, students that work the hardest, achieve the highest, and overcome any barriers that threaten their individual educational production are the ones who deserve the opportunity to assert themselves among the highest social and economic stratum. Choice, among several other conditions, has a profound impact on success, according to the ideology of meritocracy in an equal opportunity system. Proponents of neoliberal educational policies extend this assumption by arguing that when an individual's freedom to choose is maximized, and competition and accountability are required, schools will educate better and students will learn more. In this regard, KIPP does not necessarily stand out from the majority of American public schools. A critical inspection of the KIPP movement, however, reveals its deleterious underlying assumptions. Essentially, each of KIPP's Pillars to success convey the message to urban students that failure in this society will solely be a reflection of not working long and hard enough, or mere complicity with rules set and enforced by authority figures.

Moreover, contradictory notions of "choice" proffered by charter schools like KIPP convey to students that choice is virtuous only in the market-driven sense, so long as it complies with the policies and expectations of those who hold authority. For instance, students can "choose" a KIPP school over their local public school, but when it comes to choosing what to wear to school, that is not a privilege afforded to students. Regarding school uniforms, Saltman (2000) elaborates on this:

> The widespread use of uniforms in public schools to protect children from competition and choice is happening simultaneously with increasing calls for school choice. This means that even as consumerism and competition are seen as saving schools (choice), they are also understood as dangerous for students (students competing over clothing). This contradiction belies the fact that the uniforms function symbolically to suggest that the problems of public schooling derive from a lack of student discipline instead of from unequal distribution of resources in schools and communities . . . [and] that the problems themselves derive not from market-driven injustices but from individual lack and cultures of pathology and deviancy. (p. 96)

Essentially, Saltman agrees that deficit notions lay the foundation for critics who malign public education and "at-risk" children—the idea that schools are broken because individuals who patronize them are incompetent and incorrigible—while the true sources of social problems and poorly performing public schools, the unequal distribution of resources in schools and society, are equivocally couched in the principles of individualism and free will, and therefore appear as problems that can be solved by capitalistic values such as motivation, morality, competition, work ethic, and individual resilience. By signaling to those who are systematically oppressed that to escape from poverty depends solely on their willingness to embrace pro-capitalist, pro-consumer values, the true sources of social stratification remain unaddressed and are simply whitewashed as the direct result of shunning pro-capitalist values. By circumventing the causes of social inequalities and enforcing militaristic and capitalistic values upon marginalized students, KIPP schools do little to challenge subtle but nevertheless substantial forms of institutional racism and classism.

Conclusion

Summary

In spite of its ostensibly noble goals of closing the racial achievement gap and sending all of its students to college, the KIPP movement is inherently unde- mocratic because of its unabashed endorsement of capitalistic and militaristic values. While freedom and choice are important ideals associated with the American liberal tradition, the degree to which both are distributed among the citizens of this country is visibly inequitable. Choice for KIPP students is inex- tricably linked to their ability and willingness to comply with the Five Pillars and the Commitment to Excellence—both of which embody pro-capitalist ideals. Put differently, those who can't handle the "choice" to leave their zoned public middle school are driven out of KIPP because either they can't uphold the contract or because they simply decide that 62% more school time, two to three hours of busywork nightly, and the militaristic social climate are just not for them. As hopes continue to resonate that KIPP will eventually be taken to scale (in 2006, KIPP CEO Richard Barth—who incidentally is married to founder and president of Teach for America, Wendy Kopp—cited a goal of more than 100 KIPP schools and 25,000 students by the year 2011 (Robelen, 2006)), the encouraging fact is that KIPP remains only a boutique movement among the mainstream.

Implications

Ironically enough, the potential demise of KIPP might be a direct result of its pervasive capitalistic and militaristic influences: Since its inception in 1994, a majority of KIPP's total funding has come from private sources (Duxbury, 2006). Perhaps as KIPP attempts to replicate its vision nationwide, its added visibility will be accompanied by a more thoughtful and balanced critique of its mission and means of achieving that mission. In a society that is strongly built upon capitalistic and militaristic ideals, however, it is not likely that KIPP and other market-based alternatives to conventional public education will dissipate anytime soon unless the discourse about neoliberal policies that endorse such ideals are put up for public debate. Scholars and laypeople alike must seek to move these debates beyond the walls of the ivory tower, profes- sional research conferences, and academic journals, and into mainstream media. Those who support a democratic approach to schooling must seek out ways to amplify their voices, not through obscure outlets like conference presentations but in popular arenas like local, state, and federal legislative bodies, local school board meetings, editorials in the local and national newspapers and other media sources, etc. Likewise, policymakers and those who wish to reform policy must fully examine the greater social, political, and economic contexts in which struggling public schools are situated in order to make substantial attempts at bringing about positive change. As the old adage goes, it takes a village to raise a child; it's the village that deserves critical attention, not merely the school.

We would also do well to educate our potential teacher candidates about the harms of neoliberal educational policies and foster democratic practices and critique in our teacher education programs. This does not require indoctrination into leftist ideology, as many conservative critics might claim (see Gollnick, 2008) but rather a democratic approach to teaching that will ultimately make teacher candidates responsible for reflecting deeply on the social and moral implications of what and how they teach (Zeichner and Liston, 1987). Moreover, teacher education programs must realize that their responsibility for teacher education does not end with the conferring of a degree or certificate at the conclusion of a program. Teacher educators need to maintain a level of continuous, hands-on support for graduating teachers who wish to promote democratic education beliefs and practices and offer counter-narratives to those who seek to infuse market ideology into the domain of public schooling.

Notes

1. The main webpage allows you access detailed information about KIPP teaching and learning, school leadership, and general information, such as historical narratives, the Five Pillars, the KIPP Foundation, frequently asked questions, and research reports on the success of KIPP schools across the U.S. From this main site, you can also link to any of the 82 KIPP school websites.
2. New American Schools was a private non-profit organization that coalesced around the goal of improving public school performance by using "scientific research." NAS was spearheaded mostly by CEOs and other corporate representatives from Fortune 500 companies who invested in researching and developing what would later become known as "Comprehensive School Reform" designs. The No Child Left Behind Act of 2001 would later tie federal funding to low-performing schools for adopting and implementing these designs. As of 2010, the overall efficacy of Comprehensive School Reform models is generally considered inconclusive. For an excellent account of the development of NAS and notable CSR designs, see Mirel (2001). For a review of research on CSR designs, see Borman, Hewes, Overman, and Brown (2002).

References

Bailey, B. A. (2000). *Easy to love, difficult to discipline: The 7 basic skills for turning conflict into cooperation*. New York: HarperCollins.

Borman, G. D., Hewes, G. M., Overman, L. T., & Brown, S. (2002). Comprehensive school reform and achievement: A meta-analysis. Center for Research on the Education of Students Placed At-Risk (CRESPAR). Washington DC. Retrieved from http://www.csos.jhu.edu/CRESPAR/techReports/*Report59*.pdf

Boortz, N. (1998). *The terrible truth about liberals*. Atlanta, GA: Longstreet.

Brosio, R. A. (1994). *A radical democratic critique of capitalist education*. New York: Peter Lang.

Brown, E. R. (2003). Freedom for some, discipline for 'others': The structure of inequity in education. In K. J. Saltman & D. A. Gabbard (Eds.), *Education as enforcement: The militarization and corporatization of schools*. New York: RoutledgeFalmer.

Chubb, J. E., & Moe, T. M. (1990). *Politics, markets, and America's schools*. Washington DC: The Brookings Institution.

Cuban, L. (1993). *How teachers taught: Constancy and change in American classrooms, 1890–1990* (2nd ed.). New York: Teachers College.

Darling-Hammond, L. (2003). Keeping good teachers. *Educational Leadership, 60*(80), 6–14.

Doran, H. C., & Drury, D. W. (2002, October). Evaluating success: KIPP educational program evaluation. Washington DC: New American Schools. Retrieved from http://www.naschools.org/uploadedfiles/Microsoft%20Word%-%20KIPP%20Final%20Technical%20Report%2010.21.02%20_no%20embargo_.pdf

Duxbury, S. (2006, March 20). Charter mission: Don Fisher kicks $40M into KIPP schools. *San Francisco Business Times*. Retrieved from http://www.kipp.org/pressdetail.cfm?a=237&pageid=nav7b

Educational Policy Institute. (2005, August). Focus on results: An academic impact analysis of the Knowledge is Power Program (KIPP). Retrieved from http://www.educationalpolicy.org/pdf/KIPP.pdf

Feinberg, M. (2000). Interview with Christopher Lydon on September 11, 2000. [Streaming digital audio file retrieved from http://www.theconnection.org/shows/2000/09/20000911_b_main.asp]

Feinberg, M. (2005). Interview with Hedrick Smith (n. d.). Retrieved from http://www.pbs.org/makingschoolswork/sbs/kipp/feinberg.html

Finley, L. L. (2003). Militarism goes to school. *Essays in Education*, 4. Retrieved from http://www.usca.edu/essays/v0142003/finley.pdf

Glasser, W. (1998). *The quality school: Managing students without coercion* (3rd ed.). New York: HarperCollins.

Gollnick, D. (2008). Teacher capacity for diversity. In M. Cochran-Smith, S. Feiman-Nemser, D. J. McIntyre, & K. E. Demers (Eds.), *Handbook of research on teacher education: Enduring questions in changing contexts* (pp. 249–257). New York: Routledge

Goodlad, J. I. (2004). *A place called school* (20th anniversary ed.). New York: McGraw-Hill.

Headden, S. (2006, February 20). Two guys. . .and a dream. *U.S. News & World Report*. Retrieved from http://www.usnews.com/usnews/biztech/articles/060220/20leaders.htm

Hendrie, C. (2002, October 30). KIPP looks to recreate school success stories [Electronic version]. *Education Week*, 22(9), 6–11. Retrieved from http://www.edweek.org/ew/articles/2002/10/30/09kipp.h22.html

Henig, J. (2008). *What do we know about the outcomes at KIPP schools?* East Lansing, MI: Great Lakes Center for Education Research and Practice.

KIPP Foundation. (2010a). KIPP Schools. Retrieved from http://www.kipp.org/schools

KIPP Foundation. (2010b). About KIPP. Retrieved from http://www.kipp.org/about-kipp

KIPP Foundation. (2010c). KIPP Five Pillars. Retrieved from http://www.kipp.org/about-kipp/five-pillars

KIPP Foundation. (2010d). KIPP through college. Retrieved from http://www.kipp.org/students/kipp-through-college

Labaree, D. F. (2000). Resisting educational standards. *Phi Delta Kappa, 82*(1), 28–33.

Lortie, D. (2002). *Schoolteacher: A sociological study* (2nd ed.). Chicago: University of Chicago Press.

Macey, E., Decker, J., & Eckes, S. (2009). The knowledge is power program (KIPP): An analysis of one model's efforts to promote achievement in underserved communities. *Journal of School Choice, 3*, 212–241.

Mathews, J. (2004, August 24). School of hard choices. *The Washington Post*. Retrieved from http://www.washingtonpost.com/wp-dyn/articles/A27438–2004Aug23.html

Mathews, J. (2005, March 29). Assessing the KIPP schools—a new perspective. *The Washington Post*. Retrieved from http://www.washingtonpost.com/wp-dyn/articles/A9576–2005Mar29.html

Mathews, J. (2006, January 17). America's best schools? *The Washington Post*. Retrieved from http://www.washingtonpost.com/wp-dyn/content/article/2006/01/17/AR2006011700445_pf.html

Mirel, J. (2001). *The evolution of the New American Schools: From revolution to mainstream.* Washington DC: Thomas B. Fordham Foundation. Retrieved from http://www.edexcellence.net/doc/evolution.pdf

Molnar, A. (2005). *School commercialism: From democratic ideal to market commodity.* New York: Routledge.

Robelen, E. W. (2006, April 19). KIPP schools shift strategy for scaling up. *Education Week, 25*(31), 1, 19.

Robelen, E. W. (2007, June 13). KIPP student attrition patterns eyed. *Education Week, 26*(41), 1, 16.

Rosenthal, R., & Jacobson, L. (1968). *Pygmalion in the classroom.* New York: Rinehart & Winston.

Ross, S. M., McDonald, A. J., Alberg, M., Gallagher, B. M., & Calloway, F. (2005, April). Urban school reform: Achievement and school climate outcomes for the Knowledge Is Power program. Paper presented at the meeting of the American Educational Research Association, Montreal, Canada.

Rothstein, R. (2004). *Class and schools: Using social, economic, and educational reform to close the Black–White achievement gap.* Washington DC: Economic Policy Institute.

Saltman, K. J. (2000). *Collateral damage: Corporatizing public schools—a threat to democracy.* Lanham, MD: Rowman & Littlefield.

Saltman, K. J. (2003). Introduction. In K. J. Saltman & D. A. Gabbard (Eds.), *Education as enforcement: The militarization and corporatization of schools.* New York: Routledge.

Saltman, K. J. (2005). *The Edison Schools: Corporate schooling and the assault on public education*. New York: Routledge.

Sarason, S. B. (1971). *The culture of the school and the problem of change*. Boston, MA: Allyn & Bacon.

Spring, J. (2003). *Educating the consumer citizen: A history of the marriage of schools, advertising, and media*. Mahwah, NJ: Lawrence Erlbaum.

Steinberg, L. (1996). *Beyond the classroom: Why school reform has failed and what parents need to do*. New York: Touchstone.

Thernstrom, A., & Thernstrom, S. (2003). *No excuses: Closing the racial gap in learning*. New York: Simon & Schuster.

Thompson, S., McDonald, A., & Sterbinsky, A. (2005, October). KIPP DIAMOND Academy: Year 3 (2004–2005) evaluation report. Center for Research in Educational Policy, Memphis, TN: University of Memphis.

Tyack, D., & Cuban, L. (1995). *Tinkering toward utopia: A century of public school reform*. Cambridge MA: Harvard University Press.

Wells, A. S., Lopez, A., Scott, J., & Holme, J. J. (1999). Charter schools as post-modern paradox: Rethinking social stratification in an age of deregulated school choice. *Harvard Educational Review*, 69(2), 172–204.

Woodworth, K. R., David, J. L., Guha, R., Wang, H., & Lopez-Torkos, A. (2008). San Francisco Bay area KIPP schools: A study of early implementation and achievement. Final report. Menlo Park, CA: SRI International. Retrieved from http://policyweb.sri.com/cep/publications/SRI_ReportBayAreaKIPPSchools_Final.pdf

Zeichner, K., & Liston, D. (1987). Teaching student teachers to reflect. *Harvard Educational Review*, 57, 23–48.

Appendix:
Sample Commitment to Excellence Contract

TEACHERS' COMMITMENT

We fully commit to KIPP in the following ways:

~ We will arrive at KIPP every day by 7:15 A.M. (Monday–Friday).

~ We will remain at KIPP until 5:00 P.M. (Monday–Thursday) and 4:00 P.M. on Friday.

~ We will come to KIPP on appropriate Saturdays at 9:15 A.M. and remain until 1:05 P.M.

~ We will teach at KIPP during the summer.

~ We will always teach in the best way we know how and we will do whatever it takes for our students to learn.

~ We will always make ourselves available to students and parents, and address any concerns they might have.

~ We will always protect the safety, interests, and rights of all individuals in the classroom.

~ Failure to adhere to these commitments can lead to our removal from KIPP.

X _____

Please print name(s) here.

PARENTS'/GUARDIANS' COMMITMENT

We fully commit to KIPP in the following ways:

~ We will make sure our child arrives at KIPP every day by 7:25 A.M. (Monday–Friday) or boards a KIPP bus at the scheduled time.

~ We will make arrangements so our child can remain at KIPP until 5:00 P.M. (Monday–Thursday) and 4:00 P.M. on Friday.

~ We will make arrangements for our child to come to KIPP on appropriate Saturdays at 9:15 A.M. and remain until 1:05 P.M.

~ We will ensure that our child attends KIPP summer school.

~ We will always help our child in the best way we know how and we will do whatever it takes for him/her to learn. This also means that we will check our child's homework every night, let him/her call the teacher if there is a problem with the homework, and try to read with him/her every night.

~ We will always make ourselves available to our children and the school, and address any concerns they might have. This also means that if our child is going to miss school, we will notify the teacher as soon as possible, and we will carefully read any and all papers that the school sends home to us.

~ We will allow our child to go on KIPP field trips.

~ We will make sure our child follows the KIPP dress code.

~ We understand that our child must follow the KIPP rules so as to protect the safety, interests, and rights of all individuals in the classroom. We, not the school, are responsible for the behavior and actions of our child.

~ Failure to adhere to these commitments can cause my child to lose various KIPP privileges and can lead to my child returning to his/her home school.

X _____

Please print name(s) here.

STUDENT'S COMMITMENT

I fully commit to KIPP in the following ways:

~ I will arrive at KIPP every day by 7:25 A.M. (Monday–Friday) or board a KIPP bus at the correct time.

~ I will remain at KIPP until 5:00 P.M. (Monday–Thursday) and 4:00 P.M. on Friday.

~ I will come to KIPP on appropriate Saturdays at 9:15 A.M. and remain until 1:05 P.M.

~ I will attend KIPP during summer school.

~ I will always work, think, and behave in the best way I know how, and I will do whatever it takes for me and my fellow students to learn. This also means that I will complete all my homework every night, I will call my teachers if I have a problem with the homework or a problem with coming to school, and I will raise my hand and ask questions in class if I do not understand something.

~ I will always make myself available to parents and teachers, and address any concerns they might have. If I make a mistake, this means:

~ I will tell the truth to my teachers and accept responsibility for my actions.

~ I will always behave so as to protect the safety, interests, and rights of all individuals in the classroom. This also means that I will always listen to all my KIPP teammates and give everyone my respect.

~ I will follow the KIPP dress code.

I am responsible for my own behavior, and I will follow the teachers' directions.

Failure to adhere to these commitments can cause me to lose various KIPP privileges and can lead to returning to my home school.

X_____

    Please print name here.

· 5 ·

Exposing the Myths
of the Corporate City

Popular Education and Political
Activism in Atlanta

Richard Lakes, Paul McLennan, Jennifer Sauer & Mary Anne Smith

Education policymakers embrace a globalization rhetoric which claims ratcheting up academic standards will ensure that future workers can compete in a high-performance and information-saturated workplace. What has resulted is a college-for-all reform movement of public education that assumes students will be deemed job-ready, able to assume their rightful places in the global economy. Yet the labor market does not have the capacity to create an abundance of knowledge worker jobs that offer quality benefits and high pay for all. Class inequalities in America play out in sociocultural and educational life. Those who have access to a comfortable middle-class lifestyle likely will succeed in a meritocratic, globalized society. They have engendered the entrepreneurial values of individualism, responsibilization, commodification, and self-governance (Harvey, 2005). Impoverished young people, on the other hand, do not have advantages to make their way in this new social order fluidly. Failure to accumulate credentials and a portfolio and to pass standardized tests and high-stakes assessments are major impediments to their success nowadays. Many will succumb to the false promises from our political leaders that the starting line in a race to the top is uniform and even.

Globalization has enriched a few at the expense of many by creating one powerful ruling class, according to Robinson (2004, p. 48); they are a transnational managerial elite "based in the centers of world capitalism" and "at the apex of the global economy" that "exercises authority over global institutions, and controls the levers of global policymaking." For instance, the outsourcing to a variety of firms in rebuilding Iraq was conducted without proper bidding protocol, and sweetheart deals with these no-bid contractors have filled the pockets of Bechtel and Haliburton company stockholders (Saltman, 2007, p. 70). Democracy is further undermined when corporations refuse to honor collective bargaining and union agreements that have provided generations of the working classes a living wage with health benefits and promises of financial security.

The corporate model of operating institutions with a bottom line for profit margins and efficiency has influenced the way education goes about its daily business. In 1999 the public schools in Chicago turned to Sodexho Marriott as the sole food service provider as the school board consented to relinquish supervision of nutritional and dietary needs (Westbrook, 2008). Corporatization has narrowed curricular opportunity, too, under what Lipman (2004, p. 41) claimed are "new forms of educational differentiation." The spatial location of school reforms in Chicago was based upon newer gentrification patterns in the city. The wealthiest neighborhoods on the North and East sides showed the greatest numbers of innovative, challenging academic programs. Residents in the lower-income African American and Latino neighborhoods on the South and West sides of the city featured traditional lower-track offerings, basic skills literacy, and military academies. These working class neighborhoods were targeted for restructuring as charters, sanctioned by a mayoral plan endorsed by civic leaders titled Renaissance 2010, that proposes to close the large number of so-called failing schools as defined by the No Child Left Behind Act (NCLB).

Corporate privatizing schemes have resulted in termination of many unionized teaching and non-teaching personnel and support staff. After the Hurricane Katrina flood waters receded, the state of Louisiana seized the New Orleans public schools and fired all district employees, then rehired a smaller corps of teachers and staff and reopened a limited number of the schools as charters. With limited access to schooling for the poor, the recovery plan was "dictated by the urban cleansing dreams of an economic and racial elite," according to Saltman (2007), who noted, "now that the storm has done the clear-cutting, the dream of the field of economic competition can be built" (p. 60).

Hyper-accountability in the field of education requires removal of all perceived obstructions to top-down administration, such as associations with labor's historic base and teacher or staff unions—any sense of collectivity to weaken each stakeholder's input with the exception of business interests. In the current governance regime of free-market capitalists, social solidarities once openly voiced are a threat to those in control. That is why powerbrokers deeply resent unions in particular and the rank and file who engender what is considered dangerous family-like interest over mutual cares and related concerns. In this chapter, we advance the idea of popular education and political activism devoted to fighting back against the corporatization of Atlanta and its schools. We highlight the work of Atlanta Jobs with Justice, a chapter of the national Jobs with Justice, and the Atlanta Public Education Network, now called Metro Atlantans for Public Schools (MAPS). Atlanta Jobs with Justice (AJwJ) is committed to organizing against the privatization of municipal services and public institutions as well as building coalitions of labor and community groups in campaigns for workers' rights (Early & Cohen, 1994). AJwJ was founded in 1988 as a committee of the Atlanta Labor Council and, since 2002, has been engaged in local struggles with a wider social vision—a grassroots strategy that takes into account the intersectionality of oppressions and multiple issues in peoples' lives. The foundation for its good work and programs is based upon the belief that government exists to help people exercise their human rights. They believe the profit motive or market operations with their inherent injustice have no place in government or the public sector. MAPS is a more recent formation of local educators and others interested in defending public education and developing a vision of public schools that reflects democratic values and human rights.

In what follows, we explain how the corporate push to gentrify metropolitan Atlanta has resulted in a full-blown assault on the entire public sector, resulting in further marginalization of the poor and working classes. Briefly, we analyze the various crises and struggles over privatization in the city and explain the Atlanta Jobs with Justice campaign that builds a vision for organizing and resisting this corporate onslaught. We detail the formation of Metro Atlantans for Public Schools. Finally, we explain our pedagogical approach to popular education and the process of shaping consciousness around an agenda for human rights and social justice.

Privatization: A Coordinated Effort on Many Fronts

The state of Atlanta's public schools is tied inextricably to what is happening to the city's entire public sector. The public sector has traditionally been a base for employment, resources, and political power. In the South, the public sector opened up to African Americans as a result of the struggle for civil rights that brought down the walls of apartheid segregation. In addition, federal money and resources were brought to major Southern cities through programs which funded mass transit projects such as the Urban Mass Transportation Act of 1964. In the late 1970s, these advances came under attack as U.S. global capitalism began to eat away at the edges of the public sector. As global markets became more and more saturated, capital began to pursue the public sector as an untapped source of profit to exploit. Similar to what we have seen in the Global South (see Klein, 2007), Atlanta is also feeling the effects of neoliberal policies, especially privatization. Privatization is defined as the transfer of public assets and services—owned and performed by the government—to businesses and individuals in the private sector. It replaces public participation and institutional responsibility and accountability with a profit motive. This negatively impacts the human rights of the working classes and the poor, especially women and people of color.

Transit systems, hospitals, schools, libraries, police and fire departments, water and sanitation services, and even the streets and road signs are publicly defined municipal departments and city institutions. No one asks whether Atlanta's fire department made money last year or whether the sales have gone up at the local branch library. The public sector provides many of the services citizens have a right to receive because they live in a community and pay taxes. However, corporate and political elites in the city and metro Atlanta region continue to push forward with their neoliberal, privatization agenda. A few of the more notable examples of what is happening to public services:

- In 1999 Atlanta turned its water and sewer operations over to Suez, a French multi-national corporation (Koller, 2003). At the time, it was the largest water privatization deal in the U.S. Four years later, the city took it back after complaints of poor service and the failure to save money.
- The commuter bus system (C-Tran) initiated service in suburban Clayton County in October 2001. Metro Atlanta Regional Transit Authority (MARTA) had been the original operator, but Clayton commissioners decided in 2004 to turn over the operations to the private British multinational firm, First Transit. In 2007, Clayton County approved a move to return operations to the MARTA transit system that already carries 92% of transit passengers in the region.

- In 2007, the Atlanta Housing Authority announced its "Quality of Life Initiative," a plan to demolish a dozen public housing developments with about 3,000 units and 9,600 tenants. With the city facing a shortage of affordable housing for newer residents who are middle class professionals, the goal was to eliminate all public housing by 2010. This privatization of public land continues to be carried out in the interests of developers and their gentrification plans for the city.
- In 2008, the Atlanta Chamber of Commerce completed its campaign to promote the privatization of Grady Memorial, the largest public hospital in the Southeast. This resulted in the transference of operating assets valued at over $1.5 billion to the control of the new non-profit board. Grady receives no operating help from the state, a huge contributing factor to the financial crisis that led to the privatization takeover.

The forces that are privatizing and gentrifying Atlanta's public spaces and public institutions are coordinating their efforts. For the last sixteen years, the market-oriented Georgia Public Policy Foundation has promoted an agenda in favor of privatization (McCutchen, 1996). This agenda would serve corporate interests represented by the Atlanta Chamber of Commerce and their political allies and would displace and disempower the people by taking over public institutions in the name of profit.

A Campaign Centered on Human Rights

What would Atlanta look like if it were run on human rights principles? AJwJ uses the human rights agenda as a framework for its public sector campaigns. The focus is on restoring, defending, and expanding the public good. In order to achieve justice for the public good in one area, this group organizes coalitions of the most affected to fight for the public sphere as a whole. Public housing residents, public sector workers, people with disabilities, people of color, low-income families, immigrant/migrant workers, teachers, students, and faith organizations can win only when they see that their struggles are part of a larger, objective whole.

AJwJ has had to progress past an initial, single-issue focus on transit, for example, to take up broader struggles affecting the entire public sector. The multi-issue approach has meant having to overcome the obstacles of the city's historical lack of grassroots organizing, fragmentation of social justice organizations, and old-style method of group development that is centered on a single personality or leader. They understand the necessity of organizing around the day-to-day demands that arise out of all the issues that face working class and oppressed peoples in this country. This allows them to continue to be responsive to issues while simultaneously advocating a people's program that would be reflected in the city's values and institutional practices. They use the human rights campaign format as an organizing tool to build a multiracial, multi-issue, intergenerational alliance to ensure that all communities have access to services; participate in the decision-making processes of our public institutions; and fight for the resources these entities deserve. They are building power issue-by-issue, constituency-by-constituency, and neighborhood-by-neighborhood to implement a new vision for Atlanta.

Their plan is to engage a variety of constituencies in a radical, popular education process to understand the international context of human rights and what it would mean locally and in their own lives. Through a series of Leadership Institute workshops beginning in October 2008, the Universal Declaration of Human Rights has been used as a tool by community organizers and become a strong motivation for building a people-centered, human rights movement. This is the first step in what has been an unfolding, long-term campaign.

Next, a democratic, participatory mechanism such as a people's assembly will be developed to build popular support for a human rights charter in Atlanta. Used in movements around the world, peoples' assemblies (PA) are an important organizing mechanism when building multi-sector, multi-constituency consensus. They are keys to building democratic consensus and public participation. The graduates of the Leadership Institute will constitute the core-coordinating group for the assemblies. Each PA will be organized around pillars for a collective platform. They will be constructed around workers' rights, education, transportation, housing, and public health. Each PA will develop a set of core principles, platform issues, and policy recommendations. This will be a two-way process, based in a commitment to listening to and learning from the wisdom of the community or workplace while AJwJ projects a human rights vision and demonstrates what grassroots, participatory democracy actually looks like.

Human rights language becomes the connective tissue between social movements, and the charter campaign is the basis for developing a radical, people's program. In transit, for example, members of the Transit Riders Union, Amalgamated Transit Union Local 732, and Concerned Paratransit Riders (now Concerned Transit Riders for Equitable Access) worked for two years to analyze the current transit system, focusing on proposing expansions and developing their own vision for accountable, affordable, and accessible regional transit. This plan was presented to the state's Transit Planning Board in April 2008 (Atlanta Jobs, 2008). AJwJ will do the same for other aspects of the public sector, including schools, developing concrete alternatives to the neoliberal agenda dismantling Atlanta's public infrastructure, and demand a say in how our public institutions make financial decisions and set priorities that by and large exclude the democratic commons.

JwJ and MAPS believe that public education belongs to the public. Government has the responsibility to nurture and protect public education and to be accountable to the people whom it serves. In the next section we explain the beginnings of MAPS.

Metro Atlantans for Public Schools

During the spring and summer of 2007, two workshops sparked the interest of several Atlanta area teachers who wished to discuss how they might raise awareness about the impact of privatization. The first was the "Educator Roundtable" held at Georgia State University in March. Among the 100 people in attendance were two veteran Atlanta area teachers and a younger teacher working at a local charter school, all three future founders of MAPS. This daylong event was the first face-to-face meeting of U.S. education activists united against NCLB—a group which previously had communicated only through a list-serve. In late June, the same MAPS founders attended a workshop on the privatization of public education at the U.S. Social Forum, held in Atlanta and led by activists from Save our Schools DC, a grassroots nonprofit that believes in democratic education. Their leaders shared experiences and strategies at the workshop and encouraged approximately 60 participants to offer ideas about the fight to save public education. Afterwards, the teacher who had taught in a metro Atlanta area charter school proposed that the three meet soon to explore how they might raise the issue of privatization among their circles of influence.

The onslaught of the school year with its increasing demands for student accountability to the mandates of NCLB delayed the next meeting until early November of 2007. The founders were eager to become better acquainted and share their education-based "war" stories and concerns from the frontlines fighting anti-corporate, neoliberal education. For example, one teacher is an active member of her retired teachers association and regularly lobbies at the state legislature for laws that protect the public's interest in education. All agreed to meet again soon to continue their discussion. In mid-December, AJwJ asked two of these teachers for assistance in developing the education piece of their campaign. These future MAPS founders decided to involve others in this process at a meeting to be scheduled for March 8th at a neighborhood branch of the public library. They invited others to join in the exploration of public school conditions and their relationship to the process of privatization and posed the following questions: *What is happening and why? When did the privatization process in Atlanta's public education begin? What role do charter schools and NCLB play in privatization? Who benefits? How have some Atlantans successfully opposed privatization in education and in other areas of the public sector?* They included a call to engage in developing a vision of public education that is democratic and just.

In early February of 2008 one of the MAPS founders attended an AJwJ meeting on the citywide public sector human rights campaign, at which community and union activists from the public sector listened intently as Ajamu Baraka presented an orientation to human rights principles and practices. Baraka (2007), Executive Director of the U.S. Human Rights Network, has written:

> From the struggle around women's rights and racial justice to gender, sexual identity, and environmental rights, social justice activists in the 1990s turned to human rights to provide a framework and unifying umbrella for advancing social change. As a consequence, human rights discourse has moved from the margins to the center of social justice work . . . and we now have the institutional framework, mission and experience to constitute a movement. (p. 1)

This meeting provided a framework for building a social movement from the bottom up and a deeper understanding of the intersectionality of a multi-issues campaign. In preparation for the March 8, 2008 meeting, the MAPS founders utilized e-mail distribution lists of friends whom they thought might be interested in joining the network and broadened the "call" to include other school employees, parents and former students as well as those in the community with an interest in keeping public education public. They developed an agenda that began with personal introductions, followed by time for participants to write their concerns about public education on Post-it notes that were to be placed on the walls of the meeting room. The next agenda item was to brainstorm characteristics and concerns of schools that would work well for everyone. They planned to explore the subject of privatization by having participants list everything they thought they knew on large sheets of paper posted along one wall and titled charter schools, vouchers, foundation involvement, NCLB, and outsourcing. The final agenda item involved exploring the next steps.

Participants at the March 8th meeting included two college professors, two Morehouse college students, a retired elementary school teacher, two middle-school teachers and a high school teacher. Teachers represented the county school systems in Fulton, DeKalb and Gwinnett. MAPS identified three areas of concern: school culture, decision-making, and finances. At the next meeting in April the network reviewed and incorporated new contributions into the results of previous brainstorming. They discussed the types of privatization in the metro Atlanta area, including the Decatur City Schools and their reluctance to face competition from other local charter schools thanks to a new law passed by the state of Georgia. They learned about the proposed Georgia constitutional amendment allowing the creation of a TAD (Tax Allocation District) for corporate development of so-called blighted areas, and the resulting reduction in tax monies for Atlanta Public Schools. The May meeting was posted at Georgia State University and handed out and e-mailed to friends and coworkers and included a review of issues and concerns as well as characteristics of schools that would work well for all, an examination of the impact of privatization on public education as well as the role of technology in education, exploration of obstacles to change, outreach, and where to go from here. At the meeting, they planned a forum on the "school to prison pipeline" involving local activists engaged in a campaign against the Atlanta Public Schools and Forrest Hill Academy, run by the for-profit company Community Education Partners, and discussed the booklet *Keeping the Promise? The Debate over Charter Schools* (Dingerson, Miner, Peterson & Walters, 2008) published by the national educational collective Rethinking Schools. During June and July, they developed a website with information about their purpose and activities and links to organizations and resources. MAPS is becoming more knowledgeable about the complex nature of privatization and the necessity of creating a social movement to reverse this anti- democratic, neoliberal trend in Atlanta.

Talking Points about Atlanta's School Privatization Efforts

As with other areas of the public sector in Atlanta, education is also under the threat of privatization with an increase in charter schools. Recently, Georgia's governor signed House Bill 881, which will allow charter schools to petition the state for a charter even if their local school board refuses, bypassing local control altogether. This law, along with House Bill 831, which allows tax credit for anyone who donates to the improvement of a charter school, puts Georgia in the forefront of privatization efforts. The granting of charters as well as the voucher program has further exacerbated the negative impact of reduced funding for schools—about $1.5 billion since the year 2003 (Salzer, 2008). The random chartering of schools that have little or no connection to public schools or each other is fragmenting public education in metro Atlanta as well. Because Georgia's charter schools do not have to be accountable to their students and community, their creation is leading to segregation by race and assumed intellect. Charters do not have to play by the same rules as public schools and can remove students based on the parent's inability to attend meetings or complete volunteer hours.

One notable example of a privatized school in Atlanta is the Forrest Hill Academy, which is run by the for-profit company, Community Education Partners (CEP). For $6.9 million dollars a year, Atlanta Public Schools contracted this corporation to run an alternative school for students who couldn't make it in the public schools. Rather than rehabilitate students who are in need of help, CEP provided, as one American Civil Liberties Union (ACLU) attorney rightly pointed out, "little to no academic instruction and its students are treated like criminals; it is nothing more than a warehouse, largely for poor children of color" (Freeman, 2008, p. 32). The ACLU has filed a lawsuit against this company.

The boards of metro Atlanta charter schools are run by non-profit or for-profit educational management organizations (EMO) and are not as likely to be accountable to the public as elected school boards. At Kennesaw Charter School (KCS) in Cobb County, run by the second largest EMO in the country, Imagine Schools, Inc., a non-profit with 59.2 million in revenues last year, a number of questions of accountability have surfaced. For the 2007 to 2008 school year, only 12 out of the 27 teachers returned to work there (Farnsworth, 2008a). One of those teachers, also a MAPS founder, cited poor teacher support, disorderly management, and a lack of basic resources as reasons she did not return the following year. Other problems at the school included $5,500 worth of questionable charges with no receipts and the use of the school's credit card for personal items (Farnsworth, 2008b). There was also a pre-kindergarten program that was not authorized by KCS's charter which charged $600 per month per child. Because there was no license for the program, it was later shut down. According to KCS staff members, special needs students were no longer being accepted because there was not enough space or staff for them (Farnsworth, 2008c). Among the four Imagine schools in Cobb County, one upper-management leader and three principals have been forced to leave or have resigned (Farnsworth, 2008a). KCS is now threatened with losing its charter (Stevens, 2008).

There is a lack of balanced public data concerning the source of chartering schools. The city's mainstream daily press, *The Atlanta Journal Constitution* (AJC), has been the public's primary source of information about charter schools, but the newspaper celebrates rather than critiques the critical issues facing charter school start-up and sustainability. According to a study by Hankins and Martin (2006), from the years 1998 to 2004, the AJC published 50 pro-charter staff editorials, highlighting the need for educational reform and presenting these schools as the solution to the bureaucratic problems of the public school system. On the other hand, little is said about the failures of chartering, such as the fact that 11% of charter schools have closed in Georgia (higher than the national average of 7%) and 34% have gone back to operations as traditional public schools.

Amplifying the problems of tracking that already exist with many schools and school systems, charter schools moreover are fragmenting public education into class and/or race based tracks. For example, working class students tend to have charter schools in their neighborhoods that provide occupational training while middle class students are offered special academic programs in math and science. Atlanta charters such as the Knowledge Is Power Program (KIPP), an EMO, have targeted working-class students for a no-frills, basic skills curriculum. Most of the KIPP schools have longer school hours and are open Saturdays and during the summers (Hankins & Martin, 2006).

Another notable example is the Academy for America run by Charter School Administrative Services (CSAS), a for-profit EMO that has been riddled with complaints of mismanagement and high teacher turnover. CSAS has focused on recruiting minority students "with a curriculum designed to train them to be entrepreneurs and business leaders" even though it takes social and cultural capital to become mobile in a meritocratic sense (Hankins & Martin, 2006, p. 543). That is, charters can create barriers for working-class parents and their children. Students who do not fit into the charter's style of education can be expelled or simply asked to leave. Parents usually have to provide more personal resources than they would at a typical public school, such as money for transportation and student fees and time for on-site volunteering. In Atlanta's gentrified neighborhood of Grant Park, for instance, the Neighborhood Charter

School was created to provide predominantly white residents a publicly funded alternative to private schools. Hankins (2007, 2005) has shown that, since its inception, black working class family involvement in the school was dislocated by the interests of the neighborhood's professionals and volunteer middle classes. Although the charter school is zoned to include the predominately black working class neighborhood of Ormewood, about 90% of the decision-making for that charter resided among the governing board of white parents in Grant Park (Hankins, 2007, p. 123). One new MAPS participant and former employee of the Neighborhood Charter School remarked that it is the black students (who represent less than 50% of the school population) from working class homes who are asked to leave, often because parents working various hours and multiple jobs cannot attend the required meetings and accumulate enough volunteer hours to meet the school's guidelines. Although there is a special committee to support students' achievement, it is usually run by white homemakers who lack empathy for black, single mothers trying to make it in Atlanta.

Instead of properly funding all metro Atlanta schools so that no child is left behind, the granting of charters is turning public education into a marketplace of shopping mall choices. At one MAPS meeting, a participant talked about her own experience as a new teacher at an Atlanta Public School which is located near a charter school. She commented that it was hard on her students' morale to attend a school labeled a "failing school" for not making the No Child Left Behind Act mandates of annual yearly progress. Parents who leave that school usually take their children down the street to the new charter school. In fact, she has lost so many children that she teaches a class of just ten. Her students' walk daily past the charter school where they view the real-life consequences of privatization, a class- and race-based contrast that Kozol (2001) has named the sorry state of apartheid schooling. Her "failed" students could apply to the neighboring charter school, but the reality is that they are unlikely to meet its rigorous academic requirements for continued educational success.

Conclusion: Popular Education and Political Activism

In this chapter we have seized upon the idea that citizens can combat the corporatizing, neoliberal imperatives in public life through popular education and political activism. While profiling the work of community leaders at Atlanta

Jobs with Justice and the teachers engaged in start-up activities in Metro Atlantans for Public Schools, we recognize that good leaders understand their subjects, in this case working class parents and their children. Social justice organizing, after all, offers a theory of critical pedagogy, one that Paulo Freire (1995) said entailed a dialogic action between leaders and the people resulting in a mutual climate of trust and "investigation—the first moment of action as cultural synthesis" (p. 162). This does not mean that leaders impose their will upon the masses; instead, together, they build the road as they travel, and the resulting cultural synthesis (*not* cultural invasion, Freire insisted) finds both parties "somehow reborn in new knowledge and new action." The poor and working classes participate and join collective social movements to better their lives, embrace progressive political activities that are empowering and community building. By engaging in critical consciousness about their lived experiences, grassroots organizations offer an understanding of how to access information, in this case about the neoliberal landscape of privatization.

AJwJ and MAPS know how to honor counter-resistant voices while designing strategies and direct-action campaigns to resist business imperatives in their own neighborhoods. They promote a critical pedagogy—an analysis of power and privilege that deconstructs oppressive social and cultural conditions—as well as use any number of "intellectual tools to imagine and enact a different future from the one prescribed by the dictates of corporate profit and state actions to assist it" (Saltman, 2007, p. 159). Famed Chicago organizer Saul Alinsky (1971, p. 124), too, affirmed that critical pedagogy was the foundation of community organizing, when he wrote "real education is the means by which the membership will begin to make sense out of their relationship as individuals to the organization and to the world they live in, so that they can make informed and intelligent judgments."

Economic and social justice is advanced through local or regional organized opposition to the neoliberal state. In Mexico, for instance, unionized school teachers have led the fight against merit pay, standardized testing, and top-down corporatizing reforms that have closed the teacher training institutes (*normales*) in rural areas (Arriaga Lemus, 2008). The neoliberal government feared these local centers were incubators of critical pedagogy and political activism since rural teachers maintained their working class roots and taught others the need for liberating social conditions from the bottom up. Yet groups of critical teachers are committed to defending public education (sometimes with their lives) "as an expression of grassroots democracy" through a variety of tactics including "strikes, picketing, protest marches, occupations of highways and radio and television stations" (Arriaga Lemus, 2008, p. 224). These folks comprise the widening anti-globalization movement, a "Lilliput Strategy" (Brecher and Costello, 1994, p. 9), named after the tiny residents who tied down the giant Gulliver in his travels. This idea of organizing from below "requires grassroots rebellions against downward leveling, local coalition-building, transnational networking, and creating or reforming international institutions." The on-going struggle against privatization and the theft of public resources is part of a worldwide defense of the public sector.

Let us be clear: there is a full-frontal attack upon working class students and students of color. Public schools in the U.S. are defunded, re-segregated, privatized, losing public and local control, and shaping students for work rather than citizenship. As schools become more privatized, so do their services, regardless of whether they are a charter or public school. But in charter schools, most, if not all, services are privatized. Services like food, transportation, tutoring, and custodial work are compromised so that schools can save money, but at what cost?

What is needed is a larger public conversation. As long as this country's priorities are more concerned with empire than taking care of the needs of people, the public sector will be deeply affected. And, sadly, in the end we will have turned the collective responsibilities for educating the minds and hearts of our children to the stakeholders of business, the elites of corporations.

We need social justice movements that are radically democratic and led by those most affected by current conditions and that project a positive vision, not only about what we are against, but also about the change we would like to see. We need to create inclusive spaces where we can share stories, dialogue, and learn from each other as equals: teachers, students, parents, and support personnel like school bus drivers and cafeteria workers—everyone working together to advance a common program. This is how we can build power from the bottom up.

Relationship-building is central: among ourselves at the neighborhood school level, at the district level, and citywide. People do not live single-issue lives and our movement should reflect the diversity of issues and oppressions we face. Our analysis should be broad and we should seek out allies. Too often we are splintered and divided, fighting alone. When it comes to state budgets, for example, people throughout the public sector are affected. Here is where we can find potential allies.

Finally, we should use a thoughtful process of action and reflection. Take small steps. Find one more person. Do something together. Sum up the lessons learned. Go back out and try again. Engage in a permanent dialogue with the people we are organizing. Together, we can learn from our mistakes and assemble our grassroots movement.

What You Can Do

1. Start where you are. Get to know your students, parents, co-workers. For example, Springdale, an Atlanta Public School, bypassed the traditional top-down hierarchy of public schools, nurturing a relationship with a local farmer who now provides produce for school lunches. Every month they highlight a local vegetable and the farmer comes to visit.
2. You have allies. Try to create spaces of open-exchange and see where your ideas lead you. Isolating yourself does not help. Look for existing networks or start your own. Join a local union that believes in collective bargaining or an education group like the PTA and connect with other people who are working for social justice.
3. Analyze. The problems we are dealing with are complex. By giving people a chance to share their stories and experiences, we can sharpen our understandings of what is going on and who the players are. This common analysis can then guide our organizing and actions.
4. Join online discussions and blogs. Look for contacts in responses to articles about education in the newspaper. Set up your own email group.
5. Connect with people locally in order to find other progressive education activists. Attend conferences that address education issues. Do not become discouraged about not finding that for which you are looking. Always keep your eyes open and eventually you will make connections.
6. When developing an action, be creative. Know the current issues that sting and be ready to act. For example, the $15,000 pay raise for a local school superintendent outraged county education workers. Unable to bargain collectively, a local NEA affiliate called for everyone to wear black to work. For many, it was the first collective action they had ever taken. Some schools had 100% participation which far exceeded the NEA membership at those schools.
7. Expand your circle. Most people who work in education are in a good position to see that humans are affected by a multitude of issues. We are able to bring together various constituencies from other parts of the

public sector such as transportation, housing, and health. You and your group can participate in solidarity actions in support of other cross-alliance issues.

8. Be careful not to allow your movement to be co-opted by bigger fish like professional associations. While these groups are important, keep in mind that many may be more interested in increasing their membership than empowering the base. Giving up one's voice to others does not teach creative self-potential for changing this world. Do not rely upon a single, charismatic leader. Be sure that everyone around you is feeling empowered, from learning how to run meetings to participating in strategy discussions. As civil rights movement leader Ella Baker once said, *People have to be made to understand that they cannot look for salvation anywhere but to themselves.* The best answers to problems come from those most affected by the issues. Make sure they never get left out of decision-making, and you can build a real movement for transformative change.

9. Realize that people lead real and busy lives and might be unable to drop what they are doing to come to a meeting or an action. Be patient. Keep them in the loop even when they are inactive. Building a movement takes time and a lot of heart but it is ultimately rewarding.

Resources

The Advancement Project believes in making sustainable progress for those left behind in America through the use of law, policy analysis, strategic communications, technology, and research in coordination with grassroots movements. *www.advancementproject.org*

The Algebra Project is a national, nonprofit organization that uses mathematics as an organizing tool to ensure quality public school education for every child in America. *http://www.algebra.org/*

Atlanta Jobs with Justice applies a human rights framework to building movements in Atlanta that address the root causes of economic and social injustice. Its public sector campaign connects the issues in public education with those facing workers and the community in transportation, housing and health. *http://www.atljwj.org/*

The Caucus of Rank and File Educators in Chicago (CORE) seeks to democratize the Chicago Teacher's Union and turn it into an organization that fights on behalf of its members and for the students in CPS. *http://www.coreteachers.org*

The Coalition for Democracy in Education is a coalition that supports increased democracy in the D.C. Public Schools. *http://democracyineducation.net*

DeKalb County School Watch is a consortium of parents, educators, and community members who converse about improving schools in DeKalb County, Georgia, by providing quality equitable education for each student. *http://dekalb-schoolwatch.blogspot.com*

The Dignity in Schools Campaign is gathering signatures for the National Resolution for Ending School Pushout. The Resolution aims to embed these same human rights principles into our local, state and federal education laws, policies and practices in order to guarantee the human rights of all young people. *http://www.dignityinschools.org*

The Education for Liberation Network is a national coalition of teachers, community activists, youth, researchers and parents who seek to understand and challenge injustices in their communities. *http://www.edliberation.org*

Educational Justice is a collective of progressive education activists who write about teaching, thinking, parenting, social justice, desegregation, self-determination, economic justice, music, creativity, and building progressive movements. *http://edjustice.blogspot.com*

Jobs with Justice is a national organization that engages workers and allies in campaigns to win justice in workplaces and in communities where working families live. *http://www.jwj.org*

Journal of Educational Controversy is an interdisciplinary electronic journal that provides a forum for examining the controversies arising in American public education today. *http://www.wce.wwu.edu/resources/cep/eJournal*

Metro Atlantans for Public Schools (MAPS) is a progressive network of public school employees, parents, students, and others interested in ensuring that we have a free, democratic, well-funded, community-supported public education system that serves the interests of all. *http://mapsed.ning.com*

The National Center for Fair & Open Testing challenges the misuses and flaws of standardized testing to ensure that evaluation of students, teachers and schools is fair, open, valid and educationally beneficial. *http://www.fairtest.org*

New York Collective of Radical Educators (NYCoRE) is a group of public school educators who fight for social justice in the school system and society at large, by organizing and mobilizing teachers, developing curriculum, and working with community, parent, and student organizations. *http://www.nycore.org*

Quality Education as a Constitutional Right (QECR) is a national organization that works in local schools and communities to transform American public education through passage of a Constitutional Amendment guaranteeing all children the right to a quality education. *http://www.qecr.org*

Rethinking Schools expresses its commitment to equity in public education through the publication of educational materials including a quarterly magazine. An excellent listing of education-related web resources can be found on its website at: *http://www.rethinkingschools.org*

Save Our Schools is an international organization working for high quality public education that will enable all children to reach their full potential as adults, becoming active citizens who participate in an equitable, democratic and socially tolerant society. *www.saveourschools.com*

Substance News is a Chicago-based investigative newspaper about public education issues. *http://www.substancenews.net*

Susan Ohanian speaks out about national education school reform policies on her website: *www.susanohanian.org*

The US Human Rights Network is a broad array of organizations and individuals who work collaboratively to strengthen human rights work in the United States. The Convention on the Rights of the Child establishes universal standards for the human right to education which reflects the principles of dignity, full development, equity and participation. It is promoting a national resolution to embed human rights principles into our local, state and federal education laws, policies and practices. *http://www.ushrnetwork.org*

References

Alinsky, S. D. (1971). *Rules for radicals: A pragmatic primer for realistic radicals.* New York: Vintage.

Arriaga Lemus, M. (2008). In Mexico, to defend education as a social right, we must fight for union democracy. In M. Compton & L. Weiner (Eds.), *The global assault on teaching, teachers, and their unions* (pp. 221–226). New York: Palgrave Macmillan.

Atlanta Jobs with Justice (AJwJ). (2008). *Transit riders' vision for regional transit: A plan from the perspective of transit dependent riders.* Atlanta, GA: Author. Retrieved from http://www.atljwj.org/TRU%20FINAL%203.pdf)

Baraka, A. (2007, December 7). When does a movement become a movement? U.S. Human Rights Network magazine, *Twelve Ten* (Atlanta, GA). Retrieved from http://www.ushrnetwork.org/files/ushrn/images/linkfiles/USHRN_MagazineDec07_FINAL_PRINT.pdf

Brecher, J., & Costello, T. (1994). *Global village or global pillage: Economic reconstruction from the bottom up*. Boston, MA: South End.

Dingerson, L., Miner, B., Peterson, B., & Walters, S. (Eds.). (2008). *Keeping the promise? The debate over charter schools*. Milwaukee, WI: Rethinking Schools.

Early, S., & Cohen, L. (1994, Winter). Jobs with justice: Building a broad-based movement for workers' rights. *Social Policy, 25*(2), 6–18.

Farnsworth, E. (2008a, January 2). Imagine loses fourth since June. *Marietta Daily Journal*. Retrieved from http://www.mdjonline.com/content/index/showcontentitem/area/1/section/21/item/101911.html

Farnsworth, E. (2008b, December 5). Charter school's spending examined. *Marietta Daily Journal*. Retrieved from http://www.mdjonline.com

Farnsworth, E. (2008c, December 7). Kennesaw charter school pre-k to close its doors. *Marietta Daily Journal*. Retrieved from http://www.mdjonline.com

Freeman, S. (2008, May 7). Forrest Hill Academy: The children left behind. *Creative Loafing* (Atlanta). Retrieved from http://atlanta.creativeloafing.com/gyrobase/forrest_hill_academy_the_children_left_behind/Content?oid=479295

Freire, P. (1995). *Pedagogy of the oppressed*. New York: Continuum.

Hankins, K. B. (2005). Practicing citizenship in new spaces: Rights and realities of charter school activism. *Space and Policy, 9*(1), 41–60.

Hankins, K. B. (2007). The final frontier: Charter schools as new community institutions of gentrification. *Urban Geography, 28*(2), 113–128.

Hankins, K. B., & Martin, D. G. (2006). Charter schools and urban regimes in neoliberal context: Making workers and new spaces in metropolitan Atlanta. *International Journal of Urban and Regional Research, 30*(3), 528–547.

Harvey, D. (2005). *A brief history of neoliberalism*. Oxford, UK: Oxford University Press.

Klein, N. (2007). *The shock doctrine: The rise of disaster capitalism*. New York: Picador.

Koller, F. (2003, February 5). *No silver bullet: Water privatization in Atlanta—a cautionary tale*. CBC News. Retrieved from http://www.cbc.ca/news/features/water/atlanta.html

Kozol, J. (2001). *The shame of the nation: The restoration of apartheid schooling in America*. New York: Random House.

Lipman, P. (2004). *High stakes education: Inequality, globalization, and urban school reform*. New York: RoutledgeFalmer.

McCutchen, K. (1996, May 1). A response to the city of Atlanta's critique of "rescuing the city of Atlanta from fiscal crisis." Atlanta, GA: Georgia Public Policy Foundation. Retrieved from http://www.gppf.org/pub/Spending/atlresponse.pdf

Metro Atlantans for Public Schools. (MAPS). Retrieved from http://mapsed.ning.com/

Robinson, W. L. (2004). *A theory of global capitalism: Production, class, and state in a transnational world*. Baltimore, MD: Johns Hopkins University Press.

Saltman, K. J. (2007). *Capitalizing on disaster: Taking and breaking public schools*. Boulder, CO: Paradigm.

Salzer, J. (2008, March 10). Perdue decreases revenue estimate by $310 million. *Atlanta Journal Constitution*. Retrieved from http://www.ajc.com/metro/content/metro/stories/2008/03/10/revenue_0311.html

Stevens, A. (2008, September 26). Kennesaw school waiting to see if charter renewed. *Atlanta Constitutional Journal*. Retrieved from http://www.ajc.com/search/content/metro/cobb/stories/2008/09/26/kennesaw_charter_school.html

Westbrook, K. (2008). Sodexho in the Chicago Public Schools. In M. Compton & L. Weiner (Eds.), *The global assault on teaching, teachers, and their unions* (pp. 163–168). New York: Palgrave Macmillan.

· 6 ·

Ground Zero in a Corporate Classroom

Lisa Martin

AT NO TIME IN OUR NATION'S HISTORY HAS THE ASSAULT ON KIDS AND THEIR teachers been greater. In the name of standards and high stakes' accountability, we have empowered a huge apparatus that knows very little about how children effectively learn, but who seem righteous in their assertion that we must prepare workers for our competitive global society. There is a gaping hole in the current discourse on the purpose of public education. What is missing are the voices of teachers, and what they are seeing in their classrooms as testing requirements, drill and kill pedagogy, and rigid, formulaic solutions to our greatest educational challenges squeeze what little life is left in public education.

Everyone concerned with this state of affairs needs to be part of this debate. Parents in particular need to see clearly what a system that is driven by numbers looks and feels like to their child. Powerful and well-meaning policy makers also need to take a hard look at hyper-accountability and what happens when lack of transparency and administrative accountability distort the learning environment beyond all recognition. Current buzz words that we hear on talk shows and in the mainstream media sound authoritative and scholarly: teacher accountability, school choice and the charter school movement. But without debate and discussion they mask another reality that is not being acknowledged; numbers manipulation, poor decision making, data that do not reflect the learning environment or the needs of students. Those who work closest to kids have a tremendous amount to say about what is working and not working in our public schools, but they are the voices most marginalized. The voice of the disaffected teacher is often portrayed as the uninspired whiner, the individual who couldn't take the intellectual rigor of a highly complex classroom. Few people are better equipped, however, to weigh in on the effects of a system of hyper-accountability and the manic obsession with standardized test scores, than teachers and students. The effects of the system on our children, particularly those most educationally underserved, are enormous. So while this is a story of my professional experience within this system, it is also a cautionary tale of what your school could turn into, if it hasn't already. This is a system driven by numbers and burnished with a corporate veneer. This is a story of what that looks like and feels like, and what ultimately happened when I chose to challenge the system.

My Background

I started my career in 1988, teaching in a traditional high school in northern California. With two years of experience under my belt and feeling the need for adventure, I left California in 1990 and headed to the United Arab Emirates to teach history at the American Community School of Abu Dhabi. I spent four years teaching in a traditional high school environment. I wrote curriculum and developed a myriad of extra-curricular activities to supplement the high school program. This environment was marked by small class sizes, deep interaction with the families and students, rigorous curriculum, and the ability to modify and adapt this curriculum to meet students' needs. The schools were also incredibly diverse, with a dozen nationalities working and learning together and each bringing a unique world view that led to fascinating and engaging history classes. It was an exciting and stimulating teaching and learning environment. When I moved to Kuala Lumpur, Malaysia in 1998, these were the threads of my career that I picked up again: growing a high school, writing relevant, rigorous curriculum, and finding ways to engage students in their community. In 2002 I returned, with my husband and young daughter, to southern California. I taught briefly in traditional high school but soon took a position at a charter school working with students in an independent study program. Most of the students were behind and performing well below grade level.

My Charter School

I was assigned to one of the charter school's 19 classrooms spread across the county. My classroom was in a very urban area whose feeder high schools were ranked as some of the lowest in the region. My job was to oversee 40 students through an "innovative" independent study program, where students worked primarily out of textbooks and completed one or two classes at a time. They were expected to study at home for four or more hours a day and complete one class every three to four weeks. The program had been developed some 10 years earlier with the sole mission of helping the educationally underserved, those who were not succeeding in a traditional school environment. Each of our 19 classrooms had different demographics, but my site was primarily classified as Hispanic, African American and Laotian, coming from low socioeconomic backgrounds. The overwhelming majority of our students qualified for free or reduced lunch.

These social and economic parameters provide the all-critical context in which my students struggled to learn and achieve. They came to our independent study program for many reasons: they were behind academically, had gaping holes in their academic records and had the inability or unwillingness to attend an 8:00–3:00 school day. At my particular classroom we also had brutally low reading and math scores. It was very common to find 17-year-olds classified as 9th graders because they had only a handful of credits, hadn't passed the California High School Exit Exam (CAHSEE) and had a third grade reading level. My fellow teaching partners, several of them by 2008, had similar caseloads. Our school provided each of us with a teaching assistant for 25 hours a week. Their primary job was to grade papers, but they often tutored students one on one. Our classroom became a small school entity unto itself. And while my student population was a universe away from my elite international school experience, there were several key similarities: class sizes were small; I knew my community well, and the focus of my day was on meeting the needs of the entire child. My students were still tested and held accountable by those traditional metrics, but their immediate needs cried out for individualized attention, personalized education, deep engagement into their lives, and accessibility to caring teachers and staff. The mission of the school was one that I championed for many years. Many of our hardworking staff, year after year, rolled up their sleeves and worked hard, often in excess of 50 hours a week, to move kids forward, academically, socially, and emotionally. It was grueling but incredibly rewarding work.

Real Data Include More Than Numbers

Although the CEO of the school once declared that "we are not a school of social workers," teachers working in the areas of town where the needs were greatest saw a disproportionate number of problems: lower test scores, higher rates of hunger, absentee parents, transportation issues, gang and domestic violence issues. The list of concerns was very long. When these sensitive demographic topics were brought up in meetings, teachers were told not to make geographic location an excuse for poor student and teacher performance. The system had been devised to track teacher accountability as a measurement of teacher performance. Test scores (the sole measure of student performance) in part drove teacher performance, and where kids struggled, their teachers paid the price in lower professional evaluations.

Many of these lower performing students needed direct instruction: small group instruction, one-on-one tutoring, constant monitoring by instructional staff. The need in math was extremely great, and our school wisely hired certified math teachers. The allotted time these math teachers spent in classrooms was between 4 and 16 hours a week. They were required to do workshops to prepare for CAHSEE and state testing. The math instruction helped but was not entirely sufficient. The administration then directed sites to hold daily math workshops, even though teachers had neither the background nor time to do so. Again, this dilemma was raised in meetings. How were teachers to give direct and prolonged instruction when they had 40 students doing different classes and at different paces? How could a teacher devote an hour to teaching decimals to one individual when there were five students waiting at her desk for assistance? And if a teacher was required to drive the neighborhood looking for the student who wasn't coming to class, how could that same teacher conduct a language arts workshop? As the testing stakes got higher and higher, the pressure on teachers grew and grew. Teachers knew that the stakes were very high. The tension was constantly felt to balance the immediate needs of the students with the immediate need to improve test scores. At my site the average day usually consisted of crisis management first (the student being stalked, an impromptu meeting with a probation officer, the student who must leave because her bus transfer expires and she does not have enough money to get home). Deep, time-consuming remediation came second, when there was time.

The danger of this trend cannot be underestimated, since it skews all discussion on the reform agenda and makes the discussion on the problems in the system one accountability-driven by numbers (test scores, dropout rates). The discussion should be centered on many of the social ills confronting families and young people (discrimination, poverty, poor health, lack of meaningful opportunity) and how these affect what happens in the classroom. As our current political and financial sectors crisis so clearly illustrate, institutions built on beds of sand lack structural integrity, leaving their occupants in danger of being crushed by collapsing institutions. In the case of schools, it means that curricular decisions are based on test scores. Finite resources are used to improve testing outcomes, even if it runs counter to the needs of students and their communities. The data used to inform everything from course content to textbooks and support staff are driven by testing numbers. What students really need and what schools offer to them are usually two very different things. Is there any wonder that we have a generation of individuals who feel an almost total disconnect from the public education that has served them so poorly?

But I would like to challenge readers to consider what a system with limited relevant input from teachers and a manic obsession on narrowly derived data looks like from the bottom up. Students see standards and goals that are far removed from their immediate lives and needs. A teacher may have high academic standards and goals for his student but is required to focus narrowly on a math and English language agenda that may be both inappropriate and developmentally shallow. Administrators and evaluators watch the teacher's every move, making sure that the expensive testing software is used and the test prep books assigned. The students in class will have many needs, but needing to know how to factor a polynomial will usually not be one of them. And so the teacher must choose: be a 'good teacher' and fulfill the administration's agenda or be a 'bad teacher' and serve the student's immediate needs. The teachers I knew tried to do both.

The One-Way Street: Teacher Accountability on Steroids

My charter school's desire to improve test scores was no different than that of any other public school, and my administration focused on a number of steps to improve them. Departments created special classes and alternative assignments to help in the area of remediation. There was a systematic, if belated, review of teacher and student files to make sure teachers were grading rigorously and not just passing students through classes with mediocre work and effort. This did much to tighten the overall curriculum and undoubtedly resulted in better academic performance, but it did little to help the lowest achievers who needed far more than our program could give them. This action also served to protect the school from allegations of fraud, since some teachers found ways to game the system by passing off incomplete work as fully completed work. These numbers were never questioned seriously by the school's leadership as long as the bottom line—student attendance—met the school's minimum targets. That kept the money flowing from Sacramento into school coffers.

The school, from its inception, developed an educational model that stressed teacher accountability, lauded on numerous occasions by visiting accreditation teams. The very language used at the school was conscious in its corporate vernacular: students were clients, parents and teachers were stakeholders. Classrooms were meant to look uniform and business like. Of greatest importance was the monthly review of statistical data that consumed much administrative time. The data coming out of our classrooms were then shared with the school and various parties. A teacher was required to report the total amount of work that his or her students completed that month. This was the basis for our average daily attendance (ADA) and subsequent state funding. Teachers were given targets to meet monthly, targets that were raised twice in my six years at the school. The higher the attendance, the better the teacher was doing. This attendance figure was a major, if not THE major indicator, of teacher productivity. Teacher's productivity scores were assembled in a document called the Site Productivity Indicators, where monthly progress was tracked, both in statistical and graph form. Each teacher had their LPI (Learning Performance Index, a variation of ADA) scores and the number of classes their students had completed put onto a spread sheet. Teachers were then color coded based on their scores. Green was used for teachers pulling in productivity scores of 79% or greater and blue for scores between 76–78%. Red, the color of shame, was reserved for teachers pulling in less than 75%. Next to this was listed the number of courses that had been completed by that teacher's students. Again, the higher the number of courses completed, the higher the indicator. Productivity scores were based on the assumption that teachers had 40 students. If they didn't, then productivity scores ultimately went down, regardless of class size. We were told to go out and recruit students for our classrooms if numbers dropped too low.

As the years went on, additional information about a teacher's performance was added. There was the Teacher/Classroom Analysis Report, comparing numbers of credits written per month, an indicator of which teachers were moving their students through the material and to what degree the school could claim ADA. There was the Productivity Indicators Report, the Vacancy Report, the Retention Report, and the Monthly Intervention Report as well as other occasional reports for measuring test-taking participation rates. Teachers who did not bring in 100% of their students for testing were usually given a stern talking to, or were publicly, via email, reprimanded. In the winter of 2008, primarily due to poor communication, a number of teachers failed to turn in their Federal Survey cards (which required parent signatures and were often time-consuming and challenging to retrieve), prompting an angry email from the CEO "that the results of all efforts like this should be published and placed in everyone's boxes—just like LPI. Lunch forms, testing participation, all of it should be converted to percents and distributed to everyone with a mailbox. Why? Because it shows who is being *successful* (italics mine) and getting an honorable return." The email ended by sharing with us that she would be tracking these results individually, and that if people wanted to perform at a mediocre level, consistent with traditional schools and needed that (less rigorous) comfort level, then 'they ought to be on a traditional site.' The teacher most lauded was a heavily pregnant teacher who banged on student doors late at night to get those last difficult signatures. 'Beyond the call' effort was required, or your job was at stake.

Teachers across the country are finding themselves in this uncomfortable situation. Attempts are being made to tie test scores to teacher effectiveness, and in turn be a factor in determining potential merit pay. Improvements in test scores are becoming a primary indicator of a teacher's value in the classroom. As I have tried to point out, however, many of the conditions surrounding test performance were heavily influenced by factors out of individual teachers' control. Also at issue was the need to jettison test prep for more meaningful dialog and assignments. Many teachers received lowered performance evaluations because their students did not make big enough gains in testing proficiency. The best example came by way of the California High School Exit Exam, or CAHSEE. Here was an example where passing a test was not good enough for federally mandated performance targets. Passing scores were 350 but proficiency scores were 380. Students making huge gains in achievement but barely passing the CAHSEE would not help the school in their number's game. A student making a small jump from the passing to the proficient level resulted in monumentally important gains for the school. Teacher evaluations began to reflect not the overall improvement in the student's progress, but rather whether the student had tested at high enough levels to warrant a positive performance evaluation for the teacher? Test scores, therefore, played a significant role in the concept of teacher accountability, a fairly innocuous phrase when viewed from the top down but an extremely punitive and unfair label for a hard-working classroom teacher. Sadly, in some instances, teachers at our school argued articulately the expected outcomes of, say, a reduction in math teacher hours. Their concerns were ignored, and then they suffered the double injury of being slammed in their performance evaluations.

This is why there is such outspoken criticism on the part of teachers and their unions regarding merit pay and associated accolades tied to test scores. Real improvement is often punished, and strategically targeted, but less impressive improvement, is lauded as exemplary. This is a very broken dynamic and should not be replicated nationally. Derailing the merit pay movement would require a greater degree of sophistication in the public's understanding of how test scores are actually used. As teachers become increasingly disempowered through the charter movement and in non-unionized work environments, this crucial voice of dissent will be weakened.

After several years of incremental but improved test scores, the results began to plateau and the demands on teachers went up again. The school purchased an expensive computerized testing program put out by Northwest Evaluation Association (also called MAPS). Teachers then needed to find time to test students individually on three rather lengthy tests, twice a year. Our once adequate computer access was decimated by hundreds of hours of testing. Students from lower socioeconomic backgrounds were particularly ill served, since many of them did not have internet access at home and had to postpone assignments because testing became the priority. Completion rates for this testing became another measurable statistic. A full time number cruncher was added to the staff so that someone could oversee the statistical avalanche of data coming out of our classrooms. The program was meant to help teachers individualize instruction. Usually, however, this information was printed off and put in the back of a student file. With monthly attendance to bring in, student crises to deal with, and a mountain of paperwork needed from teachers, the testing data became yet another tool for the administration to show that teachers were not doing enough to target instruction. Since the school had invested in this testing program, it was explicitly stated that our test scores should go up since we could pinpoint, with laser-like precision, student deficiencies. If scores didn't improve it was because teachers were not adequately utilizing the data. The data collected provided a narrow snapshot and not even indicative of student achievement.

Students who were just below the proficient testing level (not those who were the most behind) were to be given the most attention, making a mockery of the entire concept of No Child Left Behind. We spent staff meetings pouring over class rosters, trying to identify students for whom a jump in test scores would most help the school's overall testing numbers, students for whom that extra remediation would give the biggest bang for the buck. In 2009, after the critical proficiency scores came up short, math support was actually *pulled* from low income sites. Math teachers were reassigned to areas with moderately higher passing scores, with the hopes that the extra tutoring would result in that last critical jump from passing to proficient. The school, financially solvent and with money in the bank, chose not to spend tax payers' dollars by investing in certified teachers to teach in areas with the greatest deficiencies. Instead, critical staffing needs were dictated solely by test scores, removed from the realities of what students needed. In 2009, when math scores had yet again not made significant enough gains, the CEO declared that she had wasted hundreds of thousands of dollars in math teacher salaries, and those math teachers were then reassigned to classrooms, taking away what little was left of critical math support.

Yearly, with the help of our counselors, we coded our student files with colored dots and happy face stickers to help us visualize and prioritize students in our testing hierarchy. This was done so that a teacher could tell the 'weight' or importance of that student's score at a glance. In 2003–2005, a tremendous amount of staff time was spent in meetings dissecting each reportable subgroup. Elaborate PowerPoint presentations broke down each subgroup: African-American, Hispanic, students from lower socio-economic backgrounds as well as English language learners. If the school had more than 50 students in a sub-category, we were directed to make sure that those students got every bit of help that was needed. The subtext of these meetings was that in a system with limited time and resources, some students would get more attention than others. The low point occurred when our testing administrator, the shadow of 'school improvement' designation looming over us, showed the teachers that the total number of African Americans was 53, our smallest subgroup. "If you were thinking of dropping any student who might fall into this category . . ." she said, pointing to the African American subgroup on her PowerPoint presentation, " . . . you will want to do this by the deadline. If we can get this number below 50 it will not be a reportable category and that could be extremely helpful for our school's overall score."

The importance of these stories is to draw out the very real consequences for teachers and students if an accountability system runs amok. My early inclination was to feel great pity for my school. The administrators too were victims in a system that used test scores to drive the educational agenda. That feeling changed over time when the school attempted to beat the system. If our test scores weren't going up, that meant we needed to test them more! If students were struggling in a subject, then they invested in materials for further drill and practice. What was not discussed, at least not with teachers, were the underlying problems of such a system. Would it have been too much to ask our school's leadership, once in the vanguard of alternative education and the charter movement, to use its leadership to work for a change in the test-driven accountability system? Perhaps. Since lack of administrative accountability is a troubling part of the charter movement, there are limits to the kinds of changes that can happen from within schools.

Transparency and the Two-Way Street of Accountability

As this country begins to address the political and economic costs of diminished worker rights it is ironic that the current focus on accountability finds teachers' professionalism diminished and their expertise denigrated and often ignored. Our CEO's admonishments to her staff about credit card debt and Facebook postings seem rather tame when compared to the damaging consequences of her bad decision making. Without transparency and public accountability, these bad decisions become larger than life. Teachers who advocate for changes within their program, or who even offer up mild suggestions for improvement, can face total marginalization within their schools. The voiceless teacher becomes an easy target for all that is wrong with a school.

Fear is a bad managerial style. It gives leaders, and administrators, a false sense of reality. Teachers say what the administration wants to hear, or say nothing at all. That means that teachers can't advocate for their students, or for each other. When they do, they risk the possibility of harassment, demotion or even termination. When things went wrong in our classrooms, for example, or in our dealings with the administration, teachers were left without a voice. We became isolated from support and unable to protect ourselves from administrative heavy-handedness and intimidation. Each year brought a new victim, one that could then be used to whip the staff into submission for another 12 months. The precedent for hurtful and even unethical administrative behavior had been established long before I had arrived. Early in my charter school career there occurred a personnel scandal that saw veteran teachers and their assistants verbally attacked by the CEO, en masse and individually singled out, much like the then-popular show, "The Apprentice." Teachers had their characters impugned and staff lost their jobs. It was a reaction whose ferocity was unjustified. The teachers were publically uninvited to the teacher appreciation luncheon, and a chill settled over the school.

The list of grievances and problems teachers faced ranged from the petty to the illegal. Taken together they represented a serious assault on teacher protection and rights. At my school, many of the key decision makers had no advanced education credentials to speak of, yet staff members who did were excluded from key decision-making meetings. KIPP's (Knowledge Is Power Program) attempt to unionize speaks to the need teachers have felt to protect the integrity of their programs by unionizing their schools, because, rightly, they saw that a lack of teacher input in the creation of policies for their schools both undermined the foundation of the educational program and damaged teacher morale. Similarly, the increase in administrative actions at my school was further evidence of this marginalization. This included highly personalized attacks on fellow administrators and teachers, gag orders with the threat of dismissal against teachers, refusal to verify employment for teachers seeking new employment, failure to turn over copies of signed performance evaluations, retroactive performance evaluations, non-renewal of contracts without due process or a fair and open improvement process for teacher, inability to challenge administrative actions, failure to ensure equitable and fair site transfers, particularly where student achievement would be negatively impacted. There were forced admissions of responsibility for crimes committed against school property, resulting in time off without pay, intimidation of individuals pursuing advanced degrees and a gag order on complementary discussions about the school in doctoral theses being written by staff members. There was a lack of cultural sensitivity, harassment of teachers seeking time off for adoption leave as well as personal attacks on individual teacher's intelligence and credibility.

This impacted students by creating an environment of fear and intimidation, resulting in weakened teacher's voices. When the administration's modus operandi was to isolate and intimidate teachers, the crucial flow of information regarding ways to address low student performance, for example, was not strong enough to promote educationally sound policies.

There were also issues not directly impacting students but that spoke to the administration's need to control the flow of information within the school and to put the needs of the administration first. The school, fiscally solvent, used a local charity to underwrite educational expenses that should have been covered by the school (from testing fees to graduation caps and gowns). One final method for ensuring staff acquiescence, and one that threw the issue of the administration's lack of accountability into high relief, was the use of non-renewal of contracts. In my tenure at the school this tactic was used against a highly effective administrator, a teacher assisting with the formation of our school's online program (now an assistant director at our school's competitor), a former teacher of the year, and most recently, myself. Then there were the dozen silent 'disappearances' that occurred during this same period. Gag orders were imposed, so no one quite knew why these teachers were let go. But yearly these dismissals and failure to renew contracts served as a warning to others that questioning the administration or voicing a concern would have devastating results for the teacher concerned. In my last year at the school at least four teachers were threatened with non-renewal of contracts for a myriad of reasons. A well-timed non-renewal of a contract helped the administrative team by creating a more compliant staff. The more compliant the staff, the fewer the demands and the less of a challenge posed by concerned teachers challenging bad administrative decisions. Without outside intervention, this cycle of fear would be very difficult to break.

In 2005–2006 our administrative team decided that they would put the school in the running for a Californian Achievement Performance Award (CAPE). The teachers then had the fun of watching the support team self-evaluate the internal processes of the school. When an area of weakness was discovered, flurries of warm fuzzies occurred. The themed meetings with punch and cookies returned. There was an emphasis put on getting teacher feedback and 'listening to our clients.' Monkeysurvey.com became popular, with framed questions that left little in the way of true feedback. The time and energy and money spent on this process did little to improve conditions in the classroom or to do anything that remotely helped students. After our school won a Silver in 2007, the committee presented their findings to the administration. They recommended several areas of improvement. The committee had loved the high degree of teacher accountability they had seen during their visit. They were concerned about the lack of administrative accountability and the obvious absence of a grievance process. Our CEO was personally affronted, so the story goes, and the lack of due process was brushed off as inconsequential. The school was run with the greatest level of personal integrity, she assured them. Personnel matters were handled at the individual classroom site level before there were untenable problems. News of this closed door meeting spread to parts of the school like wildfire. Understandably, the administration never shared this information with the staff.

The End

In the late spring of 2008, a veteran teacher was moved out of her classroom of many years, a move that was intended to be both punitive and an example to others. This Muslim woman had a very beloved place in the local community's heart because she had created a classroom that felt safe and culturally sensitive to a significant number of Muslim girls who called this classroom their own . The teacher's treatment by her superiors, both denigrating and rude, was followed by a transfer to the other side of town, destroying this careful crafted educational community and also triggering a domino effect of teacher reassignments throughout the city. In mid-June, weeks after I had laid out my individualized "Countdown to Graduation" plans to my 23-strong senior class, I was called into the office and told I was being reassigned to another site. Knowing that we lacked a grievance processes and had no organization or committee to assist me with my protest, I fought the reassignment with full knowledge that I was putting my job on the line. It was the utter lack of respect and concern for my student population that drove my response. Indeed, the overwhelming majority (93%) of the senior class I left behind did not graduate that year, further proof that my inability to protect the integrity of my classroom program and the needs of my students had very real and negative consequences for students. They also had negative consequences for my career.

Six weeks later, with numerous teachers assigned to new classrooms and with morale at a dangerous low, the CEO held three teas, hosted in various classrooms scattered around the city. It was billed as her opportunity to share her vision of the future and thoughts about the direction of the school. Its real purpose was sugar-coated, lace-doilied damage control, a way of sending a very clear message to the entire staff that teachers would and could be moved to any site and any time for any reason, and to fight it meant risk of dismissal. "What would you do if a teacher went over the heads of administrators to plead their case to me, and not do as they were specifically asked?" the CEO asked? The answer hung in the dead silence that followed. Furious networking for teachers wanting to leave the school began, and continued unabated for the rest of the school year.

My last months at the school were predictable. I was put under a simple but effective gag order, used against so many in the past and now against me. But unlike the rough handling, professionally speaking, that some of my co-workers got, they kept me at arm's length. I was told I didn't have to report to staff meetings. I declined this invitation. Had I chosen not to attend I would have missed the 45-minute presentation by the CEO. Here she laid out a vision of the perfect charter school teacher, and by comparison, made repeated and pointed criticisms of everything she disliked about the unnamed teachers she used as examples. She focused her repeated attacks on those she disliked and those who threatened her. Absent entirely were words that acknowledged teacher's professionalism or dedication to kids. Several weeks later when a hardworking math teacher was pulled from an extremely math deficient student population, the teacher whose students stood to be most negatively impacted accepted a new job and left. My experience has led me to conclude that when teachers are powerless and can no longer act as advocates and decision makers, students suffer. It really is as simple as that.

And Now?

With President Obama's call for an expansion of the charter school system, I feel it is imperative that charter school teachers have some degree of protection in this brave new non-unionized, hyper-accountable world. Of primary importance is this: charter schools are mainly public schools. They are funded by tax payer money and therefore should be accountable to the taxpayers and the chartering agencies who allow them to exist. Charter schools, by virtue of being charter schools, are not overburdened with an abundance of exemplary administrators. Often these administrators have proven to be underqualified, tyrannical and corrupt, unable to handle the rigors of a traditional school and unwilling to practice leadership in a more transparent environment. It is an abuse of tax payer dollars and an abdication of the trust given to alternative schools to shield and protect men and women who have no business managing the affairs of others. Every charter school in this nation should have a verifiable and transparent grievance process, and teachers should have the right to unionize their schools if administrators are abusing their power and the public's trust. Indeed, a small but growing national discussion on the shape of unionization (Ed Justice 2009) in charters finds a wide area of common interest, "with tremendous opportunity to experiment and develop new models for incorpo-

rating teacher voice into school management" (Hill et al., 2006). Many teachers gravitate towards charters because there is something special in the mission
that they chose to support, and they work hard to advance their students and
create high quality alternatives for their community. This is what so many of
my co-workers did, and it is to be applauded and emulated. I believe that even
at my school this had originally been the case: our CEO, as a once-brave
woman daring to make a difference and desiring an educational option that
would serve the most underserved in our community, created an option for students that had not existed previously. But driven by tests results and statistics,
starved of relevant and meaningful data, and shielded from scrutiny and public accountability, that vision of cutting edge alternative education died a slow
death. The school, based on current school rankings, has now become a 'school
to be improved' and ranked, next to comparable schools, near the very bottom
of the educational pecking order.

I have attempted to share what it feels like to work in a system that is both
driven by a testing regime that has little bearing on real student achievement
and where teachers cannot be an effective voice for creating a culture that promotes learning. The implications for our democracy are profound. Policy makers, in dealing with abstractions, do teachers and students a great disservice by
not recognizing the pitfalls in an accountability movement that holds only small
portions of our educational system truly accountable. The way to fix this broken system is not to do more of the same. Real change is going to require viewing teachers as professionals and asking teachers and students what's working
and what's not.

What is the hopeful message in this? There is one, although it has taken
time to find it. With a society in dire need of thinkers and builders, and many
teachers feeling they are missing an opportunity to truly educate due to the
tightening grip of testing demands, a movement of angry and frustrated reform
is growing. The goal for many now is to radically rethink the accountability system as it is now stands. Even good schools filled with higher socioeconomic students will begin to fail under the impossibly high targets of NCLB, and parents
will become increasingly involved in fighting back. In my daughter's top performing school district, the curriculum has been watered down, with much rich
curricular content stripped out. Only the veteran teachers, with protection of
tenure, quietly close their doors and create rich, vibrant classrooms with minimal drill and kill pedagogy and endless worksheets. Those students who do not
have the benefit of that teaching depth, or teachers protected enough to do
their jobs without administrative harassment, pay a steep price in dull class-

rooms and mind-numbing content. Those who have most suffered through this educational lobotomy are the very students who have traditionally been under-served by public education. My school, whose mission seemed so admirable at the start, was not coupled with the necessary courage and ethical conviction to put kids *and* teachers first. By failing in this duty they validated a corporate model where teachers were viewed as cogs in an educational machine, where students were treated as mere statistics , and the steadying hand of trust and dig-nity stripped out of the educational process.

It is a great irony that in my career I found the same student success in both the charter school classroom and the small classes in the more elite private schools I taught at overseas. Small classes, led by dedicated teachers who engaged their students and their communities, were more apt to meet with suc-cess than a purely data-driven model. If teachers are provided the luxury of working with smaller classes, then they must also be allowed the time to grow and nurture challenging students. These students might not always leave a high school with high test scores, but the very process of being engaged in learning, working with adults who held high expectations, and working within an envi-ronment ruled by dignity and mutual respect would be a refreshing change from the values of competitiveness, ranking, labeling and punishing that constant-ly dominate our schools. No publicly funded educational institution should be allowed to use taxpayer money without federally mandated fiscal transparen-cy and teacher grievance process. If greater fiscal transparency is supposedly good enough for Wall Street, is it good enough for our public schools? When the impact of poverty can be adequately discussed within the reform debate, only then can we get to the heart of many of education's most pressing prob-lems. They are society's problems, and must be addressed on a much larger stage. And teachers must be heard.

I know that these values of honesty and relevancy and engagement in stu-dent's lives work because I have seen them work with students around the word, rich and poor, privileged and not privileged. A poor student from the city and a privileged child from a gated community both want to feel that their days are not wasted, that they learn for a purpose, that the adults who monopolize their time really care about them and have something meaningful to offer. Success is more apparent when a student gets a scholarship to Georgetown or flies through college with multiple majors. Less obvious is the success of an over-weight young man who wouldn't leave his house during high school for fear of being laughed at. Thanks to a teacher he trusted and who visited him almost every day, he now loves community college and hopes to attend the University of California. Success is a student who *survives* high school, who doesn't take her own life or who begins to deal with destructive habits, relationships or addictions. Success is a young man who struggled through a deadening foster care system, but who graduated under your watch and now plans for a future that includes an advanced degree. These are all successes in spite of the fact that each and every one of these challenging students were failures according to the tests that defined and categorized them in high school. Individuals who care or who feel they have a stake in a first-rate educational system need to take a hard look at what lies beyond test scores and to question how decisions are being made within schools and for what ends. A bright light needs to be shone into the inner workings of charter schools, which are, after all, primarily public schools. And accountability, including administrative accountability, fair working conditions, and transparency, need to be the minimal prerequisites of any reform agenda. If it's fair to demand a level of accountability with teachers, then it should be demanded of administrators as well. When that occurs, a more level playing field for all in education will exist, and from that starting point, the real reform needed can begin.

Dedicated to the Shanes and Lindas, Paisleys, Rodneys and Dantes who have so enriched my career. And to Camille and my co-workers, for keeping me grounded.

References

Ayers, C. (2009, April 11). *Authentic accountability for public schools: Susan Ohanian's Outrages.* Retrieved from http://susanohanian.org/show_outrages.html?id=8507

Ed Justice. (2009). *KIPP charter school teachers organize: NYC.* Retrieved from http://edjustice.blogspot.com/2009/01/kipp-charter-school-teachers-organize.html

Emery, K. & Ohanian, S. (2004). *Why is corporate America bashing our public schools.* Portsmouth, NH: Heinemann.

Goldstein, D. (2009). *The charter barter. The American Prospect.* Retrieved from http://www.prospect.org/cs/articles?article=the_charter_barter

Hill, P. T., Rainey, L., & Rotherham, A. (2006). *The future of charter schools and teachers unions.* Retrieved from http://www.ncsrp.org/downloads/charter_unions.pdf

Obama, Barack. *The agenda: Education.* White House Website. Retrieved from http://www.whitehouse.gov/agenda/education/

Schemo, D. J. (2006). Study of test scores shows charter schools lagging. *The New York Times.* Retrieved from http://www.nytimes.com/2006/08/23/education/23charter.html?_r=1&fta=y

Wells, A. S. (2002). *Where charter school policy fails: The problems of equality and equity.* New York: Teachers College.

SECTION III
Deficit Ideology

· 7 ·

Why Aren't We More Enraged?

Virginia Lea

The United States came out of the Second World War as the greatest world power. Intent on maintaining their socio-economic and political hegemony, interwoven governmental and corporate interests were increasingly active in influencing formal educational policy and practice, as this was seen as the key to preparing a work force that would sustain the nation's international superiority. In today's educational system, government and corporate spokespersons have appealed to a similar logic to justify hyper-accountability[1] measures. These measures have resulted in the standardization of formal public education. They have not, however, eliminated the huge opportunity gap, commonly referred to as the "achievement" gap, that remains between poor students, disproportionately of color, and middle/upper middle class students, disproportionately white (NCES, 2005). This inequality is, of course, as old as the United States. However, after World War II, from the 1950s to the early 1970s, it did seem possible to some people that the country would take a different direction. At that time, legal and educational activists used increased federal government willingness to become involved in local politics to win some important civil rights decisions. Their actions exemplified the diverse ways in which hegemonic structures might be harnessed for social justice ends. It appeared, for a moment, that a new zeitgeist, one President Johnson called

"The Great Society," had arrived—one in which deficit policies, practices and thinking might be interrupted and rendered unacceptable to the nation as a whole.

One of these early victories was the end to de jure segregation brought about by the 1954 Supreme Court decision in *Brown versus Board of Education*. However, the *Brown* decision did not result in an immediate end to segregation in schooling—or indeed in an end to segregation at all. The subsequent (1955) *Brown II* decision gave power to those opposed to integration to create impediments to the implementation of *Brown I*. While Chief Justice Warren urged localities to act on the new statute promptly and to move toward full compliance with its principles "with all deliberate speed," the Supreme Court held that the problems identified in *Brown I* required varied local solutions. Therefore, the Court *legalized* delay in implementing the original Brown decision on the part of local courts that had heard the school segregation cases, as well as local educational authorities (Van Delinder, 2004)—and these institutions were led by some of the very people who supported segregation. Indeed, *Brown I and II* resulted in decades of deliberation and school desegregation lawsuits in both the North and the South. However, where desegregation *was* implemented, "integration" frequently represented cultural hegemony and racist educational environments, replete with deficit discourses about students of color. As a result, integration, *also*, has failed to meet the needs of many children of color (*Time*, 1970; Tatum, 1997). I will return to a discussion of the curriculum as cultural hegemony later in this chapter.

In the chapter, I begin by looking at some current deficit practices in education, evidenced with a few findings from my recent research, in which I compare qualitative case studies of two multi-ethnic, working class high schools, one in northern California and the other in south east England. Framed within a complex critical multicultural theoretical lens, this research addressed ways in which hegemonic, deficit narratives have shaped educational practice in these institutions.

Next, I look back at the myth of a golden age in education in United States society (Bastian et al., 1993), prior to World War II, pinpointing some of the most egregious, hegemonic deficit discourses in practice—those laws, socioeconomic practices, cultural and psychometric ideas based on pseudo-science that rendered "normal" and common sense the idea that adults and students of color and people from low-income backgrounds were biologically and/or culturally inferior to whites of a higher socioeconomic class. I intersperse my discussion of this process with a description of some of the many ways people have challenged these discourses. I then further describe some of the civil rights laws and policies of the 1960s and early 1970s, and some of the reasons for their failure to interrupt the increasing socioeconomic inequalities that have been shaped by the neo-liberal, socio-economic structures that had begun to be built after World War II (Loury, 2002; Arrow, Bowles, & Durlauf, 2000).

Finally, I suggest one of the ways in which teacher educators can assist pre-service teachers to interrupt any deficit discourses they may hold about poor students and students of color in low-income schools, in the interest of developing a more equitable, empowering, and liberatory educational process.

Current Deficit Discourses in Education

Hegemony is the process whereby elites "manufacture consent" for their agenda (Chomsky, 1993). Hegemonic control works best when people are unaware that control is being exerted over them. Therefore, elites expend huge efforts to conceal the origins of their power and influence. Indeed, the effectiveness of modern, hegemonic strategies, like surveillance technologies and the ability of elites to control a power-knowledge nexus (Foucault, 1977), may explain in large measure why the efforts of civil rights, social, and educational activists have not had more impact on bringing about a more equitable society. Modern hegemonic technologies of power are "imbued with aspirations for the shaping of conduct in the hope of producing certain desired effects and averting certain undesired ones" (Rose, 1999, p. 52).

Surveillance

We are familiar with Jeremy Bentham's 1795 prison design, the *panopticon*, which allowed guards to observe prisoners at all times without their being aware of being watched. As Foucault observed (1977), this model was a break from the methods of discipline and punishment used by power elites in the past. It was a disciplining strategy that allowed those in power to control the bodies of target populations *unobtrusively*. Such technologies have been and continue to be very effectively used as a way of exerting control over students in public schools.

As part of a research project I undertook in 2007 and 2008, I interviewed twenty teachers in two urban high schools, one in southeast England and one in California, and observed the ways in which current hegemonic discourses were playing out in the teachers' classrooms and schools. I found that surveillance was, indeed, one cog in the wheel of coherent, technologically powerful systems of control emanating from the mandates of governments committed to neo-liberal, hegemonic processes. For example, in Britain, under the so-called Labour Party and Prime Minister Tony Blair, the national government invited corporations to build and run for profit the infrastructure of public schools. Apart from generating an apparent conflict of interest between the corporation expecting to make profit on real estate and the government expecting to provide a meaningful educational experience to students for no profit, the partnership accomplished something else. The school infrastructure was built in the form of a panopticon, allowing administration and teachers to survey their students at all times. The illusion that education was about critical and creative thinking outside of the lines seemed ridiculous in this space. The seeds of past hegemonic projects advocating the re-privatization and deregulation of education were flowering blatantly in the present.

Power over Knowledge

Surveillance was not the only technology of power that I found to be operating in different ways in the two schools in my study. Power was also associated with control over knowledge in the form of "hyper-accountability" (Mansell, 2007; Berlak, 2003). Mandated by the 2001 Elementary and Secondary Education Act No Child Left Behind, (NCLB) in the United States, and the 2004 Children Act in the United Kingdom (Every Child Matters), hyper-accountability is a technique of power that uses high stakes, standardized tests to *normalize* certain academic outcomes. In this way, under the guise of improving failing schools, hyper-accountability contributes to constituting *cultural hegemony*. Both of the public schools in my study were obliged to meet the standards set by their high stakes tests, to respond or risk losing financial support from their governments. Although this one-size-fits-all approach to the curriculum and pedagogy was anathema to most of the teachers in my study, few felt it was possible to resist standardizing their practice to meet the demands of these high stakes tests. In spite of this complicity, I recorded teachers in both schools expressing their frustration in the following terms—"Exams, exams, exams!"; 'It's about control!"; "The Borg!"—although they felt helpless to resist. One teacher said to me about the national educational agenda in Britain that was unabashedly preparing workers to fit into the increasingly hierarchical, political economy: "If this is not the purpose of education, then what we are doing is absurd."

Whiteness, Racism, and Classism

Whiteness, racism, and classism are *normalizing* and *dividing strategies* that have long been used as disciplinary technologies of power to serve the traditional hierarchical system in the United States and Britain (Foucault, 1977). They perform the functions of normalizing certain physical appearances, and ways of thinking, feeling, believing, and acting to the disadvantage of other expressions and those who inhabit them. Whiteness is a *racialized* hegemonic process whereby white privilege—physical signifiers and cultural codes—becomes the invisible norm at all levels of the dominant/mainstream culture, including that of the public school. Whiteness and racism are dynamic. They are sets of ideological cultural discourses that people construct, reconstruct, internalize and practice to reproduce white privilege and social, economic, cultural, political, and educational advantage (Lea & Sims, 2008a). Classism associates deficit with poor people or people from low-income backgrounds. It constitutes unequal socio-economic, political, cultural and educational relations, and justifies hierarchy.

Since the inception of the public school in the U.S., before and after the emergence of the common school, elites have engaged in whiteness, racism, and classism to dominate the school curriculum (Spring, 2008; Anderson, 1988), gain consent for their authority, and conceal this process by making it seem normal and natural (Apple, 1993). In terms of the written curriculum, control was first obtained through puritanical religious texts. More recently, history texts include examples of historical myths, "manufactured" and presented to students as truths, securing their political allegiance to school and the state (Loewen, 1996). The recent "textbook curriculum massacre" in Texas is a case in point (Smith, 2010).

Action and narrative research (Lea & Helfand, 2004; Lea and Sims, 2008b), and analyses of the work of self-styled poverty 'experts' like Ruby Payne (Gorski, 2007; Bohn, 2007; Payne, 1996), have indicated the depth to which current deficit thinking is embedded in and justified by whiteness, racism, and classism. Through the familiar, unobtrusive, common sense, "normal" discourses of whiteness, racism, and classism, the complicity of some teachers and the wider public with deficit, normative curricular and pedagogical discourses has been re-established and maintained in an on-going fashion.

In my study, I observed how the whiteness, racism, and classism embedded in NCLB in the United States and Every Child Matters in the United Kingdom were playing out in classrooms. The curriculum and pedagogy in both schools, while ostensibly open to a full range of critical multicultural perspectives on reality, were in practice privileging ideas and strategies more culturally relevant to students from the dominant culture: Eurocentric, standardized curricula, communication styles, and participation structures. On occasion, the schools actually mandated practices that did not disrupt the status quo. I observed some teachers in both schools with low academic expectations of their students, also expecting their students to *give up* familiar relationships and cultural expectations and move to a middle class, Eurocentric, neo-liberal norm (Payne, 1996). In addition, several were also intent on controlling the class agenda by circumscribing the subject matter to be discussed and disallowing dialogue about controversial issues. Since my own daughter attended the California school, I was reminded of the many occasions on which she came home frustrated by the same lack of freedom of expression.

As agents of powerful states with which they identify, many if not most teachers are loath, even afraid, to challenge official policy. They are also aware that their jobs may be on the line. In carrying out their roles, many come to embody the very disciplinary technologies of power and represent the very tools of neo-liberal forces that function to maintain a socio-economic hierarchy in the interests of the wealthy.

The Myth of a Golden Age: Deficit Thinking in Historical Perspective

Deficit narratives about low income students and students of color, telling us that it is normal and natural to expect these groups to do poorly in school, have always been part of the dominant cultural landscape in the United States. Following independence, many of the "giants" of the U.S. political system, and advocates of the nascent educational system, clearly expressed their belief in the merits of a hierarchical, caste-based, U.S. social order, characterized by white "race," upper/middle class and male privilege. For example, historian "Eric Foner writes that in the minds of the 'founding fathers' was a view of human nature as susceptible to corruption, basically self-interested and dominated by passion rather than reason" (Fresia, 1988). According to this discourse, if human nature is depraved, then democracy needs to be kept in check so that the wise, honest "philosopher kings" of the age can remain in power. Although some have seen James Madison's fear of the power of the masses as wisdom leading to "the tripartite American system of government" (Grandin, 2010), oth-

ers have seen his pronouncement on faction in *Federalist Paper* #10 as an example of the individualist, classist, and racist self-preservation that gripped the
leaders of the new nation based on conquest, slavery and indenture (Fresia,
1988):

> Among the numerous advantages promised by a well constructed Union, none deserves
> to be more accurately developed than its tendency to break and control the violence
> of faction. . . .By a faction, I understand a number of citizens, whether amounting to
> a majority or a minority of the whole, who are united and actuated by some common
> impulse of passion, or of interest, adverse to the rights of other citizens, or to the per-
> manent and aggregate interests of the community. (Madison, 1787).

Another founding father, Thomas Jefferson, like Madison a slave owner, also
used his deficit assumptions to justify the socio-economic framework for the new
nation. While advocating that white male children receive three years of free
education, Jefferson

> felt women ought to have enough education to direct that of their daughters, and if
> need be, their sons "should their fathers be lost, or incapable, or inattentive." He did
> not believe blacks had the mental capacity to warrant much education and would
> always need caregivers. Although he had higher expectations for the Native American
> capacity to learn, Native Americans first and foremost must be taught Euro-American
> culture and give up their own before any attempt at formal education would be made
> (Tozer, Violas, & Senese, 1995, pp. 37–38).

In his own words, Jefferson "advance(d) it therefore as a suspicion only, that
the blacks, whether originally a distinct race, or made distinct by time and circumstances, are inferior to the whites in the endowments both of body and
mind" (Jefferson, 1787). Such a discourse is a powerful justification for the system of slavery of which he took full advantage.

While the War of Independence and the Civil War in the United States
are considered by many to be "sacred wars" (Zinn, 2009), off limits to genuine
critique from multiple perspectives, the supposed father of emancipation,
Abraham Lincoln, contributed the following deficit discourse to the national
psyche in 1858, again justifying segregation if not slavery:

> I will say, then, that I AM NOT NOR HAVE EVER BEEN in favor of bringing about
> in any way the social and political equality of the black and white races—that I am
> not, nor ever have been, in favor of making voters or jurors of negroes, nor of quali-
> fying them to hold office, nor to intermarry with White people; and I will say in addi-
> tion to this that there is a physical difference between the White and black races which

will ever FORBID the two races living together on terms of social and political equality. And inasmuch as they cannot so live, while they do remain together, there must
be the position of superior and inferior, and I, as much as any other man, am in favor
of having the superior position assigned to the White race. (Lincoln, 1858)

However, in spite of the deficit discourses held by revered leaders of the nation,
de jure civil rights initiatives in the United States date back to the end of the
Civil War. Affirmative Action in response to deficit discourses may be said to
have begun with the (1865) Thirteenth Amendment to the Constitution
designed to make slavery illegal. This was followed by the 1866 Civil Rights Act
guaranteeing every citizen "the same right to make and enforce contracts . . .
as is enjoyed by white citizens . . ." (Sykes, 2005). Then, in 1868, the Fourteenth
Amendment to the Constitution was enacted. It was designed to guarantee
equal protection under the law, although technically allowing segregation.
Two years later the Fifteenth Amendment to the Constitution was passed, for-
bidding discrimination in access to voting (1870). Yet, in spite of this amendment, which gave Congress the authority to enforce voting rights and regulate
the voting process, state laws barred African Americans, other citizens of color,
and poor whites from voting through biased literacy tests. This legal situation
was upheld by the United States Supreme Court from the post-Reconstruction
era to 1959 (justicelearning.org, 2010).

Then, in 1989, the *Plessey vs Ferguson* Supreme Court decision upheld the
"separate but equal doctrine" and was followed by Jim Crow laws that enabled
racist practices, exposed by Douglas Blackmon in his (2008) book, *Slavery by
Another Name*. Blackmon, Atlanta bureau chief of the *Wall Street Journal*, told
us about historical details that have rarely been included in the curriculum in
U.S. schools:

Southern convict labor policies perpetuated slavery for almost a century after the
Emancipation Proclamation. . . .Almost as soon as the Civil War ended, powerful white
politicians, plantation owners and industrialists began reinstituting slavery through laws
intended "to criminalize black life.". . .Countless thousands of blacks were arrested on
the flimsiest of charges, thrown into jail and, in effect, sold to plantations, railroads,
mines, factories, mills and lumber camps. . . .In addition, millions of blacks, if they
wanted to work, were forced to do so under labor contracts that prevented them from
leaving without written permission from their employers. Many of these men and
women were also treated like slaves, subject to the harshest discipline. (Barnes, 2008)

Deficit discourses leading to discriminatory, oppressive socioeconomic practices
also impacted immigrants in the early twentieth century. The first large wave
of immigration from Mexico began in 1910 and federal policy against Mexicans

was debated for the first time in 1921. Japanese and Chinese immigrants were also victims of anti-immigrant sentiment, resulting in the Chinese exclusion act in the late 1800s and the Japanese exclusion act in 1924. In 1916, Ellwood P. Cubberley, "Dean of the Stanford University School of Education, describing the goals of the Americanization campaign" insisted that,

> Our task is to break up [immigrant] groups or settlements, to assimilate and amalgamate these people as part of our American race, and to implant in their children, as far as can be done, the Anglo-Saxon conception of righteousness, law and order, and our popular government. (Nunberg, 2007)

From his position of relative power, Cubberley believed in the hegemonic discourse that proclaimed that the "Anglo-Saxon conception of righteousness, law and order, and our popular government" was "common sense," and anyone who did not share this dominant way of thinking, feeling, believing and acting—the culture of power—should be expected to adopt it (ibid.). This included knowing one's place within the dominant culture and the social structure that upheld it. A few years later, in 1925, Dr. Lewis Terman, also of Stanford University, riding the wave of the eugenics movement, reported that "mental tests given to nearly 30,000 children in Oakland prove conclusively that the proportion of failures due chiefly to mental inferiority is nearer 90 per cent than 50 percent" (Epstein, 2006, p. 20; Tyack, 1974). Terman clearly felt justified in declaring that the vast majority of students were deficient by virtue of the standardized tests he had contributed to developing. His stance demonstrates the extraordinary power and longevity of hegemony that continued to shape or attempt to shape popular belief in a Platonic, idealistic notion that human beings were made of different metals and, as a result, should fulfill different roles in the ideal republican state (Spring, 2003). This notion had played out in Madison's, Jefferson's, Lincoln's, Cubberley's, and Terman's "democratic" United States. As research indicates, it plays out still in our consent to technologies of power, like high stakes testing and tracking (Oakes, 2008), that reproduce the status quo. I discuss this further later in this chapter.

It was not until 1941 that another federal initiative, responding to the exigencies of war, was enacted to outlaw discrimination in the workplace. This was Executive Order 8802, signed by President Franklin D. Roosevelt, outlawing segregation in defense-related industries that held federal contracts. Subsequently, in 1953, the Committee of Government Contract Compliance urged the Bureau of Employment Security "to act positively and affirmatively to implement the policy of nondiscrimination . . ." (Sykes, 2005). The year after this action, which was a precursor to the 1965 Affirmative Action law, the Supreme Court's 1954 decision in *Brown v Board of Education* overturned the *Plessy v Ferguson* decision. The *Brown* decision was influenced by the 1950s UNESCO statement that "included both a scientific debunking of race theories and a moral condemnation of racism" (and) suggested in particular to "drop the term 'race' altogether and speak of 'ethnic groups'" (Wikipedia, 2008). However, even though, from then on, de jure segregation no longer existed, segregation was not widely eliminated in practice. According to Steinhorn and Diggs-Brown (1999):

> The fact that some of us dreamed of integrating does not mean it was ever close to happening. The civil rights movement ended legal segregation in America. It created unprecedented opportunities for black political power and economic mobility. It established a social norm that no longer tolerated or condoned overt discrimination and bigotry. . . . it simply couldn't build an integrated America. As much as we like to blame the southern strategy, the silent majority, affirmative action, busing, race riots, multiculturalism, black power, or the precipitous rise of inner-city violent crime for poisoning the "beloved community," the evidence shows that the infrastructure of a separated America had already been established by the time any of these factors even entered the realm of race relations.

Post World War II Laws and Policies: The Promise of Civil Rights

> Over the next thirty or so years of the Cold War, real and imagined threats from the Soviet Union profoundly changed the political, social, and economic life and the cultural landscape of the American nation, including its educational policies and practices. Less than a year after the Sputnik launch, Congress passed NDEA, the National Defense Education Act. This legislation was the first in a series of legislative moves that turned on its head a foundational assumption of US democracy since Colonial times—that schooling of the young was to be a strictly local affair, and pedagogical and curricular decisions were to be left to teachers, principals, districts, and locally elected governing boards. (Berlak, 2003, p. 1)

The promise of a federal affirmative action law, the implementation of the *Brown* desegregation decision, and the 1958 National Defense Education Act gave impetus to the civil rights movement and had a huge impact on American national discourse during the next few decades (Van Delinder, 2004). We saw the growth of the Black Power, Black Panther, civil rights, feminist, and anti-war movements associated with Johnson's (1965) escalation of the Vietnam War. "New Left," youth, disproportionately white, questioned and defied the culture of their parents in what has been called a "cultural revolution." This included challenging sexual mores, as well as the power structure, and traditional norms and values. "Other identity movements—La Raza, Native and Asian American, Latino, gay rights, and ethnic studies movements—emerged challenging corporate and white male dominance of the political process, the culture, and the economy" (Berlak, 2003).

The extraordinary courage of civil rights and local education activists was rewarded with a number of the civil rights laws in the 1960s, including the Equal Pay Act of 1963; the Civil Rights Act of 1964, Title VII prohibiting employment discrimination based on race, sex, national origin, or religion, and Title VI prohibiting public access discrimination, and Title VIII amounting to the original "federal fair housing law," later amended in 1988; the 1965 Executive Order 11246 requiring government contractors to engage in affirmative action; the 1967 ADEA prohibiting age discrimination; and the 1973 Rehab Act barring disability discrimination in employment. In 1965, President Johnson signed the Elementary and Secondary Education Act, or ESEA. This legislation replaced the NDEA in authorizing federal funding for schools and teacher education that had previously been state and local expenditures.

In spite of or perhaps because of the increased involvement of the federal government in insuring civil and education rights, the tight hegemonic web that had enveloped citizens appeared to be strung a little looser. For those committed to integration in schools, however short lived, federal involvement in local educational policy was welcomed. Technology played an increasingly important role in the dissemination of knowledge and communication between activists. For example, when Black citizens and their allies took to the streets to claim their civil rights, denied for over 300 years, citizens who owned televisions gained a visual image of their brutal treatment by some Whites. It appeared to some that deficit discourse was losing momentum. After more than three hundred years of ideological and physical struggle for social justice in what had become the United States of North America, people who had little or nothing to lose and their allies stood up against a racist and classist social system that had failed abysmally to live up to the promise of the Bill of Rights and amendments to the Constitution. Students in large numbers challenged the expansion of the war in Vietnam that was claiming American, Vietnamese and other lives for no purpose they could support or understand. Four white students were shot dead senselessly in 1970 by National Guard at Kent State during one such protest, followed ten days later by the murder, in a similar context, of two Black students by police at Jackson State University. This murder received little media attention in a racist climate, illustrating the depth of the ideological divisions besetting the nation. Poets and musicians of the time expressed the souls of the oppressed in their inspiring lyrics. Latinos, American Indians, Asians, and African Americans had particular reason to sing. Marvin Gaye sang, "Brother, brother, there are too many of us crying/dying," and Edwin Starr asked and answered the question still salient at the time of imperial US wars at the beginning of the 21st century: "War, what is it good for? Absolutely nothing!" These anti-war narratives, juxtaposed with music that engaged the soul, inspired listeners to recognize and challenge the dominant culture of the time.

In 1968, as a white, upper middle-class, immigrant, teenage student, of French, Irish, Arab and Scandinavian origin, raised in England, I was amongst those who observed and participated in this protest. I fell in love with a young Black musician, who is now my husband, and experienced, vicariously, for the first time in my life, what it meant to encounter, on a systematic basis, the deficit discourses about people of color that white people embodied. I learned that if I was to truly live a life committed to social justice I would have to begin to come to terms with and learn to interrupt the ways in which I inhabited these discourses that were deeply embedded in the society's institutions and gave me social and cultural privilege on a daily basis.

Why the US Public Has Not Yet Interrupted the Normalization of Deficit Discourses about Poor Students and Students of Color

While the recognition of injustice, at home and abroad, ignited the action of many civil rights activists at this time, it also ignited to arms entrenched conservative and neo-liberal interests—secular, Christian, and xenophobic (Kumashiro, 2008). The latter were not about to let control of the economy they had collectively defined slip away from them as a result of this wave of egalitarian ideas. Indeed, neo-liberal, transnational capitalism is a socioeconomic system that is not served by the extension of power to the people. According to Harold Berlak (2009):

> The fears that the 1960s movements provoked in the halls of government, big business and culturally right wing sectors of America society are difficult to exaggerate. As the 1970s began, the major US corporations were experiencing what the business pages call a 'profit squeeze.' The World War II enemies of the US, Germany and Japan, were

seriously challenging the economic dominance of the US. All moves toward liberal, social democracy that would restrict corporate power were portrayed by its leaders as serious threats to corporate profitability, economic recovery and growth. To Christian fundamentalists the cultural transformations of the sixties were nothing less than a frontal assault by the godless on their cherished values and beliefs about family, sexuality and country. (p. 4)

Indeed, far from allowing a genuinely free market, neo-liberalism relies on central government ensuring that the socioeconomic playing field is supportive of corporate profitability. The civil rights and anti-poverty activism of the 1960s and early 1970s had not transformed the economic structures of US society so as to prevent the escalation of neo-liberal policies that began to be put into place after the Second World War. The need to curtail government spending after the disastrous over-expenditure on a Vietnam War became a pretext for cutting back on implementing programs supporting equality of educational opportunity and a war on poverty (Klein, 2007). Most importantly, conservative and neo-liberal interests played on enduring deficit discourses and parental fears that mediocre schools were failing to prepare their kids to be competitive in the existing capitalist market—a pretext that is playing out again today.

In the 1970s, then, coporate and business elites began to successfully reframe multicultural, civil rights efforts in education as inadequate to meet the needs of middle class and low-income children. As Harold Berlak (2003) explained, full-blown standardization in US education, representing cultural hegemony, would not be realized until the administration of George W. Bush with the passage of the 2002 version of the Elementary and Secondary Education Act, No Child Left Behind. However, the journey to this increased neo-liberal federal government and corporate control of schooling began during the administration of Ronald Reagan under Secretary of Education, Terrel Bell. The 1982 report, A Nation at Risk, laid the groundwork for future public discourse on education by focusing on "excellence" as opposed to equity and "high standards" as opposed to critical multicultural education. The report also co-opted the educational debate by linking education to an economy that was said to need to become more competitive internationally (Berlak, 2003). As mentioned, this call is being echoed mercilessly by President Obama today.

The fact that today we have a Black president, a person of color at the top of a socioeconomic, hierarchical system in deep depression, is no doubt associated with the changes in social norms and values that took place during this "civil rights period" in history. Yet, at the same time we have the Tea Party

Movement that is resisting what they perceive as the president's "socialist" policies. While a very long way from the truth, this predominantly white male, largely middle class interest group, an entitled sector of the population, is against any initiative that impacts and detracts from their individual rights.

> At the heart of Tea Party history is the argument that "progressivism is fascism is communism." Conceptually, such a claim helps frame what many call "American exceptionalism," a belief that the exclusive role of government is to protect individual rights—to speech, to assembly, to carry guns, and, of course, to own property—and not to deliver social rights like health care, education, or welfare. US society remains hugely divided and greater race and class equity seems a distant reality. (Grandin, 2010)

Moreover, President Obama receives on average 300 death threats a day (*Democracy Now*, 2009) and presides over a society that was described by Michael Yates in 2005, three years *before* the current depression, as follows:

> (Except for the Clintonian years between 1995 and 2000), the working class has been taking a beating for the last 30 years. . . . There is a great deal of wage inequality in the United States, and it has been growing since the late 1970s. . . . Two important aspects of wage inequality are the decline in the real value of the minimum wage and the runaway inflation of the salaries of top corporate officials. . . . The ratio of CEO pay to the wage of the average worker went from 24 to 1 in 1967 to 300 to 1 in 2000. (pp. 17–18)

In summary, federal government intervention in U.S. society after World War II was clearly influenced by the demands of the people for equal rights in the society for which they fought in that war and subsequently in Korea and Vietnam. However, it is also clear in retrospect that the *Brown* and subsequent civil rights decisions did not represent sufficient societal transformation to ensure the development of an equitable U.S. educational system and society. As Derrick Bell (2004) noted:

> Generating an emotionally charged concoction of commendations and condemnations, the *Brown* decision recreated the Nineteenth Century's post-Civil War Reconstruction/ Redemption pattern of progress followed by retrogression. It stirred confusion and conflict into the always-vexing questions of race in a society that, despite denial and a frustratingly flexible amnesia, owes much of its growth, development, and success to the ability of those dominant members of society who use race to both control and exploit most people, whatever their race. (p. 5)

Alternatives to Deficit Approaches to Teaching: Recognizing and Re-cognizing² Our Own Deficit Discourses

In this chapter, I have argued that the *Brown* decision, and the subsequent passage of civil rights laws signed by President Johnson in the mid-1960s, did not represent sufficient societal transformation to ensure the development of an equitable U.S. society. So, what will it take to interrupt the historical normalizing of deficit discourses about poor students and students of color? A first step would be to recognize the ways in which these narratives are not only situated in institutions but at the nexus of our relationships with one another. They form part of our identities, deeply held in ourselves as unconscious and/or less than conscious knowledge (Berlak, 2008; King, 1991).

Critical multicultural alternatives to deficit approaches to teaching owe much to Paulo Freire (1993/1970) and to those who have contributed to his humanist and transformational educational teachings (Au, 2009; Darder et al., 2003; Steinberg, 2009). Critical pedagogical narratives help students to understand the culture of power and the relationship between power and knowledge. They help students understand themselves and their own social and cultural worlds in relation to the culture of power (Delpit, 1995; 1988). Such narratives encourage students to engage in praxis—the act of "reflection and action on the world in order to transform it" (Freire, 1970, in Glass, 2001, p. 16). In fact, according to Freire, praxis is necessary to freedom. It allows all human beings to engage in "intentional, reflective and meaningful activity" that is historically and culturally situated (Glass, 2001, p. 16).

Given this agency we, as teachers, have the opportunity to structure learning experiences for our students through which we can come, reciprocally, to recognize and re-cognize or rethink our own deficit narratives. In my own as a critical multicultural teacher educator, I involve my pre-service teachers in a number of different experiences towards this end. They include a cultural portfolio (Lea, 2004), a Mask assignment (Lea, 2010), a Whiteness Artifact exercise (Lea & Sims, 2008a), a Culture Shock experience, (Lea & Sims, 2008a; Lea, 2009), "educultural" experiences (Lea & Sims, 2008b), and a "Funds of Knowledge" assignment (Moll et al., 1992; Lea, 2010).

I have also engaged my disproportionately white and middle class, pre-service teachers in a *Problem-Posing approach* (Freire, 1993/1970) to enable their own students, often from lower income backgrounds and of color, to find meaning in developing literacy tools to "read *their* world." In this course, the pre-service teachers worked in teams with second language learners and African

American students who attended after-school programs run by Migrant Education and other local community organizations. After several weeks of getting to know their students, and working on developing a level of critical consciousness in which they were able to affirm difference, work in solidarity with their students, and critique hegemony as it was embodied by society, school, and themselves (Nieto & Bode, 2007), my pre-service teachers began to develop critical literacy and community action projects. They asked their students what "problems" they wished to resolve or interests they wished to realize in their lives or communities. Once the problems and/or interests had been identified, the pre-service teachers helped their students to develop the literacy, numeracy, historical, scientific, artistic or other tools (critical literacy project: linking the "word" with the "world") that they might apply to realize their goals in a community action project: implementing the "word" to better "read the world."

In critical multicultural literacy terms, the pre-service teachers are building on their students' generative themes, engaging them in dialogue, and developing their voices and critical consciousness. They are helping their students to read "texts" (written/film/performance) critically; recognize hidden, hegemonic scripts and interlocking systems of oppression; analyze motives and interests; synthesize two or more "texts"; evaluate the word in terms of ethical standards that *they*, the students, develop; and construct hybrid ideas. The students and their pre-service teachers develop identity and agency. Throughout this work, through readings, film, and dialogue, the pre-service teachers continue to work on identifying and transforming in practice and praxis their own deficit assumptions. They check their stereotypes and become cognizant of power relations. They grow awareness of their own "positionality," and how white, upper/middle class/males have been advantaged by historical and current policies and practices. They become committed to ongoing dialogue with and empowering the families of the students with whom they are working. Through problem-posing education, their students are facilitated in understanding and developing ways of using literacy to help identify and act on real alternatives to the "limit situations" in which they find themselves (Freire, 1993/1970).

Conclusion

Resistance to real change for equity is, then, deeply embedded in U.S. historical practice. Building on ancient "common sense" understandings—including

Plato's notion that human beings were made of different "metals" and were therefore of differential worth (Rouse, 1956)—governmental and corporate discourses and propaganda have constituted a patriotic citizenry, the majority of whose members consent to the nascent neo-liberal, capitalist state. While this citizenry is currently divided in terms of who is to blame for the recent financial crisis, most people perceive the institutions and culture of the military-corporate state as essentially benign, and view its maintenance as a normal and natural process. Whiteness, racism, and classism, amongst other deficit narratives, still govern this process, aided by modern disciplinary technologies of power.

While my classroom work does not replace the need for change at the socio-economic and policy level to transform socio-economic and educational structures towards more equitable, sustainable models, my own on-going action research indicates that the above *problem-posing* process shows promise in undoing deficit thinking and preparing teachers to build deep and committed relationships with their students. As the course developed, an increasing number of my pre-service teachers began to develop a vision of human possibility that transcended the stereotypical shadows portrayed by deficit theorists like Ruby Payne. Some of them have come to see their own students as agents of social transformation in their own right, capable of socially constructing liberatory knowledge—quite a change given the conservative, segregated backgrounds of many of my white, upper middle class teacher candidates. A few radically re-imagine themselves, their relationships, and the categories they use to make sense of the world. They understand and feel how whiteness, racism and classism have led them to falsely generous, color-blind, culturally hegemonic relationships with students of color (Freire, 1993/1970; Bonilla-Silva, 2006). They are better able to identify the oppressive policies and practices of the past and commit to becoming agents in the service not of the state but of their own students. They reject complicity with hegemony on the terms of "experts" like Ruby Payne, who expects students to become "good student subjects" by giving up their languages and home cultures.

If we are to build a society based on genuine socio-economic, racial, and gender justice, as was envisioned by some in the 60s, we still need to work collectively, in solidarity. However, today's activists must also learn the lessons of the last fifty years. We must understand how the hegemonic deficit discourses of whiteness, racism, classism, neo-liberalism and other disciplinary technologies of power work to reproduce systemic inequities within the educational system and wider society. We must be aware of how we embody these discourses, and how easily our emancipatory, creative and critical actions can become indi-vidualized and un-tethered from their social justice moorings by policies and practices serving dominant, corporate and political interests. We must active-ly search for collective and individual ways to engage in a new civil rights move-ment for the 21st century and continue to imagine socio-economic and inter-ethnic relationships that will result in a fairer and kinder quality of life for all people. As Martin Luther King said on April 4, in 1967, in New York City:

> We were convinced (in forming the *Southern Christian Leadership Conference*) that we could not limit our vision to certain rights for black people, but instead affirmed the conviction that America would never be free or saved from itself until the descendants of its slaves were loosed completely from the shackles that they still wear. In a way we were agreeing with Langston Hughes, the black bard of Harlem, who had written ear-lier:
>
> *O, yes, I say it plain,*
> *America never was America to me,*
> *And yet I swear this oath—*
> *America will be!*

Notes

1. Hyper-accountability refers to the testing and accountability measures mandated by recent government legislation: the 2001 Elementary and Secondary Education Act, No Child Left Behind in the United States, and Every Child Matters in the United Kingdom.
2. I have borrowed these terms from my brilliant colleague and friend, Jean Ishibashi.

References

Anderson, J. (1988). *The Education of Blacks in the South, 1860–1935*. Chapel Hill: The University of North Carolina Press.

Apple, M. (1993). Constructing the Other: Rightist Reconstructions of Common Sense. In C. McCarthy & W. Crichlow (Eds.), *Race, Identity and Representation in Education*. New York: Routledge.

Arrow, K., Bowles, S., Durlauf, S. (Eds.) (2000). *Meritocracy and Economic Inequality*. Princeton: Princeton University Press.

Au, W. (Ed.). (2009). *Rethinking Multicultural Education: Teaching for Racial and Cultural Justice*. Milwaukee: Rethinking Schools.

Barnes, H. (March, 2008). Slavery by Another Name. *St. Louis Post-Dispatch*. Retrieved March 25, 2008, from http://www.stltoday.com/stltoday/entertainment/reviews.nsf/book/story/5299116F8715402386257415007A5F83?OpenDocument

Bastian, A., et al. (1993). Three Myths of School Performance. In H. Svi & D. Purpel (Eds.), *Critical Social Issues in American Education: Toward the 21st Century*. NewYork: Longman.

Bell, D. (2004). *Silent Covenants: Brown v. Board of Education and the Unfulfilled Hopes for Racial Reform*. New York: Oxford University Press.

Berlak, A, (2008). Challenging the hegemony of whiteness by addressing the adaptive unconscious. In V. Lea & E. J. Sims, *Undoing Whiteness: Critical Educultural Teaching for Social Justice Activism*. New York: Peter Lang.

Berlak, H. (2003, 17 October). From local control to government and corporate takeover of school curriculum: The No Child Left Behind Act and the 'Reading First' program. v.1.

Berlak, H. (2009). Education policy 1964–2004: The No Child Left Behind Act and the assault on progressive education and local control. *Rouge Forum*. Retrieved July15, 2009 from http://www.pipeline.com/~rougeforum/PolicyandNCLB.htm

Blackmon, D. A. (2008). *Slavery by Another Name: The Re-enslavement of Black Americans from the Civil War to World War II*. New York: Doubleday.

Bohn, A. (2007).*A Framework for Understanding Ruby Payne*. Milwaukee, WI: Rethinking Schools.

Bonilla-Silva, E. (2006). *Racism without Racists: Color-blind Racism and the Persistence of Racial Inequality in the United States*. Lanham, MD: Rowman & Littlefield.

Chomsky, N. (1993). *Year 501: The Conquest Continues*. Boston: South End Press.

Cochran-Smith, M. & the Boston College Evidence Team (2009). "Re-culturaling" teacher education: Inquiry, evidence, and action. *Journal of Teacher Education*, 60 (5), 458–468.

Darder, A., Baltodano, M., & Torres, R. (2003). *The Critical Pedagogy Reader*. New York: RoutledgeFalmer.

Delpit, L. (1995). *Other People's Children: Cultural Conflict in the Classroom*. New York: The New Press.

Delpit, L. (1988, August).The silenced dialogue: Power and pedagogy in teaching other people's children. *Harvard Educational Review*, 58 (3), 280–298.

Democracy Now (2009). August 4 Broadcast. Podcast retrieved from www.democracynow.org/

Epstein, K. K. (2006). *A Different View of Urban Schools: Civil Rights, Critical Race Theory, and Unexplored Realities*. New York: Peter Lang.

Foucault, M. (1977). *Discipline & Punish: The Birth of the Prison*. New York: Random House.

Freire, P. (1993/1970). *Pedagogy of the Oppressed*. New York: Continuum.

Fresia, J. (1988). *Toward an American Revolution: Exposing the Constitution and Other Illusions*. Boston, MA: South End Press.

Glass, R. (2001). *Educational Researcher*. Washington, DC: American Educational Research Authority.

Gorski, P. (Spring, 2007). The question of class. Teaching for Tolerance, 31. Retrieved from the Teaching for Tolerance website: http://www.tolerance.org/magazine/number-31-spring-2007/question-class

Grandin, G. (2010). Glenn Beck, America's historian laureate: The Tea Party's guide to American Exceptionalism (It is all about race). Retrieved May 17th, 2010:http://www.tomdispatch.com/post/175247/tomgram%3A_greg_grandin%2C_does_the_tea_party_run_on_race

Jefferson, T. (1787). from Notes on the State of Virginia. *Jefferson on Race and Slavery*, Retrieved online June 15, 2009: http://pasleybrothers.com/jefferson/jefferson_on_race_and_slavery.htm

justicelearning.org (2010). Retrieved May 11, 2010: http://www.justicelearning.org/justice_timeline/Amendments.aspx?id=15

King, J. (1991). Dysconscious racism: Ideology, identity, and the miseducation of teachers. *Journal of Negro Education* 60 (2), 1–14.

King, M. L. (1967). Beyond Vietnam speech in New York City. Retrieved online: http://www.stanford.edu/group/King/publications/speeches/Beyond_Vietnam.pdf.

Klein, N. (2007). *The Shock Doctrine: The Rise of Disaster Capitalism*. New York: Picador.

Kumashiro, K. (2008). *The Seduction of Common Sense: How the Right Has Framed the Debate on America's Schools*. New York: Teachers College Press.

Lea, V. (2004, March/April). The reflective cultural portfolio: Identifying public scripts in the private voices of white student teachers. *Journal of Teacher Education*, 55 (2), 116–127.

Lea, V. (2009). Unmasking Whiteness in the Teacher Education College Classroom: Critical and Creative Multicultural Practice. In S. Steinberg (Ed.), *Diversity & Multiculturalism: A Reader*. New York: Peter Lang.

Lea, V. (2010). Empowering pre-service teachers, students and families through critical multiculturalism: Interweaving social foundations of education and community action projects. In S. May & C. Sleeter (Eds.), *Critical Multiculturalism: From Theory to Practice*. New York: Routledge.

Lea, V. & Helfand, J. (Eds.). (2004). *Identifying Race and Transforming Whiteness in the Classroom*. New York: Peter Lang.

Lea, V. & Sims, E. J. (2008a). Imaging whiteness and hegemony in the classroom: Undoing oppressive practice and inspiring social justice activism. In V. Lea V. & E. J. Sims (2008). *Undoing Whiteness in the Classroom: Critical Educultural Teaching for Social Justice Activism*. New York: Peter Lang.

Lea V. & Sims, E.J. (2008b). *Undoing Whiteness in the Classroom: Critical Educultural Teaching for Social Justice Activism*. New York: Peter Lang.

Lincoln, A. (1894). Spoken at Springfield, Illinois on July 17th, 1858. *Abraham Lincoln: Complete Works*, 1, p. 273, Retrieved online: http://www.civilwarhistory.com/_/lincoln/Abraham%20Lincoln%200n%20Race.htm

Loewen, J. (1996). *Lies My Teacher Told Me: Everything Your American History Textbook Got Wrong*. New York: Touchstone.

Loury, G. C. (2002). *The Anatomy of Racial Inequality*. Cambridge, MA: Harvard University Press.

Madison, J. (1787, November 22). *The Federalist* No. 10: The Utility of the Union as a Safeguard Against Domestic Faction and Insurrection (continued). *Daily Advertiser*, Retrieved July 30, 2009 from http://www.constitution.org/fed/federa10.htm.

Mansell, W. (2007). *Education by Numbers: The Tyranny of Testing*. London: Politico's.

Moll, L. C., Amanti, C., Neff, D., Gonzales, N. (1992, Spring), Funds of knowledge for teachers: Using a qualitative approach to connect homes and classrooms. *Theory into Practice*, XXXI (2).

NCES (2005). Dropout rates in the United States. Retrieved May 17th 2010, from the NCES website: http://nces.ed.gov/pubs2007/dropout05/NationalEventDropout.asp.

Nieto, S. & Bode, P. (2007). *Affirming Diversity: The Sociopolitical Context of Multicultural*

Education. Boston: Allyn & Bacon.

Nunberg, G. (2007). Afterword: The official English movement: Reimagining America. Quoted in J. Crawford, *Bilingual Education: History, Politics, Theory, and Practice*, 3rd ed. Los Angeles: Bilingual Educational Services, p. 27.

Oakes, J. (2008). Keeping track: Structuring equality and inequality in an era of accountability. *Teachers College Record*, 110 (3) 700–712. Retrieved from http://www.tcrecord.org, ID Number: 14610, 2/3/10.

Payne, R. (1996). *A Framework for Understanding Poverty*. Highlands, TX: aha! Process, inc.

Rose, N. (1999) *Powers of Freedom: Reframing Political Thought*. Cambridge: Cambridge University Press.

Rouse, W. H. D. (1956). *Great Dialogues of Plato*. Denver, CO: Mentor.

Smith, E. (April 26, 2010). The Texan curriculum massacre: What a conservative rewriting of history tells us about how Texans view the world, which is, for them, Texas. *Newsweek*.

Spring, J. (2003). *American Education*. New York: McGraw-Hill.

Steinberg, S. (Ed.). (2009). *Diversity and Multiculturalism: A Reader*. New York: Peter Lang.

Steinhorn, L. & Diggs-Brown, B. (1999, November/December). By the color of our skin: The illusion of integration and the reality of race. *Poverty & Race*. Washington, DC: Poverty & Race Research Action Council.

Sykes, M. (2005, August). The origins of Affirmative Action. *National Organization of Women*. Retrieved 26 March 2008 from http://www.now.org/nnt/08–95/affirmhs.html

Tatum, B. D. (1997). *"Why Are All the Black Kids Sitting Together in the Cafeteria? And Other Conversations about Race*. New York: Basic.

Time (1970, July 13). The bad side of integration. *Time*. Retrieved July 30, 2009 from http://www.time.com/time/magazine/article/0,9171,909450,00.html

Tozer, S. E., Violas, P. C., and Senese, G. B. (1995). School and society: Historical and contemporary perspectives. In M. Brulatour, *Transcendental Ideas: Education. Background for the State of Education in New England: Post-Revolutionary War to Mid-19th Century*, Retrieved January 17th, 2009 from American Transcendentalism Webpage: http://www.vcu.edu/engweb/transcendentalism/ideas/edhistory.html

Tyack, D. B. (1974). *The One Best System: A History of American Urban Education*. Cambridge, MA: Harvard University Press.

Uribe, M. & Nathenson-Mejia, S. (2008). *Literacy Essentials for English Language Learners: Successful Transitions*. New York: Teachers College Press.

Van Delinder, J. (2004, Spring). *Brown v. Board of Education of Topeka*: A landmark case unresolved fifty years later. *Prologue Magazine*, 36 (1). Retrieved July 30, 2009, from *The National Archives.Gov* website: http://www.archives.gov/publications/prologue/2004/spring/brown-v-board-1.html)

Wikipedia (2008). Voting Rights Act. Retrieved 25 March 2008 from http://en.wikipedia.org/wiki/Voting_Rights_Act#Background

Yates, M. D. (2005, April). A statistical portrait of the U.S. working class. *Monthly Review*, 56 (11), 12–31.

Zinn, H. (2009, May 13). I wish Obama would listen to MLK. *Democracy Now*. Retrieved July 30, 2009, from http://www.democracynow.org/2009/5/13/howard_zinn_i_wish_obama_would

· 8 ·

Unlearning Deficit Ideology and the Scornful Gaze

Thoughts on Authenticating the Class Discourse in Education

PAUL C. GORSKI

IT IS POPULAR IN THE EDUCATION MILIEU TODAY TO TALK ABOUT THE DANGERS of assuming a *deficit perspective,* approaching students based upon our perceptions of their weaknesses rather than their strengths. Such a perspective deteriorates expectations for students and weakens educators' abilities to recognize giftedness in its various forms (Ford & Grantham, 2003). The most devastating brand of this sort of deficit thinking emerges when we mistake *difference*— particularly difference from ourselves—for *deficit.* If one concentrates best while sitting still it may be difficult to imagine that somebody else—a student or colleague, perhaps—concentrates more effectively while pacing or tapping a pencil. Similarly, if one always has lived among people who speak a certain language variation, such as what people commonly refer to as "standard English," she or he might mistake somebody's use of a different variation, such as the Appalachian variety spoken by my grandmother, as an indication of intellectual inferiority or, worse, deviance (Collins, 1988).

Over the past ten or so years a critical discourse challenging the deficit perspective has emerged among educators. Some insist that "every student is gifted and talented." Others urge us to "find the gift in every child"; to "focus on student strengths." Unfortunately, like many discourses in the education milieu, the one surrounding the deficit perspective occurs largely outside of what Nieto and Bode (2008) call the *sociopolitical context* of schooling, "the unexamined ideologies and myths that shape commonly accepted ideas and values in a society" (p. 7). So while this discourse involving deficit perspective focuses on individual attitudes and biases, it rarely addresses the ideologies or conditions which underlie and perpetuate the deficit perspective.

Like most repressive dispositions, the deficit perspective is a symptom of larger sociopolitical conditions and ideologies born out of complex socialization processes. We can no more quash the deficit perspective without acknowledging, examining, and quashing these processes than we can eliminate racism without comprehending and battling white supremacist ideology. Otherwise we are dealing merely with symptoms, as we do when we attempt to redress racism with programs that celebrate diversity but ignore systemic racism or when we respond to class inequities by studying a fictitious "culture of poverty" rather than attacking, or at least understanding the educational implications of, the sociopolitical context of economic injustice.

The ideology underlying the deficit perspective has been described as "deficit theory" (Collins, 1988; Dudley-Marling, 2007; Gorski, 2008a), "deficit ideology" (Sleeter, 2004), and "deficit thinking" (Ford & Grantham, 2003; Pearl, 1997; Valencia, 1997; Yosso, 2005). I have chosen to use the term "deficit ideology" in this chapter in order to emphasize that it is, in fact, an ideology, based upon a set of assumed truths about the world and the sociopolitical relationships that occur in it. Despite variations in terminology, scholars who have studied deficit ideology similarly refer to something deeper than individual assumptions and dispositions. They describe an institutionalized worldview, an ideology woven into the fabric of U.S. society and its socializing institutions, including schools. They describe an ideology *which shapes individual assumptions and dispositions* in order to encourage compliance with an oppressive educational and social order. As Sleeter (2004) explains, "the long-standing deficit ideology still runs rampant in many schools . . . despite the abstraction that 'all children can learn'" (p. 133).

Briefly, deficit ideology is a worldview that explains and justifies outcome inequalities—standardized test scores or levels of educational attainment, for example—by pointing to supposed deficiencies within disenfranchised individuals and communities (Brandon, 2003; Valencia, 1997; Weiner, 2003; Yosso, 2005). Simultaneously, and of equal importance, deficit ideology discounts sociopolitical context, such as the systemic conditions (racism, economic injustice, and so on) that grant some people greater social, political, and economic access, such as that to high-quality schooling, than others (Brandon, 2003; Dudley-Marling, 2007; Gorski, 2008a; Hamovitch, 1997). The function of deficit ideology, as I will describe in greater detail later, is to justify existing social conditions by identifying the problem of inequality as *located within*, rather than as *pressing upon*, disenfranchised communities so that efforts to redress inequalities focus on "fixing" disenfranchised people rather than the conditions which disenfranchise them (Weiner, 2003; Yosso, 2005).

Dudley-Marling (2007) has warned of a recent resurgence of deficit ideology in the U.S., particularly visible in discourses related to low-income people's access to public services such as high-quality education, welfare, and healthcare. In the case of education, the class discourse tends to focus on outcomes in educational "achievement," and more specifically on how to "close" achievement gaps between low-income students and their wealthier peers, a framing which is, itself, a symptom of deficit ideology (as I will explain later). It is my intention here to describe the nature of this current wave of class-based deficit ideology, the ways in which it has come to dominate today's discourses on the education of low-income people, and the consequences thereof. In the process of doing so I hypothesize a process by which people in the U.S., including teachers, are socialized to comply with deficit ideology. I then discuss ways to "spot" and interrupt class-based deficit ideology in educational contexts.

Conceptualizing Deficit Ideology

Deficit ideology is a remnant of imperial history (Shields, Bishop, & Mazawi, 2005), a mechanism for socializing citizens to comply with a host of oppressions, from colonization to enslavement, educational inequities to unjust housing practices. In the most basic terms, deficit ideology can be understood as a sort of "blame the victim" mentality applied, not to an individual person, but systemically, to an entire group of people, often based upon a single dimension of identity. At the core of deficit ideology is the belief that inequalities result, not from unjust social conditions such as systemic racism or economic injustice but from intellectual, moral, cultural, and behavioral deficiencies assumed to be inherent in disenfranchised individuals and communities (Brandon, 2003; Gorski, 2008a, 2008b; Valencia, 1997; Yosso, 2005). The deficit ideologue justifies this belief by drawing on stereotypes already well established in the mainstream psyche—stereotypes which paint disenfranchised communities as intellectually, morally, and culturally deficient or deviant (Villenas, 2001; Weiner, 2003). *Why are poor people poor? They're lazy. They don't care about education. They're substance abusers. . . .* These stereotypes, however untrue—and, as we will see, considerable amounts of research clarify that people in poverty are not, in fact, lazier, less likely to value education, or more likely to be sub-stance abusers than their wealthier counterparts—are the deficit ideologue's ammunition. She or he uses them, in a process Rank (2004) calls "labeling," to draw a clear us/them distinction. Apple (2006) explains,

> We are law-abiding, hardworking, decent, and virtuous. 'They'—usually poor people and immigrants—are very different. They are lazy, immoral, and permissive. These binary oppositions act to exclude indigenous people, women, the poor, and others from the community of worthy individuals. (p. 22)

This sort of binary encourages all people, including those who otherwise might identify strongly with the "they," to associate with the "we," particularly upon witnessing the consequences of not doing so. It becomes easier, then, to train the mass consciousness to pathologize disenfranchised communities—to, in effect, blame them for their own disenfranchisement. Once that scornful gaze down the power hierarchy is in place, so the justification is established for main-taining existing social, political, and economic conditions, such as gross inequities in access to healthcare or educational opportunity, or the waning of social programs and supports for disenfranchised communities. After all, if poor communities are to blame for their own poverty, they are more easily paint-ed as being unworthy or undeserving of a fair shake (Apple, 2006).

Consider, for example, the stereotype that low-income families do not value education. This stereotype often is propagated within school walls, not by educators who intend to act unjustly, but by those who have been socialized by the deficit hegemony to buy into and perpetuate it (Yosso, 2005). Rarely have I participated in a conversation with a roomful of educators about class and poverty in schools without observing multiple and impassioned attempts to frame the conversation primarily, if not completely, in reference to low-income families' supposed disinterest in, lack of motivation for, and disengage-ment from their children's education. We must recognize, first of all, that this stereotype is fallacious. Studies have shown since the late 1970s that low-income families have the same attitudes about the value of education as their wealthier counterparts (Compton-Lilly, 2003; Lareau & Horvat, 1999; Leichter, 1978). But we must recognize, as well, that facts and evidence are of little mit-igating consequence against mass perception. Once the justifying stereotype is socialized into the mainstream consciousness, the foundation for mass compli-ance is set.

Mass compliance with deficit ideology can be witnessed most clearly, per-haps, in the way we, in education, have responded to the "problem" of the "socioeconomic achievement gap." We comply by employing a deficit perspective and, as a result, demonstrating low expectations of low-income students (Sleeter, 2004). We comply by locating the problem of the socioeconomic achievement gap within low-income families and communities (Ladson-Billings, 2006). We comply by demonizing the most powerless people among us (Weiner, 2003)—*those people don't care about education!* And, as a result, we comply by attempting to redress the socioeconomic achievement gap by offering parenting classes and mentors to low-income families and students, measures that assume the chief problems to be what low-income communities lack, rather than by understanding and addressing the larger sociopolitical context of class inequity in the U.S. and its schools (Lipman, 2008; Weiner, 2003; Yosso, 2005). And this is the surest sign of deficit ideology: the suggestion that we fix inequalities by fixing disenfranchised communities rather than that which disenfranchises them.

This, then, is the *function* of deficit ideology: to manipulate popular consciousness in order to deflect attention from the systemic conditions and sociopolitical context that underlie or exacerbate inequities, such as systemic racism or economic injustice, and to focus it, instead, on recycling its own misperceptions, all of which justify inequalities (García & Guerra, 2004; Jennings, 2004). It deflects our scornful gaze from the mechanisms of injustice and the benefactors of these mechanisms, and trains it, instead, on those citizens with the least amount of power to popularize a counter-narrative, just as the dominant "achievement gap" discourse draws attention away from underlying systemic conditions, such as growing corporate control of public schools, and pushes it toward "at-risk" youth from "broken" homes whose "culture of poverty" impedes them from "making it." Deficit ideology defines every social problem in relation to those toward the bottom of the power hierarchy, trains our gaze in that direction and, as a result, manipulates the popular discourse in ways that protect and reify existing sociopolitical conditions (Brandon, 2003; Yosso, 2005).

This phenomenon is not new in the U.S. Slavery, American Indian genocide, Jim Crow: these and countless other atrocities have been perpetuated against people through a similar socializing process. Writing about one popular target of deficit ideology in the U.S., Jennings (2004) explains,

> Dominant imagery depicts single mothers on welfare as women who lack an 'appropriate' orientation to the Protestant work ethic and to mainstream family values. Consequently, reform discourse emphasizes resocialization; it encourages the formation of programs that aim to inculcate an 'appropriate' (read White, middle class, heterosexual) orientation to work and family. (p. 114)

Similarly, a litany of atrocities within the education milieu, from the withering away of bilingual education to inequitable school funding, have been aided by deficit socialization processes that frame the least powerful communities as deficient and, as a result, undeserving of equal opportunity. Brantlinger's (2003) study of middle class attitudes toward educational equity illustrated this point. She found that middle class parents supported equitable educational access in theory but almost universally retracted their support when faced with the possibility of resources being redistributed out of their children's schools and into those of lower-income communities. Her study raised important questions about the sorts of cognitive tensions people experience when their worldviews are informed by conflicting value systems and socializations. But it also demonstrated how deficit ideology can be a strategic wedge or buffer protecting the economic elite: it encourages the middle class to see poor and working class people as threats to the meager levels of access they have been granted, despite the fact that their lot is much more similar to that of poor and working class people than to that of wealthy people. As a result, as Kivel (2006) explains, the middle class and even the working class, by scornful gazes trained down the wealth hierarchy, in effect police compliance with the corporatocracy by keeping each other and the poor in line with, among other behavior management tools, the threat of the "them" label, evident in the "othering" power of brands like "socialist" or "communist." Unfortunately, as long as these sorts of deficit discourses dominate conversations about class and poverty, the notion will dominate that we "fix" problems like poverty by "fixing" those most devastated by them (Villenas, 2001). And so long as we apply our resources and energies in this manner, we ignore the sociopolitical conditions that underlie poverty and its implications in and out of schools: the scarcity of living wage jobs, the scarcity of access to quality health care, and so on.

Complicating matters, schools, as the common refrain goes, are only microcosms of the larger society. They are micro-contexts into which individuals and groups carry their socializations, behaving accordingly. The false stereotype that low-income families do not value education can be seen, then, as a symptom of broader social conditioning to which current and future educators are susceptible. For example, the insinuations of laziness and irresponsibility underlying the stereotype that low-income people do not value education is propagated commonly by policy-makers who want to pinpoint the "problem" of class inequities *outside* of the systems they control and the larger sociopolitical conditions that have facilitated their own ascents to power. So although Berliner (2006) and others have argued rightly that we cannot assign schools the full responsibility for undoing systemic economic injustices such as the scarcity of living wage jobs or growing corporate influence on schools, a task for which they are neither intended nor equipped, these conditions are integral to the socializing processes of current and future educators and the experiences of students and their families. And, as Berliner (2006) demonstrated, they substantially influence educational outcomes. So we cannot engage low-income and working class families equitably if we do not at least understand that these families are coming to us, in part, through the repression of this sociopolitical context. Nor can we identify and institutionalize effective strategies for dealing with the symptoms of these inequities which *are* in the purview of schools and their practitioners—low expectations, disproportionality, formulations of family involvement in ways that are not accessible to many low-income families—if we do not understand the ideologies and conditions that bare these symptoms. Deficit ideology quiets this discourse and discourages this deeper understanding (Brandon, 2003; Valencia, 1997), an additional layer of repression leveled against the dispossessed.

Breeding Deficit Ideology: Layers of Socialization

Unfortunately, the class discourse in the U.S. education milieu, like that in the larger U.S. society, reflects the capitalist and consumerist hegemony through which educators, like everybody else, are socialized. In other words—and this is a critical point—I am not referring here to purposefully repressive educators acting in purposefully oppressive ways. Instead, I am referring to a socializing process that conditions educators (as well as education scholars), like everybody else, to buy into certain myths and stereotypes that inform educational philosophies and practices but which also inform individuals' and communities' levels of commitment to, and willingness to struggle for, social, economic, and educational justice for low-income and other disenfranchised people.

Certainly counter-discourses exist, both in the larger theoretical landscape (Blaney & Inayatullah, 2009; Chomsky, 2003; Gans, 1995; hooks, 2000; Klein, 2008) and in the education milieu (Books, 2004; Gabbard, 2003; Giroux, 2008; Kozol, 1992). However, as mentioned earlier, these discourses continue largely to be marginalized as anti-American, socialist, or communist, the conflation of which is, in and of itself, a product of capitalist hegemony and the deficit paradigm employed to help protect it. Enforcement of this hegemony and socialization for compliance with the deficit paradigm begin at birth, after all—a process powerfully detailed, in part, in *Consuming Kids*, Adriana Barbaro's (2008) film about the increasing commercialization of childhood in the U.S.

These conditions, like any sociopolitical context, present formidable challenges to those who are attempting to offer or engage with counter-discourses, including critically oriented teachers, teacher educators, and staff development specialists. One function of class hegemony is to ensure constant self-reproduction so that its outcomes—socialization for compliance with itself, for example—are mistaken as organic and natural rather than purposeful and manipulative.

My examination over the past several years of the origins and implications of deficit discourses in education (see Gorski, 2009, 2008a, 2008b, 2008c, 2006) and my review of others' critical contributions on this topic (Collins, 1988; Dudley-Marling, 2007; Gans, 1995; García & Guerra, 2004; Ladson-Billings, 2006; Pearl, 1997; Sleeter, 2004; Valencia, 1997; Yosso, 2005) have led me to understand this process of socialization for complicity with economic injustice, deficit ideology at its core, as a two-dimensional process of social conditioning and compliance enforcement, each dimension informing and providing support for the other. This process, depicted in Figure 1, prepares individuals to comply with the dominant discourse—the *deficit* discourse—on class and poverty in education and the larger society. But it also prepares us to enforce compliance by marginalizing counter-discourses.

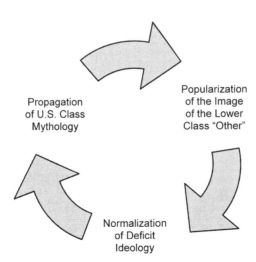

Figure 1. Cycle of social conditioning for compliance with deficit ideology.

Propagation of the U.S. Class Mythology

The base layer of socialization for compliance with deficit ideology is the prop-agation of a complex class mythology that frames the U.S. as a meritocratic land of opportunity while simultaneously reifying the popular conception of a defi-cient, undeserving underclass (Gans, 1995). The popular discourse about the U.S. opportunity structure, grounded firmly in notions of rugged individualism, the Protestant ethic of hard work and sacrifice, the conflation of democracy and capitalism, and an imaginary level playing field of meritocracy remains domi-nant even as wealth inequality increases—even as the wealth inequality in the U.S. exceeds that of most every other "advanced democracy."

An implication of the propagation of this mythology in education can be observed in the growing sense of urgency, even among many people ostensibly committed to educational equity and social justice, to "close" an "achievement gap" measured almost exclusively by standardized test scores while a grossly un-standardized educational *opportunity structure* receives considerably less atten-tion. An implicit assumption underlying this discourse appears to be that the opportunity structure is relatively solid, that the playing field is relatively level, that the system is relatively equitable (Yosso, 2005). Otherwise, a problem like the "achievement gap" would be seen as precisely what it is: an outcome, *and only one of many outcomes*, of economic injustice—a symptom of gross inequities, of a playing field that is, in Kozol's (1992) language, "savagely" un-level.

High-poverty schools are more likely than low-poverty schools to have inadequate facilities, insufficient materials, substantial numbers of teachers teaching outside their licensure areas, multiple teacher vacancies, inoperative bathrooms, and vermin infestation (National Commission on Teaching and America's Future [NCTAF], 2004). Studies point to less rigorous curricula (Barton, 2004), fewer experienced teachers (Barton, 2004; Rank, 2004), high-er student-to-teacher ratios (Barton, 2003), larger class sizes (Barton, 2003), and lower funding (Carey, 2005) in high-poverty schools than in their low-pover-ty counterparts. The NCTAF (2004) concludes,

> The evidence . . . proves beyond any shadow of a doubt that children at risk, who come from families with poorer economic backgrounds, are not being given an opportuni-ty to learn that is equal to that offered to children from the most privileged families. The obvious cause of this inequality lies in the finding that the most disadvantaged children attend schools that do not have basic facilities and conditions conducive to providing them with a quality education. (p. 7)

Broaden the view, and the picture is even bleaker. Low-income people bear the brunt of almost every imaginable social ill in the U.S. (Books, 2004): limited access to healthcare, to safe and affordable housing, to living wage work, to clean air and water. But how often are conversations about the economic achievement gap informed, for example, by data on access to prenatal care? How often do these discourses consider the percentages of jobs that pay a living wage in neighborhoods feeding into a particular school district? Wouldn't these sorts of concerns be evident, if not central, if the popular class discourse in education did not assume the existence of a meritocratic playing field?

But again, the reality of a savagely un-level playing field means little to a popular consciousness molded to hold the notion of meritocracy as a defining tenet of the U.S. and its education system. And so critical to grasping this layer of socialization for compliance with deficit ideology is understanding that, in order to buy into this class mythology—in fact, in order to be seen as a "real" American—I need to ignore, or be wholly miseducated about, sociopolitical context. And this, precisely, is the groundwork laid by the propagation of the U.S. class mythology.

Popularization of a Stereotyped Image of the Lower Class "Other"

Making matters worse, the imposition upon mainstream consciousness of a structural class mythology—the solidification of this sort of class hegemony— happens simultaneously with that of an equally inaccurate mythology that paints low-income communities (as well as communities of color, LGBTQ communities, communities in which English is not a primary language, and other disenfranchised communities) as morally, culturally, and intellectually deficient. As a result, as sociopolitical context—economic injustice, racial injustice, and so on—fades into the backdrop of popular discourses on problems like the "achievement gap," those who are most disenfranchised by existing conditions and by the discourse itself are thrust into the spotlight, rendered indistinguishable from the problems themselves.

Consider this: Since the mid-1970s most people in the U.S. have believed that poverty is caused by insufficiencies or deficiencies among poor people (Feagin, 1975; Gilens, 1999; Kaiser Family Foundation, 2001; Kluegel and Smith, 1986; Rank, Yoon, & Hirschl, 2003). For example, a 2001 Kaiser Family Foundation study revealed that a majority of people considered poverty to be a result of low-income people not doing enough to help themselves overcome poverty. People who made more than twice the poverty level ranked "drug abuse" and "a decline in moral values" as the most prominent causes of poverty. Furthermore, demonstrating the power of socialization, although a slightly smaller majority of low-income people believed that poverty resulted from a lack of effort among the poor to escape poverty, low-income respondents were *more likely* than their wealthier counterparts to identify "drug abuse," "poor people lacking motivation," and "a decline in moral values" as prominent causes of poverty (Kaiser Family Foundation, 2001). Take a step back, now, and consider that this was not always the case. Prior to the mid-1970s, the popular perception was that poverty resulted, not from deficiencies within low-income individuals and communities but from social conditions and repression (Rank et al., 2003).

In order to understand the manufactured nature of this shift, we might recall the introduction to mainstream consciousness of a single deficit depiction of a disenfranchised community during the 1976 presidential primaries. During his unsuccessful campaign for Republican endorsement, Ronald Reagan often repeated the story of Linda Taylor, a woman from the south side of Chicago who defrauded the government out of roughly $8,000 in welfare claims by using four aliases. Again, the legitimacy and accuracy of Reagan's claims appear to have mattered little. He exaggerated considerably, suggesting that she had collected more than $150,000 and used more than 80 aliases, a mischaracterization uncovered immediately by *The Washington Star* ("'Welfare queen' becomes issue in Reagan campaign," 1976). The article concluded: "The 'welfare queen" item in Mr. Reagan's repertoire is one of several that seem to be at odds with the facts" (par. 12). Despite failing to survive past the Republican primary, Reagan left an indelible mark on the popular class and poverty discourse with the strategic and repeated use of "welfare queen." Reagan did not coin the term. But his habitual use of the idiom established it, with all of its insinuations, firmly in mainstream U.S. cultural and political lexicons, where it has remained for more than thirty years.

Broadening the sociopolitical context even further, it surely is no coincidence that Reagan used this strategy in the mid-1970s. Only fifteen years earlier Oscar Lewis (1961), one of the most prominent social scientists of his era, introduced the "culture of poverty" hypothesis, which he based on observational studies of small high-poverty Mexican and Puerto Rican communities. Lewis argued based on these studies that poor people shared a universally consistent, predictable set of values and behaviors: emphasis on the present and neglect of the future, violent tendencies, a lack of a sense of history, and so on. Once again, the rigor and accuracy of Lewis's work, which initially was challenged empirically by social scientists in the early 1970s and largely dismissed by them shortly thereafter (Abell & Lyon, 1979; Billings, 1974; Harris, 1976; Van Til & Van Til, 1973; Villemez, 1980) as the product of unsupported extrapolation, seemed to be of negligible consequence. Despite the fact that Lewis identified strongly as a champion of the downtrodden and associated with the emerging progressive segment of the social science community (Ortiz & Briggs, 2003), his culture of poverty hypothesis was endorsed and employed over the next couple decades most vigorously by Reagan and other members of the right-wing establishment, including the mass media. They found the culture of poverty hypothesis a useful paradigm for encouraging support for, or at least discouraging resistance to, their goal of reversing a litany of progressive programs, such as social welfare programs, intended to shift modest amounts of resources from the elite to the poor. And it worked: by the mid-1970s, social scientists began identifying a shift in mainstream U.S. attitudes about the primary cause of poverty, from social conditions and repression to deficiencies within low-income communities (Rank et al., 2003).

By the late 1970s, as Reagan launched his successful campaign for president, his "welfare queen" terminology was established firmly in the mainstream lexicon and low-income people who collected welfare were being blamed for the very social ills that repressed them the harshest, from national deficits to urban decay. In pure deficit ideology form, this was especially true for low-income African American single mothers, those with little power to popularize a counter-narrative to the increasingly dominant, highly racialized and gendered, "welfare queen" one. As the political landscape has shifted increasingly rightward, U.S. politicians, whether Republican or Democrat, have engaged this narrative through three decades of "welfare reform," withering programs created, not to eliminate poverty but merely to sustain people in poverty. In the process, these politicians, as well as the corporations which have funded both these sustenance programs and political campaigns, have been able to frame themselves as socially responsible saviors of the "undeserving" poor (Gans, 1995).

Again, the key to this process was in training the mainstream scornful gaze down, rather than up, the socioeconomic hierarchy by popularizing the "welfare queen" image—the surest way to avoid demands for substantial social change. In fact, policymakers on the political right today employ a related deficit tactic—the repeated use of the term "entitlement class" to refer to peo-

ple benefitting from welfare programs in the U.S.—in order to turn the scornful gaze from those with, perhaps, the greatest entitlement complexes (including bailed-out banks and other corporations) and onto poor and working class
people.

Like mass indoctrination with the U.S. class mythology, the implications
of this "othering" of economically dispossessed people can be observed in educational chatter about the economic achievement gap "problem," which tends
to point most vigorously to insufficiencies or deficiencies in the rearing and
home lives of low-income students (Weiner, 2003; Yosso, 2005). *Their parents
don't care about education. They're lazy and have weak work ethics. They have poor
language skills because of language-deficient home lives.* Ladson-Billings (2006) has
argued that this sort of chatter reflects the common fabrication of "them" that
occurs constantly in education, where all variety of problems are attributed to
the amorphous "culprit" of *those students'* "cultures" (p. 105), perhaps a reflection of the continued popularity of the "culture of poverty" concept. She
explains,

> . . . culture is randomly and regularly used to explain everything. So at the same
> moment teacher education students learn nothing about culture, they use it with
> authority as one of the primary explanations for everything from school failure to prob-
> lems with behavior management and discipline. (p. 104)

Once again, the fact that these assumptions of laziness, ambivalence about education, language deficiencies, and so on, are baseless—that research refutes virtually every common stereotype about poor people, including those that form
the basis of the "culture of poverty" paradigm—appears to be of little consequence against relentless socialization. In fact, in a previous examination of
research on these stereotypes (Gorski, 2008b), I found that:

- There is no evidence that poor people have weaker work ethics than
  their wealthier counterparts. In fact, evidence suggests that socioeconomic status is no indicator of work ethic (Iversen & Farber, 1996;
  Wilson, 1997). The shortage of living-wage jobs necessitates that
  many low-income adults work multiple jobs. As a result, according to
  the Economic Policy Institute (2002), poor working adults spend more
  hours working each week on average than their wealthier counterparts.
- Studies have shown consistently that low-income parents possess the
  same attitudes about the value of education as their wealthier peers
  (Compton-Lilly, 2003; Lareau & Horvat, 1999; Leichter, 1978). While

it is true that low-income parents are less likely to attend school functions or volunteer in their children's classrooms (National Center for Education Statistics, 2005), there is no indication that this is because they care less about education. In fact, they believe just as strongly in the value of education as wealthier parents despite the fact that opportunities for school involvement usually are structured in ways that are not accessible to people who are likely to work multiple jobs, to work evenings, to have jobs without paid leave, and to be unable to afford child care or public transportation if necessary.

- Drug use is distributed equally across socioeconomic brackets (Saxe, Kadushin, Tighe, Rindskopf, & Beveridge, 2001). Meanwhile, Chen, Sheth, Krejci, and Wallace (2003) found that alcohol use is significantly higher among upper middle class white high school students than poor black high school students. Overall, alcohol abuse is far more prevalent among wealthy people than among poor people (Diala, Muntaner, & Walrath, 2004; Galea, Ahern, Tracy, & Vlahov, 2007).
- Linguists have known for decades that all language varieties are highly structured with complex grammatical rules and syntaxes (Gee, 2004; Hess, 1974; Miller, Cho, & Bracey, 2005). What often are assumed to be deficient varieties of English—varieties spoken by some poor people in Appalachia, perhaps—are no less sophisticated than so-called "standard English."

Ruby Payne's (2005) decade-long dominance of the class and poverty discourse in education, despite the inaccuracy of the culture of poverty paradigm and the many false stereotypes, like those listed above, that her framework propagates, is another important symptom of this layer of socialization (Dudley-Marling, 2007; Gorski, 2008a). Because several scholars recently have mined Payne's work in great detail, uncovering its deficit bases (Bohn, 2007; Bomer et al., 2008; Dudley-Marling, 2007; Kunjufu, 2007; Ng & Rury, 2006; Osei-Kofi, 2005) and critically examining its "culture of poverty" grounding, and because this book contains three chapters detailing these and other oppressive dimensions of Payne's work, there is little need to reproduce those analyses here. But a cursory reading of most any example of her work reveals the ways in which the culture of poverty paradigm continues to be used to socialize people—in this case, teachers—into deficit-laden misperceptions about poverty and low-income people.

For example, in one single-page essay Payne (2006) wrote in response to

Hurricane Katrina, she managed to support dominant U.S. class discourses by reifying several popular deficit stereotypes about the economically repressed people most devastated by the hurricane. "The violence was to be expected," she wrote. After all, "Words are not seen as being very effective in generational poverty to resolve differences; fists are" (¶ 3). Poor people lack the "necessary language" (¶ 3) to communicate effectively. In addition, she argued that in poor neighborhoods "prostitution and drugs" constitute "two of the primary economic systems" (¶ 4). Meanwhile, in classic deficit ideology form, her essay contained not a single reference to government inaction or mis-action before, during, or after the hurricane; not a single note about ineffective communications regarding the hurricane and its aftermath among government officials; not one mention of the horrid economic conditions—the scarcity of living wage work, the lack of access to healthcare, and so on—that plagued low-income communities in and around the affected region before Hurricane Katrina struck. And again, this silence on sociopolitical context, married with the relentless reification of the lower class "other," reaffirms readers' perceptions that the "problem" to be fixed, that the deficiency to be remedied, exists within the disenfranchised community rather than in the conditions which disenfranchise the community. Howley, Howley, Howley, and Howley (2006) have shown that teachers trained using Payne's deficit model demonstrate a keen propensity for "othering"—for drawing a clear and deficit-drenched distinction between themselves and their low-income students—because Payne reaffirms their stereotypes, because she reifies class hegemony.

A telling symptom of this process of socialization lies in the most common response I receive from people raising questions about my own critiques of Payne's work (see Gorski, 2008a). Rarely is the content of my critique questioned. Instead, I am met most often with comments like, "Payne's model rings true for me. It reflects my experience with students in poverty." In this sense, Payne is, if nothing else, a brilliant businesswoman. Her work has joined a long history of educational programs, pedagogies, and practices which, however unsupported or contradicted by research, won popular approval because they spoke to a certain mass sensibility which, in and of itself, was the result of socialization. (Consider how a supposed loss of U.S. global competitiveness in math and science has been used, among other things, to justify standardization and high-stakes testing, neither of which have been shown to improve students' math or science competencies.)

Again, the scornful gaze is trained down the power hierarchy, at a fictional "them," where it poses no threat to existing inequities. As a result, the policies, programs, and practices engaged in order to redress educational problems focus, as well, down the power hierarchy, aimed at fixing the most disenfranchised students and families rather than that which disenfranchises them (Brandon, 2003; Weiner, 2003). Instead of addressing school funding discrepancies, we implement more standardization and testing. Rather than fighting for fair wage work for all families, we offer parenting workshops. Rather than insisting as an *educational imperative* that all students have equitable access to healthcare, we offer tutoring and mentoring programs. Certainly this is not to say that we should not offer tutoring and mentoring programs for any students who need them, as long as we do not fall into the deficit-inspired "savior syndrome" or use "mentoring" as code language for "assimilating." But in the end, these programs and practices pose no threat to educational inequities, much less economic injustice. They simply sustain disenfranchised people within a disenfranchising system.

The implications are devastating for a variety of reasons. First, by complying with deficit ideology we contribute to the very stereotypes and repressions we ought to be eliminating. Secondly, by doing so we dutifully play the role of buffer class (Kivel, 2006), protecting elite class interests by shifting attention from systemic injustice and locating the sources of social problems as existing within economically disadvantaged communities. Thirdly, even if we do not imagine the destruction of injustice on a systemic scale as our purview, by failing to understand the sociopolitical ramifications of institutionalized racism, economic injustice, and other systemic conditions, we all but ensure our failure at facilitating and sustaining equity, even at the individual classroom level. After all, how can I facilitate and sustain an equitable classroom environment if I do not comprehend fully the very inequities I am attempting to unravel?

Defeating Deficit Ideology

How, then, might we encourage and facilitate this understanding in ourselves and others? How might we begin to see that which we are socialized not to see? Based upon my ongoing process of grappling with this topic and my own complicity with it, I have identified five strategies for defeating deficit ideology—for loosening its hold on educational discourses related to class and poverty.

The first step toward uprooting any ideology is in learning to "spot" it—a challenging task when it envelops us, when it has infested most every social and political discourse. Drawing on my experience uncovering deficit ideology in education discourses and a review of the literature on the topic, I have located three common discursive hallmarks of socioeconomic-based deficit ideology: three discursive signs that alert me that deficit ideology is being employed in conversations about class and poverty in education. These include: (1) an unnamed assumption of shared stereotyped thinking (between author and reader, speaker and listener, and so on), (2) identification of the "problem" of inequality, or of poverty itself, as existing within working class and low-income families and their "cultures," and (3) failure *or refusal* to acknowledge sociopolitical context. In order to defeat deficit ideology, both in my own thinking and in those around me, I must learn to recognize these signs. Often they appear implicitly in what has become common language in education: "at-risk," "remedial," "culturally deprived," "disadvantaged"—the very normalization of these idioms, the way they slide so easily off the tongues of many of us who count ourselves among equity advocates, demonstrates the hegemonic power of mass socialization. I must challenge this language and ask questions of the overall class discourse: How are issues like the socioeconomic achievement gap being framed in the context of professional development? How is the problem being defined? Do proposed solutions focus on remedying supposed deficiencies in poor and working class families? Are concerns regarding contextualizing factors, including systemic inequities and the ways those inequities are reflected in school policy and practice, suppressed or ignored? Posing these sorts of questions can help us make sense of class and poverty discourses in education and whether they show the signs of deficit ideology. But beyond mere recognition, I must be willing and able to name the limitations of these discourses and to offer a counter-narrative.

Secondly, I must reflect critically upon my own class socialization; on how and by whom my gaze has been trained. I must recognize that the very perception of something "ringing true" for me could be a symptom of manipulative socialization—that my perceiving it is so does not make it so and might be the best evidence that it is not, in fact, so. How do I, intentionally and unintentionally, reify the myth of meritocracy or stereotypes of low-income people in my educational practice? What assumptions or biases might keep me from demonstrating the highest possible expectations of all of my students?

Additionally, and in a similar vein, I must refuse, despite the dominant discourses, to locate any problem in the "cultures" of disenfranchised communities. Doing so is, in and of itself, a disenfranchising practice. But it is also the surest way to misdirect strategies for redressing inequities. For example, when we locate the "problem" of lower rates of family involvement among low-income families than their wealthier counterparts as existing within those families, we ignore critical sociopolitical context. We fail to ask very basic questions, such as whether opportunities for family involvement are even accessible to parents and guardians who are most likely to work multiple jobs, to work nights, to be unable to afford child care or public transportation, or to experience schools as hostile environments. When we fail to ask these questions, it becomes too easy to assume that we "fix" this problem by fixing low-income families rather than by addressing systemic inequities in access to opportunities for family involvement, much less the larger sociopolitical context of, for example, the scarce jobs that pay a living wage. In addition, by locating this "problem" in low-income families, we solidify the presumptive and supremacist notion that the only way to be an involved parent or guardian is to do so in ways that reflect dominant norms of involvement (i.e., through parent-teacher conferences and other school visits). As a result, we distract ourselves from the opportunity to develop deeper understandings of the problems we are attempting to solve. And without this deeper understanding, we continue to develop solutions that demonize our most disenfranchised neighbors rather than those that offer new possibilities for equity.

As a final, longer-term, strategy for defeating deficit ideology, I must teach about economic injustice and poverty. In doing so, it is critical that I refuse to frame "poverty" as a culture rather than an oppressed condition. The former suggests choice and intimates deficiency. And I must teach about socializing forces like deficit ideology, providing my students opportunities to practice the competencies of media and propaganda literacies.

Conclusion

In *Following the Equator*, a travel book full of scathing anti-imperialist commentary, Mark Twain wrote, in response to the deficit ideology employed by Europeans to justify the oppression of indigenous Australians, "There are many humorous things in this world; among them the white man's notion that he is less savage than the other savages" (p. 213). Still, here we are, all these years later, grappling with deficit ideology, hegemonically buried in it, using it implicitly as the basis for conversations about myriad social problems from health care disparities to educational outcome inequalities.

Hegemony is a difficult thing to break. In order to break it, we must consider our own complicity with it and our socialization for compliance. We must avoid the quick fix and the easy answer. We must bear the price of refusing compliance, knowing that by looking up, by training our gaze toward the top of the power hierarchy, we might strain our necks, not to mention our institutional likeability, more so than we do when we train it downward, where we pose no threat to the myths that power the corporate-capitalist machine. But if we do not break hegemony, if we do not defeat deficit ideology, we have little chance of redressing, in any authentic way, its gross inequities. This, we must realize, is the very point of the redirected gaze: to ensure and justify the maintenance of inequity and to make us—educators—party to that justification and maintenance.

Collins (1988) has called deficit ideology "a social pathology model" (p. 304) because of how it pathologizes disenfranchised communities. I argue that it is equally accurate to refer to deficit ideology as a social pathology model because it is symptomatic of a mass pathology born of socialization and psychosocial coercion. It is we, the people engaging deficit ideology, who are pathological, who push aside so much evidence to comply with a world view of which each of us, in one way or another (class, race, gender, sexual orientation, language, religion, size, age, or something else), eventually becomes a target.

References

Abell, T., & Lyon, L. (1979). Do the differences make a difference? An empirical evaluation of the culture of poverty in the United States. *American Anthropologist, 6*(3), 602–621.

Apple, M. (2006). Understanding and interrupting neoliberalism and neoconservatism in education. *Pedagogies, 1*(1), 21–26.

Barbaro, A. (Producer), & Barbaro, A., & Earp, J. (Directors). (2008). *Consuming kids.* [Motion picture]. Northampton, MA: Media Education Foundation.

Barton, P. E. (2004). Why does the gap persist? *Educational Leadership 62*(3), 8–13.

Barton, P. E. (2003). *Parsing the achievement gap: Baselines for tracking progress.* Princeton, NJ: Educational Testing Service.

Berliner, D. (2006). Our impoverished view of educational reform. *Teachers College Record, 108*(6), 949–995.

Billings, D. (1974). Culture and poverty in Appalachia: A theoretical discussion and empirical analysis. *Social Forces, 53*(2), 315–323.

Blaney, D. L, & Inayatullah, N. (2009). *Savage economics: Wealth, poverty, and the temporal walls of capitalism.* New York: Routledge.

Bohn, A. (2007). A framework for understanding Ruby Payne. *Rethinking Schools, 21*(2), 13–15.

Bomer, R., Dworin, J., May, L., & Semingson, P. (2008). Miseducating teachers about the poor: A critical analysis of Ruby Payne's claims about poverty. *Teachers College Record, 10*(11). Retrieved from http://www.tcrecord.org/content.asp?ContentsId=14591

Books, S. (2004). *Poverty and schooling in the U.S.: Contexts and consequences.* Mahwah, NJ: Lawrence Erlbaum.

Brandon, W. W. (2003). Toward a white teachers' guide to playing fair: Exploring the cultural politics of multicultural teaching. *Qualitative Studies in Education, 16*(1), 31–50.

Brantlinger, E. (2003). *Dividing classes: How the middle class negotiates and rationalizes school advantage.* New York, NY: RoutledgeFalmer.

Carey, K. (2005). *The funding gap 2004: Many states still shortchange low-income and minority students.* Washington, DC: The Education Trust.

Chen, K., Sheth, A., Krejci, J., & Wallace, J. (2003, August). *Understanding differences in alcohol use among high school students in two different communities.* Paper presented at the annual meeting of the American Sociological Association, Atlanta, Georgia.

Chomsky, N. (2003). The function of schools: Subtler and cruder methods of control. In K. Saltman & D. Gabbard (Eds.), *Education as enforcement: The militarization and corporatization of schools* (pp. 25–36).New York: RoutledgeFalmer.

Collins, J. (1988). Language and class in minority education. *Anthropology & Education Quarterly, 19*(4), 299–326.

Compton-Lilly, C. (2003). *Reading families: The literate lives of urban children.* New York: Teachers College Press.

Diala, C. C., Muntaner, C., & Walrath, C. (2004). Gender, occupational, and socioeconomic correlates of alcohol and drug abuse among U.S. rural, metropolitan, and urban residents. *American Journal of Drug and Alcohol Abuse, 30*(2), 409–428.

Dudley-Marling, C. (2007). Return of the deficit. *Journal of Educational Controversy, 2*(1). Retrieved from http://www.wce.wwu.edu/Resources/CEP/eJournal

Economic Policy Institute. (2002). *The state of working class America 2002–03.* Washington, DC: Author.

Feagin, J. R. (1975). *Subordinating the poor: Welfare and American beliefs.* Englewood Cliffs, NJ: Prentice Hall.

Ford, D. Y., & Grantham, T. C. (2003). Providing access for culturally diverse gifted students: From deficit to dynamic thinking. *Theory into Practice, 42*(3), 217–225.

Gabbard, D. A. (2003). Education *is* enforcement!: The centrality of compulsory schooling in market societies. In K. Saltman & D. Gabbard (Eds.), *Education as enforcement: The militarization and corporatization of schools* (pp. 61–80). New York: RoutledgeFalmer.

Galea, S., Ahern, J., Tracy, M., & Vlahov, D. (2007). Neighborhood income and income distribution and the use of cigarettes, alcohol, and marijuana. *American Journal of Preventive Medicine, 32*(6), 195–202.

Gans, H. J. (1995). *The war against the poor: The underclass and antipoverty policy.* New York, NY: Basic.

García, S, & Guerra, P. (2004). Deconstructing deficit thinking: Working with educators to create more equitable learning environments. *Education and Urban Society, 36*(2), 150–168.

Gee, J. P. (2004). *Situated language and learning: A critique of traditional schooling.* New York: Routledge.

Gilens, M. (1999). *Why Americans hate welfare: Race, media, and the politics of antipoverty policy.* Chicago: University of Chicago Press.

Giroux, H. A. (2008). *Against the terror of neoliberalism: Politics beyond the age of greed.* Boulder, CO: Paradigm.

Gorski, P. C. (2009). What we're teaching teachers: An analysis of multicultural teacher education coursework syllabi. *Teaching & Teacher Education, 25*(2), 309–318.

Gorski, P. C. (2008a). Peddling poverty for profit: Elements of oppression in Ruby Payne's framework. *Equity & Excellence in Education, 41*(1), 130–148.

Gorski, P. C. (2008b). The myth of the 'culture of poverty.' *Educational Leadership, 65*(7), 32–36.

Gorski, P. C. (2008c). Good intentions are not enough: A decolonizing intercultural education. *Intercultural Education, 19*(5), 515–525.

Gorski, P. C. (2006). Complicity with conservatism: The de-politicizing of multicultural and intercultural education. *Intercultural Education, 17*(2), 163–177.

Hamovitch, B. (1997). *Staying after school.* Westport, CT: Praeger.

Harris, D. (1976). The culture of poverty in Coconut Village, Trinidad: A critique. *Sociological Review, 24*(4), 831–858.

Hess, K. M. (1974). The nonstandard speakers in our schools: What should be done? *The Elementary School Journal, 74*(5), 280–290.

hooks, b. (2000). *Where we stand: Class matters.* New York, NY: Routledge.

Howley, C. B., Howley, A. A., Howley, C. W., & Howley, M. D. (2006). *Saving the children of the poor in rural schools.* Paper presented at the Annual Meeting of the American Educational Research Association, San Francisco, California.

Iversen, R. R., & Farber, N. (1996). Transmission of family values, work, and welfare among poor urban black women. *Work and Occupations, 23*(4), 437–460.

Jennings, P. K. (2004). What mothers want: Welfare reform and maternal desire. *Journal of Sociology and Social Welfare, 31*(3), 113–130.

Kaiser Family Foundation. (2001). *Poverty in America.* Menlo Park, CA: Author.

Kivel, P. (2006). *You call this a democracy?: Who benefits, who pays, and who really decides?* New York, NY: Apex.

Klein, N. (2008). *The shock doctrine: The rise of disaster capitalism.* New York: Picador.

Kluegel, J. R., & Smith, E. R. (1986). *Beliefs about inequality: Americans' views of what is and what ought to be.* New York: Aldine de Gruyter.

Kozol, J. (1992). *Savage inequalities: Children in America's schools.* New York: HarperCollins.

Kunjufu, J. (2007). *An African centered response to Ruby Payne's poverty theory.* Chicago: African American Images.

Ladson-Billings, G. (2006). It's not the culture of poverty, it's the poverty of culture: The problem with teacher education. *Anthropology & Education Quarterly, 37*(2), 104–109.

Lareau, A., & Horvat, E. (1999). Moments of social inclusion and exclusion: Race, class, and cultural capital in family-school relationships. *Sociology of Education, 72,* 37–53.

Leichter, H. J. (Ed.). (1978). *Families and communities as educators.* New York: Teachers College Press.

Lewis, O. (1961). *The children of Sanchez: Autobiography of a Mexican family.* New York: Random House.

Lipman, P. (2008). Mixed-income schools and housing: Advancing the neoliberal urban agenda. *Journal of Educational Policy, 23*(2), 119–134.

Miller, P. J., Cho, G. E., & Bracey, J. R. (2005). Working-class children's experience through the prism of personal storytelling. *Human Development, 48,* 115–135.

National Center for Education Statistics. (2005). *Parent and family involvement in education: 2002–03.* Washington, DC: Author.

National Commission on Teaching and America's Future (2004). *Fifty years after* Brown v. Board of Education: *A two-tiered education system*. Washington, DC: Author.

Ng, J. C., & Rury, J. L. (2006). Poverty and education: A critical analysis of the Ruby Payne phenomenon. *Teachers College Record*. Retrieved from http://www.tcrecord.org/Content.asp?ContentID=12596

Nieto, S., & Bode, P. (2008). *Affirming diversity: The sociopolitical context of multicultural education* (5th ed.). Boston, MA: Pearson.

Ortiz, A. T., & Briggs, L. (2003). The culture of poverty, crack babies, and welfare cheats: The making of the "healthy white baby crisis." *Social Text, 21*(3), 39–57.

Osei-Kofi, N. (2005). Pathologizing the poor: A framework for understanding Ruby Payne's work. *Equity & Excellence in Education, 38*(4), 367–375.

Payne, R. K. (2005). *A framework for understanding poverty*. Highlands, TX: aha! Process.

Payne, R. K. (2006). *Reflections on Katrina and the role of poverty in the Gulf Coast crisis*. Retrieved http://www.ahaprocess.com/files/Hurricane_Katrina_reflections.pdf

Pearl, A. (1997). Democratic education as an alternative to deficit thinking. In R. R. Valencia (Ed.), *The evolution of deficit thinking* (pp. 211–241). London: Falmer.

Rank, M. R. (2004). *One nation, underprivileged: Why American poverty affects us all*. New York, NY: Oxford University Press.

Rank, M. R., Yoon, H., & Hirschl, T. A. (2003). American poverty as a structural failing: Evidence and arguments. *Journal of Sociology and Social Welfare, 30*(4), 3–29.

Saxe, L., Kadushin, C., Tighe, E., Rindskopf, D., & Beveridge, A. (2001). *National evaluation of the fighting back program: General population surveys, 1995–1999*. New York: City University of New York Graduate Center.

Shields, C.M., Bishop, R., & Mazawi, A.E. (2005) *Pathologizing practices: The impact of deficit thinking on education*. New York: Peter Lang.

Sleeter, C. E. (2004). Context-conscious portraits and context-blind policy. *Anthropology & Education Quarterly, 35*(1), 132–136.

Valencia, R. R. (1997). Introduction. In R. R. Valencia (Ed.), *The evolution of deficit thinking* (pp. ix–xvii). London: Falmer.

Van Til, S. B., & Van Til, J. (1973). The lower class and the future of inequality. *Growth & Change, 4*(1), 10–16.

Villemez, W. J. (1980). Explaining inequality: A survey of perspectives represented in introductory sociology textbooks. *Contemporary Sociology, 9*(1), 35–39.

Villenas, S. (2001). Latina mothers and small-town racisms: Creating narratives of dignity and moral education in North Carolina. *Anthropology & Education Quarterly, 32*(1), 3–28.

Weiner, L. (2003). Why is classroom management so vexing to urban teachers? *Theory into Practice, 42*(4), 305–312.

'Welfare queen' becomes issue in Reagan campaign. (1976, February 15). *The Washington Star*. Retrieved from ProQuest Historical Newspapers.

Wilson, W. J. (1997). *When work disappears*. New York: Random House.

Yosso, T. J. (2005). Whose culture has capital? A critical race theory discussion of community cultural wealth. *Race, Ethnicity and Education, 8*(1), 69–91.

SECTION IV
Ruby Payne

· 9 ·

A Framework for Maintaining White Privilege

A Critique of Ruby Payne

MONIQUE REDEAUX

> I am a Black youth. I teach Black youth. I am attentive to the way these youths are described, portrayed, perceived. Because I teach "these children." And I am one of "these children."

I DO NOT LOCATE MYSELF OUTSIDE MY PRACTICE. MY EXPERIENCES—AS A BLACK student in classrooms where race was never discussed except when we came to that one paragraph in the Social Studies book on Martin Luther King, Jr. and the Civil Rights Movement, as one of the only students of color in Honors and Advanced Placement courses, as one out of five Black students to graduate from a public university teacher education program designed to prepare teachers for "urban environments," as a teacher of low-income students of color tracked into the "lower" grade level class—have influenced my cognitive and social development and inevitably seep into my teaching. But rather than distance myself from these experiences, I cling to them because they define me. They make me the teacher that I am and drive me towards the teacher I want to be. I embrace my vested interest in this work and argue that it makes for a more passionate and effective educator than one who has only book knowledge.

I readily acknowledge my stake in this work. As teachers and researchers, we are taught to be objective, to teach what we know, not who we are. But all teaching is autobiographical.

* * * *

"Happy Birthday, Ms. Redeaux." Ellis handed me a small box.

"Oh, thank you," I said, somewhat surprised. I was turning 23, and half way through my first year of teaching 7th grade. It was only around 8:00, but Ellis and I always arrived at school around 7:30. In fact, Ellis usually beat me to school. He would wait in the gym or by the security desk until I arrived to open our classroom. While we had a pretty good relationship due to our early morning ritual, I had not expected a gift for my birthday. I was even more surprised as I opened the box and found a thin gold necklace with a diamond-shaped yellow topaz stone. It was beautiful. "Thank you," I said again, this time in a quiet, strained voice, unsuccessfully trying to hold back tears.

Today, as I wear that chain, tears well up in my eyes for a different reason. Tears of sadness are immediately followed by tears of anger as I remember the newspaper headlines and the reports from TV journalists: "Police Investigation Says Officer Justified in Shooting Boy Who Pointed Gun at Officer"; "He refused to stop, take his hands out of his pockets and he subsequently raised the weapon and pointed it at the officer"; "The boy also matched the description of a robbery suspect."

The Cabrini-Green neighborhood was frantic. One of their residents, a 13-year-old boy named Ellis Woodland, had been shot three times by Chicago police. The police stated that the boy was about to be questioned regarding a robbery that had recently taken place in the area. When asked to stop, they said, Ellis proceeded to raise a semiautomatic weapon at the officers, who then shot at him five times, hitting him three. On later review, the semiautomatic turned out to be a BB gun, and witnesses argued that Ellis was not pointing the gun at the officers but attempting to place the gun down on the ground. Whatever the case, there was a child critically wounded and a community with a history of bad relations with the CPD in an uproar. I looked down at the chain on my chest and imagined Ellis lying on the hot pavement writhing in pain as the police handcuffed his helpless body. I wondered if the Ellis I knew was, in fact, the one being described in the news. Was he the offender, the victim, the cause of what had happened? After all, as Police Superintendent Phil Cline remarked, "The police officer has seconds to make a decision when he sees that gun pointed at him." Regardless of whether or not the gun was pointed at the officers or whether they simply saw Ellis reaching for the gun in an effort to put it down, the superintendent is correct: police officers only have a split second to make a life-changing decision. But something said by Ellis' father while questioning the police board still rings in my ears: "As the father of that boy, I want to ask one question: Did his race or community have a part in that split second decision?"

* * * *

Ellis is Black, young, male and a resident in a low-income housing project. To many in education, these criteria classify Ellis as an "at-risk" student: at risk of failing or dropping out of school, being placed in special education, being incarcerated, being the victim of a homicide—the list of potential "destinies" continues. And statistically, these evaluative judgments are not without merit. It is a fact that Black males drop out at higher rates than males from any other racial group and the probability of school failure or of dropping out increases exponentially when the Black male is of low socioeconomic status. The same is true when examining the demographics of special education placements and incarceration rates (Ladson-Billings, 1994; Shihadeh & Flynn, 1996; Land & Legters, 2002; Patrick, 2004; Glenn, 2004; The Civil Rights Project at Harvard University, 2005). The plight of these students has therefore led to increased efforts to supposedly help and assist this "endangered species."

Enter Ruby Payne. I first heard of Payne from a friend who teaches at a suburban high school that serves a high percentage of Black youth from low-income backgrounds. My friend was quite disturbed by Payne's theories about the behaviors and characteristics of these particular students. According to my friend, Payne was a "self-proclaimed expert" on the "mindset of poverty," using her limited experiences as the basis for broad generalizations. As an educator within a school where 98% of the student body is comprised of low-income students of color, I decided I should take a look at education's latest phenomenon. I found that Payne holds workshops all over the country, has produced several best-selling books, and is the founder and president of her own publishing company which distributes countless products—from CDs to audiocassettes to Simulated Classroom Scenarios (SIMS)—designed, she says, to help educators and professionals work effectively with children and adults who live in poverty. Her success demonstrates how much the field yearns for answers to the questions regarding how poverty and social class affect students in the classroom. But as I read Payne's (1996) work, I did not see answers but more insidious and pernicious problems. In fact, I was appalled. What had been accepted as doctrine by many teachers and administrators was the belief that there is a "culture" of poverty characterized by certain behaviors:

- **fun-loving** ("one of the main values of an individual to a group is the ability to entertain," p. 18),
- **loud** ("the noise level is high, the TV is always on and everyone may talk at once," p.18),
- **inherently criminal** ("the line between what is legal and illegal is thin and often crossed," p. 36)
- **sexually deviant** ("males are in and out in no predictable pattern," p. 74)

Payne argues that these behaviors hinder the success of people living in poverty, so they must be taught how to behave in middle-class society. In addition, they must be taught to *want* to escape the grasp of poverty since, according to Payne, it is a position they choose to be in. As I read Payne's beliefs about how violence and prison are considered a part of life to people in poverty (p. 18), I thought about Ellis. I thought of that split second in which the police officers had to make that decision. I wondered if they looked at Ellis and saw the person Payne describes: inherently violent, seeing "jail as a part of life that's not always bad" (p. 36). What if they, like educators all over the world, were being taught about what to expect from children of poverty? And then one night as I casually surfed through Payne's website, through a list of workshops conducted by her and her representatives, I saw it. It virtually jumped off the page and held me in a choke hold: "Understanding Class for Law Enforcement: A Customized Workshop for Officers and Administrators." And I knew that I could no longer remain silent.

* * * *

The widespread consumption of Payne's theories across disciplines highlights the salience of race and class inequities and speaks to the absence of practical educational strategies that confront these inequities. But while Payne and her "framework for understanding poverty" may be a new phenomenon in the education community, the ideology that forms the basis for her "practical solutions" is not new. In fact, the ideology has framed (and has been framed by) sociological and anthropological theories that have caused controversy for decades. In an effort to provide insight on the persistent usage of poverty theory within our society, this chapter examines how Payne and the "culture of poverty" discourse promote the dominant narrative of race, class, sexuality, and gender.

A Historical Look at the "Culture of Poverty"

The term "culture of poverty" was a term coined by anthropologists and sociologists to describe a distinct segment of the population. Culture, in this context, can be defined as a "systematic, integrated pattern for living" (Irelan et al., 1969, p. 405). The patterns that define a culture also make it distinct and separate from other cultures. Hence by referring to a "culture" of poverty, the assumption is that patterns and behaviors of living for poor people are systematic or similar. Though the term "poor" usually refers to socioeconomic status and a lack of some measure of financial resources (i.e., wealth, income, etc.), the "culture of poverty" is most clearly defined by a set of behaviors and assumed beliefs held by poor people that are viewed as counter to that of the dominant culture. Oscar Lewis and Ken Auletta, key scholars in the early work on this "underclass" culture, agreed that poverty *and* antisocial behavior serve as the qualifications for membership into the "culture of poverty." Reed (1992) quotes from Auletta who argued that there is nothing new about the twentieth century "culture of poverty" because there have always been "pirates, beggars, vagrants, paupers, illiterates, street criminals and helplessly, hopelessly damaged individuals" (Reed. 1992, p. 23). Though he recognizes that individuals from poverty suffer from a lack of financial resources, Auletta emphasizes that "the underclass suffers from behavioral as well as income deficiencies." In fact, he continues that "they are often set apart by their 'deviant' or 'antisocial' behavior, by their bad habits, not just their poverty" (Reed, 1992, p. 23). Kelley (1997) takes this even further and argues that behavior is the ultimate signifier of the underclass: "The general agreement is that a common, debased culture is what defines the underclass . . . what makes it a class is members' common behavior—not their income, poverty level, or the kind of work they do" (p. 18). By framing the "culture of poverty" in behavioral terms rather than economic ones, scholars advocating poverty theory suggest that it is poor people's behavior more than their economic plight that is problematic.

The "culture of poverty" paradigm has been examined, analyzed, and critiqued since anthropologist Oscar Lewis coined the term in the 1960s. But both empirical and qualitative studies have suggested that the "culture of poverty"—the assumption that poor people abide by a different value/belief system—is, in fact, a myth (Miller, 1959; Irelan et al., 1969; Davidson & Gaitz, 1974; Abell & Lyon, 1979; Corcoran et al., 1985; Katz, 1989; Reed, 1992; Bomer, Dworin, May, Semingson, 2008). Opponents of poverty theory assert that the values and beliefs of poor people are not significantly different from their middle and upper class peers, and the difference in their behavior patterns is a result of their circumstances and not of inherent differences in their value systems. Yet the "culture of poverty" paradigm continues to exist. Payne herself has created an empire based on the concept: she conducts seminars and workshops worldwide on how to successfully deal with poor people in schools, in churches, in intimate relationships, and even in situations that require law enforcement; school districts across the nation pay thousands of dollars for her workshops, and she has developed her own publishing company which distributes her books, workbooks, DVDs, and computer simulations. The widespread success of Payne attests to the fact that society has legitimated poverty theory as a valid and credible explanation for class inequities—despite its being disproven time and again.

"Culture of Poverty" and Ruby Payne

Ruby Payne not only uses the term "culture of poverty" directly, she quotes from Oscar Lewis and Daniel Moynihan, known supporters of the "culture of poverty" concept. She describes those in poverty as exhibiting certain behaviors and values. Payne (1996) argues that it is often poor students' cognitive or psychological deficiencies that are to blame for their behavior (p. 124). Their "culture" at home is different than that of the school culture, hence, they find it nearly impossible to succeed academically. What should be done to remedy this situation? According to Payne, the solution is not increasing resources within schools. No, the key is for educators to "teach a separate set of behaviors" (p. 100). Payne's "framework for understanding poverty" is helping students acknowledge that there are hidden rules in whatever class they "wish" to live in. In order to move from one class to another, there must be someone to model and teach students the hidden rules of that particular class (p. 18). Thus, for Payne, the key to transcending poverty is two-fold: students must first make a personal decision about which class they wish to live in and then they must change their behavior in order to fit into that class. By locating poverty as a choice that students can choose to remain in or transcend, Payne, like her "culture of poverty" counterparts, overemphasizes the role of individual behavior as the reason for poverty and virtually ignores the role of structures and institutions in the process.

Ng & Rury (2006) found that the claims Payne makes about poor people essentialize their values and behaviors and are unsubstantiated by contemporary social science work. Bohn (2006) argues that Payne's work is popular because it places blame on individuals and their culture while underemphasizing the role of institutional and systemic factors that facilitate social, economic, and political exclusion. Critics often highlight that promoting commonly held racial stereotypes and maintaining current power structures are key contributors to Payne's success. But the discourse around "race" and "racial" stereotypes usually revolves around people of color. This, however, ignores a critical component of racism: Whiteness and the facilitation of White privilege and White supremacy.

"Culture of Poverty"—Maintaining White Power and Privilege

Bonilla-Silva (2003) highlights that a society's racial structure is "the *totality* of the social relations and practices that reinforce white privilege" (p. 9). Thus, when discussing race, it is essential that Whiteness be unmasked and explicitly identified as it is what allows racism to exist. The marginalization of people of color is not racism in itself but represents the *result* of White privilege and White supremacy. The "culture of poverty" theory advocated by Payne is rooted in a gendered and sexualized discourse of Whiteness. Bonilla-Silva argues that such discourses and ideologies will remain in place, despite being disproven theoretically, because "the actors racialized as 'white' receive material benefits from the current racial order and therefore struggle to maintain their privileges" (p. 9). Examining Payne's work using this lens may provide insight on why such discourses as the "culture of poverty" continue to be recycled and consumed by society.

"Racism without Racists"—Colorblind Ideology

Before embarking on a discussion of race, it is important to note that Payne herself admittedly does not explicitly discuss race in her "framework." During a training session, she justified this omission by saying that race was only one factor influencing class. She enumerated several other factors including age, gender, and disability. To talk about one, she argued, would mean she would have to discuss them all; hence, she preferred to simply talk about class. Furthermore, she argued that race and class are not the same and can be discussed separately because there are poor people in every race. While this statement is true, it masks a hidden racism. By focusing only on class, Payne fails to acknowledge how class, race, gender, and sexuality intersect and create remarkably different material realities. By not acknowledging the socially constructed benefits of Whiteness, Payne makes it seem as if all poor people have the same experience. To illustrate that class is often built on constructions of race, however, consider one of the major determinants of class: home ownership. According to a comprehensive study conducted by the Boston Federal Reserve Bank (1992) on mortgage loan bias, after controlling for some 38 different risk factors, Blacks were still 56 percent more likely to be rejected for a mortgage loan than Whites with the same credit worthiness (Tootell,1993). A similar study in Louisville had Black and White "testers" enter banks with equal credit ratings and financial characteristics and had them request conventional mortgages for the very same housing. The Black participants were repeatedly given less information or encouragement to apply and were oftentimes told that their credit or income made them ineligible for the loan. Their white counterparts, while having the same income and credit, were told they were eligible (Wise, 2005). Quoting the *Wall Street Journal*, Tim Wise (2005) highlights that nearly 70 percent of Whites with poor credit are able to receive a mortgage loan compared to only 16 percent of Blacks with equally bad credit. More recently, the Housing Research and Advocacy Center in Cleveland, Ohio, found that, according to mortgage rejection rates from 2007, 33 percent of higher income Blacks were rejected for mortgage loans compared to only 28 percent of lower income Whites (2009). This instance demonstrates how race often subsumes class. While she acknowledges that poor people have different resources—emotional, financial, spiritual, physical, and mental—by not mentioning race as a factor that limits or provides access to these resources, Payne paints a picture of a monolithic "poor experience." When critiquing women's history as representing only *White* women's history, Higginbotham (1992) asserts that by universalizing "woman's culture and oppression" with no regard to racial differences, White women are able to ignore their own "investment and complicity in the oppression of other groups of men and women" (p. 255). Similarly, by negating or omitting race from the discourse on poverty, Payne facilitates in masking White privilege. Whites, then, *from all classes* including the poor, fail to see how their Whiteness grants them unearned privileges and advantages and they remain complicit in a system of inequality.

When reflecting on the privileges she enjoys but often never recognized as a White woman, Peggy McIntosh (1990) admits that she was never taught to acknowledge her role as an oppressor of others. Instead, she states, "I was taught to see myself as an individual whose moral state depended on her individual moral will" (p. 1). The focus on the individual and on individual "choice" is another expression of colorblind racism. In her best-selling *Framework for Understanding Poverty*, Payne asserts that remaining in poverty is a choice and many choose not to live a different life. For others, she adds, alcoholism, laziness, lack of motivation and drug addiction, make the choices for the individual. Payne argues that it is the responsibility of educators and others who work with the poor to teach the skills that will allow the individual to make the choice (p. 148). In quoting Kinder and Sander, Bonilla-Silva (2003) states that prejudice today is expressed in the language of American individualism (p. 6). By situating poverty with individuals, Payne leaves current power structures intact. Though she admits that the system is indeed discriminatory, by not being explicit about the integral role the system plays, the assumption is that people with "moral will" have the ability to usurp this system and "behave themselves" out of poverty. This assumption does not recognize that race-based discrimination results in some groups being dominant while others are subordinate. Hence if minorities face group-based discrimination and Whites have group-based advantages, demanding individual treatment for all can only benefit the advantaged group (Bonilla-Silva, 2003, pp. 35–36). In addition, if poverty is an individual choice and people of color are disproportionately poor, the "logical conclusion," according to many poverty theorists, is that there is something pathological or dysfunctional about the culture that keeps them from making "proper choices."

Cultural Racism—Class Meets Race

Though Payne has argued that her analysis of poverty is one devoted strictly to class, her behavioral indicators are laden with racial prejudices. She attempts to show that poverty transcends race by providing scenarios in which poverty affects Whites, Blacks, and Latinos. But even as she describes different races and their unique experiences with poverty, she promotes and reinforces common racial stereotypes and White norms. For example, John is described as an eight-year-old White boy whose father is a doctor but has no contact with him. His mother is a twenty-nine-year-old White woman who quit college in her sophomore year to support her husband as he went to medical school. After her husband finished his residency, he decided to divorce her, leaving his two children and their mother with only a $300.00 weekly income, which includes child support but does not include taxes. Now juxtapose this scenario with that of Otis, a nine-year-old Black boy. His mother conceived her first child at 14, dropped out of high school, and is on welfare. She is now twenty-three, still on welfare with four children, the last being born when she was eighteen and the oldest being a gang member. She lives in a crime-infested neighborhood where drive-by shootings are not uncommon and survives on a weekly income (including food stamps) of $215.00 (pp. 19–23).

The two scenarios describe women heads-of-households living in poverty, but the women occupy remarkably different social locations. The Black mother exhibits most, if not all, the deviant behavioral characteristics described by "culture of poverty" theorists: birthing children out-of-wedlock, pregnant as a teen, dependent on welfare, low level of education, surrounded by crime (Reed, 1992; Corcoran et al., 1985). The White mother, however, does not exhibit any of these deviant behaviors. She was married when she conceived both her children, college educated, and only dropped out to support her husband. Her only sin is that she is an alcoholic and Payne makes a point to explain the cause of her addiction: during the time her husband was a medical intern, she found that a drink or two in the evening calmed her down. There is no such explanation for Otis' mother. Instead Payne makes sure to emphasize her deficiencies and bad decision-making: she is uncomfortable reading because she dropped out of school; she has a boyfriend who sometimes works, but who also must be bailed out of jail on occasion; she is unmarried and unemployed with four children. The White mother is a victim of circumstance; her callous husband left her for another woman. The Black mother is the victim of her own bad choices and behavior. In the first situation, poverty is the result of a change of economic circumstance which calls for our empathy. In the second scenario, though, poverty is pathological and a cause for disgust. Hence even as she uses the scenarios to deemphasize race, Payne reifies and promotes stereotypical perceptions of race and illustrates how class is racialized. She locates poverty in the most convenient place: among poor people of color and their pathological "culture." This location is convenient for the status quo because it means that societal structures and institutions that maintain and facilitate their power are not to blame. Rather, it is individuals who must alter their behavior because their behavior is the cause of their poverty.

"We're All In This Together"
The Intersections of Race, Class,
Sexuality, and Gender

While the scenarios represent many racial stereotypes, it is important to emphasize that they promote racialized definitions of sexuality and gender. Let's revisit the scenario of Otis mentioned above. Payne's first mention of Otis' mother, Vangie, is one that describes her sexuality or sexual behavior. The first mention of Vangie reveals that she conceived Otis when she was 14. This piece of information is key because it evokes immediate assumptions about Vangie's character that are both political and historical.

In her categorization of people in poverty, Isabel Sawhill (Reed, 1992) points out that these individuals fail to live up to the "consensual obligations that society demands of its members." One of these societal norms is conceiving children only after first completing school (Reed, 1992, p. 25). Individuals who do not do this, Sawhill argues, fail to live up to their end of America's bargain (Reed, 1992, p. 25). Nicholas Lemann more specifically racializes the "underclass" and describes them as a "strongly self-defeating culture *which has its roots in the sharecrop system* whose centerpiece seems to be out-of-wedlock birth" (italics mine, Reed, 1992, p. 24). Sawhill and Lemann indirectly name perceived sexual deviance as a characteristic of poverty. Lemann, who identifies the underclass as Black, more specifically indicts Black sexuality in his condemnation of the poor. Because sexuality and sexual relations are the process by which a culture or people reproduces itself, labeling a culture as sexually deviant delegitimizes the culture and the persons it produces. Hence Sawhill, Lemann and the proponents of poverty theory by categorizing the poor as a "culture," indict the sexuality of poor women, particularly poor Black women.

In Payne's scenario regarding Otis' mother, two details are key: Vangie was a teenage mother and an unwed mother. Let's first take up her status as a teenage mom. Reed (1992) highlights that teen pregnancy is a symbol of condescension; "it is the big trump in the underclass pundits arsenal of pathologies" (p. 34). The power behind the symbol, however, does not lie in the frequency of teenage *pregnancy* but in teenage *childbearing*. While the "epidemic" of teen mothers is seen to be a phenomenon among people of color, this does not take into consideration the number of teens who become pregnant *but do not actually give birth to children*. Fine and McClelland (2006) poignantly highlight that those who have insurance, confidential relationships with medical practitioners, and access to other community supports are able to hide or terminate their pregnancies privately. However, for young teens without such class privileges, "these outcomes become publicly known and, as a result, only certain groups of youth become publicly known as 'failures'" (p. 321). Thus youth of color bear the brunt of ridicule and condemnation, not so much for engaging in sexual activity but for their inability to keep their "immorality" hidden. And even though the frequency of teen pregnancy has decreased among Black youth in the past 30 years, the perception of Black promiscuity has nonetheless remained fixed in the public and scholarly discourse.

The discourses of racism have developed and reified stereotypes of sexuality (Higginbotham, 1992, p. 265). The perception of Black females as hypersexual, lascivious, and promiscuous has remained intact since the days of slavery. This perception facilitated White domination of the Black female body. While Black females were biologically women and therefore entitled to protect and defend their bodies, their class position as property as well as the perception of them as promiscuous and sexually licentious facilitated White violence and aggression against their Black bodies. In addition, it allowed their potential allies, White women, to turn a deaf ear to their cries for help. White women, as pure, virtuous, and passionless, could not identify with these hypersexualized Black females. Instead they felt threatened by them; they considered Black women as competitors with them for White men. Even more importantly, White women's class and race privilege was reinforced by the degradation and sexual subjugation of Black women (hooks, 1994). As long as Black women were represented as "whores," White women could maintain their status of "ladies." By drawing on the stereotypes of Black women as sexually deviant, therefore, Payne reinforces White privilege by situating poverty at the feet of Black sexuality.

Let us now focus on the second detail in the description of Vangie: she is an unwed mother. Along with teenage pregnancy, children born out-of-wedlock is another mantra that classifies the supposed "'underclass." In describing people of poverty, Payne highlights that men are often in and out but in no predictable pattern so that mothers are always at the center, though they may have multiple sexual relationships (p. 73). It is true that poverty is gendered: women and their children are more likely to be victims of poverty. However, Payne and other poverty theorists fail to explain this phenomenon as being the result of a sexist and patriarchal system. They make no mention of the fact that one-parent households are more likely to be poor because they are overwhelmingly female-headed households, and women earn significantly less than men.

Instead, the "culture of poverty" paradigm insists that these female-dominated homes are inferior and pathological. Reed (1992) contends that this belief is promoted by those who want to "impose female economic dependence on men under the pretext of restoring traditional family values" (p. 34). By ignoring the role of sexism and patriarchy as crucial factors affecting the economic status of households supported by women, Payne and poverty theorists again facilitate the maintenance of inequitable power systems. The issue therefore becomes not how to eliminate a gendered labor market and wage discrimination but how to strengthen two-heterosexual-parent households (Reed, 1992, p. 34).

Even in regard to female-headed households, though, gender does not stand isolated from race, class, or sexuality. In regard to out-of-wedlock birth, Reed adeptly illustrates that one's social location dictates how this particular behavior will be perceived:

> How exactly does out-of-wedlock birth become an instance of social pathology? If a thirty-five year-old lawyer decides to have a baby without seal of approval from church or state or enduring male affiliation, we quite rightly do not consider her to be acting pathologically; we may even properly laud her independence and refusal to knuckle under patriarchal conventions. Why does such a birth become pathological when it occurs in the maternity ward in Lincoln Hospital in the South Bronx, say, rather than within the pastel walls of an alternative birthing center? (p. 27)

Hence, the "culture of poverty," while founded on a set of assumptions that are based on the frequency of certain behavioral occurrences, is heavily influenced by societal biases and prejudices. The thirty-five-year-old mother in Reed's example, while exhibiting what many poverty theorists classify as deviant behavior, mothering a child out of wedlock, would not be viewed as an expression of pathology because of her class position within the social hierarchy. By juxtaposing her position with a woman from the South Bronx, a region typically occupied by people of color, Reed implicates race and class as being key in how "behaviors" are accepted or despised.

"White Domination, Black Criminality"

Crime is also one of the behavioral indicators poverty theorists use to identify the underclass. In conjunction with welfare and teenage mothers, Auletta describes ex-convicts and drug addicts as completing the trinity of key identifiers of the underclass (Reed, 1992, p. 23). Lemann and his description of the Black underclass include gang members and drug-pushers (Reed, 1992, p. 23).

In describing the life patterns of the poor, Payne, too, makes the claim tha,t for poor people, "the line between what is legal and illegal is thin and often crossed . . . the poor simply see jail as a part of life and not necessarily always bad" (p. 36). In the two scenarios that involve males of color within Payne's *Framework*, crime and violence are a consistent part of their everyday lives. In the case of Otis, his oldest sibling is a gang member, his mother's boyfriend is in and out of prison, and there were two drive-by shootings in his neighborhood last week (pp. 22–23). In the case of Juan, his father's killing was gang-related, his mother is in jail for gang-related activities, and his uncle and legal guardian, Ramon, is the leader of a gang and sells drugs to support the family. Ramon often has to leave Juan with his grandmother because he has to hide from the police (pp. 31–32). Such stereotypical depictions of poor males with no systemic analysis of crime masks how the criminalization of poor people of color serves to justify White domination and social control.

In the two scenarios of Otis and Juan, Payne not only describes the violence surrounding each of the boys, but she emphasizes the gang activity that is prevalent all around them. This is not something Payne has invented; the "Black/Latino gang member" is a common image in America's vision of the urban poor. Hence it is important that we examine this gangbanger persona. There is no doubt that violence has plagued the residents in many low-income communities and that this violence is at times gang-related. But violence is often sensationalized in the media, and the results are similar to that of the promiscuous Black Jezebel phenomenon: the implementation of policies that are discriminatory and a false perception of young Black males as violent, "shoot-first" drug dealers that we must "chain or expel from our midst" (Takaki, 1993, p. 56). Such a perception facilitates the social control of youth of color. For example, there is a gang loitering ordinance in Chicago that enables the police to order a group of 2 or more people to disperse from a public place if it is believed that one of these people is a gang member. Any person that disobeys can be jailed for up to 6 months and fined up to $500. During the first 3 years the ordinance was enforced, 89,000 orders were reportedly issued and 42,000 individuals were arrested, most being young Black or Latino males. Even the Supreme Court ruled that the ordinance allowed for "arbitrary and discriminatory enforcement by the police" (http://gangresearch.net). There is generally no accepted methodology for identifying gangs, gang members, or gang-related crime (http://www.streetgangs.com). Yet the media, including Payne, and the police saturate us with horrific statistics of gangs, their activities, and their so-called members. Vertner and Chang (2000) argue that "gang" is simply a racialized code word. John Crew of the California ACLU agrees that "the 'gang label' has everything to do with race: "Frankly, we do not believe that this tactic (a database with suspected gang affiliates) would have spread so widely, and come to be accepted within law enforcement generally if it was not being applied almost exclusively to people of color" (http://www.arc.org). In at least 5 states simply wearing baggy pants, having a tattoo, and/or wearing a certain brand of athletic shoe is sufficient enough "evidence" to be classified as a gang member. In the Chicago Crime Commission's book on gangs in Chicago, there is a glossary of often-used slang terms used by gang members. Words such as "hood" and "homie" are described and defined. Indeed, more than half the words in the book are Black English terms that can be heard amongst white youth in suburbia due to the widespread popularity of hip-hop culture. But this language, characteristic of black, urban youth, is being used to further vilify and control them.

White domination and social control of Black bodies necessitate the criminalization of those bodies, particularly of Black males. The criminalization and subsequent arrest of people of color serve many purposes, one being economic. It fuels the massive, multimillion-dollar expansion of the prison-industrial complex. Beyond the construction and maintenance of prisons, subsidiary industries that include food, furniture, and medical care make huge profits for corporations providing these products and services (Kelley, 1997, p. 98). In addition, prisoners, who are disproportionately Black and Brown, are invaluable sources of cheap labor. Prison inmates are employed in a variety of occupations—telemarketing, manufacturing, textiles, construction, and street and highway maintenance. These are all jobs that would normally require at least minimum wage and benefit packages for employees. But by "outsourcing" these positions to "criminals," corporations make the same profit for less than half the expense. Hence the criminalization of people of color serves as a crucial component of the U.S. economy.

Black criminalization not only serves to benefit Whites economically, it also serves to maintain White hegemony physically and psychologically. Just as one's position within society—which is based on class, race, sexuality, and gender—determines whether behavior is pathological or deviant, Wilson (1990) highlights that crime, too, has socially constructed definitions: "Crime and criminal behavior occur not in a vacuum, but within a complex matrix of interpersonal, social, intergroup relations" (p. 11). "Crime" and "criminal acts" are racialized to ensure the criminalization of people of color while masking White criminality and privilege.

Wilson asserts that criminal acts are far more equally distributed across racial lines than are acts of punishment (p. 18). In other words, while all races may participate in criminal activity, certain groups are disproportionately punished for their participation. Thus, equating "crime" only with those who are arrested or convicted creates the illusion that "crime is fertilized by the slums and nurtured by low socioeconomic status" since these groups are the ones most often arrested and accused of criminal acts (Wilson, 1990, p. 9). In addition, Black and Brown neighborhoods are more often surveyed by police and law enforcement than are White neighborhoods, through physical police presence or the new phenomenon of blue light cameras. Since they are most frequently watched, it is only logical that they are also the ones most often caught participating in criminal activity. Wilson (1990) sums this up poignantly:

> There is no substantial relationship between social class and the commission of crimes, but there is a very marked relationship between class and conviction for crime. The lesson of all this is plain: the fact that half or more persons arrested for crimes of personal violence, and that forty to fifty percent of all prisoners in jails and penitentiaries are black says nothing at all about the criminality of black people. And that an even higher proportion of persons arrested are poor and imprisoned sheds no light whatever on the criminality of the poor. *These facts only identify the objects of police and court activity.* There are law violators and there are law violators; one kind gets arrested, the other kind is usually left alone (italics mine, p. 19–20)

Thus, the disproportionate surveillance of communities of color is in part due to the racialization of what is perceived as "crime."

The "War on Crime" enacted in the early nineties has in many ways been a war on Black youth, Black males, and the Black community. It resulted in heavier sentences, increased surveillance, and the expansion of prisons primarily for men of color. Societal definitions of "crime" facilitate this social control. White collar crime exemplifies how "crime" is socially constructed and therefore has different implications depending on one's position within the system. Corporate crime robs Americans of billions of dollars each year and is committed primarily by upper class Whites, yet it is rarely considered "crime"; perpetrators get relatively light prison sentences and receive virtually no air time on the news. Most often, when we think of crime or see images of crime in the news, we see examples of "street crime" which is perceived to be a Black monopoly (Wilson, 1990, p. 18). If media images are the only ways in which we define and identify criminals, then our images will be gendered and racialized because media "grossly distort the average citizen's image of what crime is all about. It minimizes and deflects attention from one kind of crime and exaggerates and spotlights another" (Ryan, 1971, p. 46). Again, this serves a two-fold purpose: to criminalize poor people of color, thereby justifying White domination, while simultaneously ignoring or overshadowing the criminal acts of Whites. The common perception of the Black male as criminal enabled White criminals such as Charles Stuart and Susan Smith to get away with murder (albeit temporarily) by blaming their crimes on a Black assailant (Kelley, 1997, p. 99). These criminals not only knew and understood the stereotypes regarding Black criminality, but they understood how deeply these stereotypes were inscribed on the hearts and minds of Americans and they counted on that inscription to escape from blame. Similarly, Chicago police sought to absolve themselves from the blame of shooting a child by constructing Ellis as a gang member and a robbery suspect, a criminal who brought such brutality on himself.

Just as a decrease in Black teenage pregnancy has not curbed societal perceptions of Black sexuality, the decrease in violent crimes committed by Blacks in America has not helped to resist the stereotypes of Black criminality. In fact, the stereotype has become more ingrained as the number of Blacks in prison continues to escalate due largely to racial disparities in sentencing. But instead of addressing such racial inequities in the criminal justice system, Payne and poverty theorists attribute criminal behavior to the pathological culture of poor people of color. By tapping into stereotypes of criminality in her descriptive scenarios and in the claims she makes about the poor, Payne not only promotes and further inscribes these stereotypes into our subconscious, she legitimizes the racist and classist system that accuses, convicts, and incarcerates people of color based on racialized definitions of "crime."

Conclusion

Children of color represent 30% of public school students. In the twenty largest urban school districts in the U.S., over 70% of the student population are students of color. In 1999, the U.S. census estimated that over 33.1% of Black children and 30.3% of Latino children lived in poverty. It is fair to say, then, that in urban public schools, there is not only an overwhelming population of children of color, but many children from low socioeconomic status as well (Ladson-Billings, 1994; Payne, 1996).

Poor students are more likely to drop out of school, be placed in special education, be suspended or disciplined in school, and be under the control of the criminal justice system (Ladson-Billings, 1994; Shihadeh & Flynn, 1996; Patrick, 2004). To say that we as a nation and as an educational system need to address this crisis is an understatement. However, when doing so, we must be careful to examine not only our intentions and motives, but the biases and assumptions we bring about poor students and the families they come from.

Ruby Payne and her "framework for understanding poverty" represent one of education's latest attempts to address the needs of students from low socioeconomic backgrounds. But her solutions and practical strategies are rooted in a discourse that promotes the racist, sexist, and classist system that results in exclusion, isolation, and deprivation. While Payne insists that she is an economic pragmatist and therefore is only interested in class, such thinking masks the reality that class is socially co-constructed along with race, sexuality, and gender. The underlying assumptions about the "culture of poverty" that ooze from Payne's work exemplify how race, class, gender, and sexuality intersect. The scenarios, puns, anecdotes, and truth-claims Payne makes about the poor reflect racist, classist, and sexist societal stereotypes of women and people of color, and couches poverty in terms of "individual choice" and "moral will." Such a framework does not help us eradicate poverty or "understand" it. On the contrary, it helps to maintain White hegemony by shifting the blame away from White privilege and patriarchy and onto individuals who "choose" not to do better. Educating students to simply change their "dysfunctional and pathological behavior" in favor of a "morally superior one" does not change or disable the system of inequality but gives it the needed fuel to continue running smoothly.

* * * *

My subjectivity—the fact that I know and care for Ellis, worked with him on a regular basis, and am a Black educator who works with the "culturally deficient" children Ruby Payne describes—does not weaken my work but strengthens it. I occupy a unique position; I see things others cannot. While most can only read about Ellis and draw conclusions based on the media's portrayal of him, I am able to draw from my real life, everyday experiences with him. I can therefore locate inconsistencies that others cannot. While the papers describe a robbery suspect with gang affiliations and no respect for law enforcement, I can juxtapose this with the highly intelligent, soft-spoken young man who came to school at 7:30 every morning, carried my bags up the stairs, and drew cartoon characters for my bulletin boards. This insider's perspective, while not free of contradictions, makes for a more holistic and messy version of "reality"—where problems and solutions are not black and white, obvious, or self-evident, but are different shades of gray, complicated, and subjective. It is this perspective that provides us with insight and understanding as the process necessitates a cycle of inquiry, analysis, critique, and articulation.

This cycle must be perpetuated by us first—teachers. While Ruby Payne refers to the kids we teach as "those students," we understand that these are *our* students. And our students are indeed "at risk": at risk of being labeled as culturally deficient, at risk of receiving instruction that reinforces that they are inferior, at risk of being stifled by a system that would have us believe they need to be fixed because it is they and their communities that are broken. Yes, it is easier to diagnose them as having the problem than to indict the present social order which is founded on the exploitation and exclusion of poor people of color.

As teachers, we must understand the history of American education. It has never been the goal of the American educational system to interrupt the cycle of poverty, alleviate crime, or equalize society. The educational system, like the criminal *in*justice system, is a billion-dollar industry. Ruby Payne herself is a self-made millionaire. She has made millions by situating poverty within the dominant narrative of cultural deficiency and individual choice. She is successful, not because her work has proven effective, but because it reconfirms the "reality" that it is indeed poor people of color who are the problem. Their situation, being poor and of color, makes them inherently "at risk." But our students are not inherently at-risk of failure, they are, in fact, *the* risk. To provide these students, who are the majority in urban school districts, with a quality education runs the risk of educating a new generation of Malcolm Xs, Emiliano Zapatas, Assata Shakurs—a generation of critically literate persons who seek to eradicate systems of injustice rather than simply "understand the framework."

Those who promote the master narrative of individual choice and accountability understand the framework. So they attack us first, the people who educate "these children." If they can influence our perceptions of who these students are and how they behave, they will inevitably affect students' beliefs about who they are and what they can achieve. So they convince us that these students are deficient, lacking completeness, but that we can help them out of their deprived state. They tell us that schools are the only places where students can learn the choices and rules of the respected middle class, and because we want so badly for our children to succeed, we busy ourselves with trying to assimilate them into a system that benefits from their exclusion and failure. We forget that it is the system that is flawed and attribute the defects to these children, their families, and their culture. We recognize these students as "at-risk" and we vow to help them recover, to save them from their present condition, as long as they are willing to be saved. And in doing so, we forget that they are not sick. We forget that they are not lab rats or science experiments with universal characteristics and uniform behaviors. We forget that they are whole, not deficient or incomplete. And we forget that *these* children are *our* children.

* * * *

Ellis' physical wounds have healed. His body has made a full recovery. But he will never be the same child as before. He has been robbed of his innocence and his emotional wounds will take much longer to heal. Every day that I teach, I see potential Ellises and I am saddened. Because I realize that as teachers, we can inflict wounds on our students that last longer than even Ellis' physical scars: every time we teach to assimilate rather than liberate, to maintain rather than deconstruct this defective system, every time we imagine our students to be broken and ourselves to be repairmen, when we uncritically accept racist policies and ideologies, every time we forget that these children are our children.

We cannot afford to forget. Because we teach "these children." And we are "these children."

References

Abell, T. & Lyon, L. (1979). Do the differences make a difference? An empirical evaluation of the culture of poverty in the United States. *American Ethnologist, 6*(3), 602–621.

Bohn, A. (Winter 2006). *A framework for understanding Ruby Payne*. Retrieved from www.rethinkingschools.org

Bomer, R., Dworin, J.E., May, L., & Semingson, P. (2008). Miseducating teachers about the poor: A critical analysis of Ruby Payne's claims about poverty. *Teachers College Record*. Retrieved from www.tcrecord.org

Bonilla-Silva, E. (2003). *Racism without racists: Color-blind racism and the persistence of racial inequality in the United States*. Lanham, MD: Rowman & Littlefield.

Carr, J. & Megbolugbe, I. (1992). The Federal Reserve Bank of Boston study on mortgage lending revisted. *Journal of Housing Research, 4* (2), 277-313.

The Civil Rights Project at Harvard University (2005). *Confronting the graduation rate crisis in the South*. Retrieved from www.eric.ed.gov

Corcoran, M., Duncan, G., Gurin, G., & Gutrin, P. (1985). Myth and reality: The causes and persistence of poverty. *Journal of Policy Analysis & Management 4*(4), 516–536.

Davidson, C. & Gaitz, C. (1974). "Are the poor different?" A comparison of work behavior and attitudes among the urban poor and nonpoor. *Social Problems, 22*(2), 229–245.

Fine, M., & McClelland, S. (2006). Sexuality education and desire: Still missing after all these years. *Harvard Educational Review, 76*(3).

Glenn, D. (2004). The train has left: The No Child Left behind leaves Black and Latino literacy learners waiting at the station. *Journal of Adolescent and Adult Literacy, 47*(8), 297–338.

Gorski, P. (February 9, 2006). *The classist underpinnings of Ruby Payne's framework*. Retrieved from www.tcrecord.org

Gorski, P. (2005). *Savage unrealities: Uncovering classism in Ruby Payne's framework*. Retrieved from www.edchange.org/publications.html

Higginbotham, E. (1992). African-American women's history and metalanguage of race. *Signs: Journal of Women in Culture and Society, 17*(2), 251–274.

hooks, b. (1994). Holding my sister's hand. *Teaching to transgress: Education as the practice of freedom*. New York: Routledge.

The Housing Research and Advocacy Center (2009). Racial and ethnic disparities remain in Ohio mortgage lending. Retrieved from www.thehousingcenter.com.

Irelan, L., Moles, O., & O'Shea, R. (1969). Ethnicity, poverty, and selected attitudes: A test of the "culture of poverty" hypothesis. *Social Forces, 47* (4), 405–413.

Jones, R.J. & Luo, Y (1999). The culture of poverty and African-American culture: An empirical assessment. *Sociological Perspectives, 42*(3), 439–458.

Katz, M. (1989). *The undeserving poor: From the war on poverty to the war on welfare*. New York: Pantheon.

Kelley, R. (1997). *Yo mama's disfunktional: Fighting the culture wars in urban America*. Boston, MA: Beacon.

Ladson-Billings, G. (1994). *The dreamkeepers: Successful teachers of African American children*. San Francisco, CA: Jossey-Bass.

Land, D. & Legters, N. (2002). The extent and consequences of risk in U.S. education. In S. Stringfield & D. Land (Eds.), *Educating at-risk students* (pp. 1–28). Chicago, IL: University of Chicago Press.

McIntosh, P. (1990). Unpacking the invisible knapsack. *Independent School, 49*(2), 31–36.

Miller, W. (1959). Implications of a lower class culture. *Social Service Review, 12*, 12–16.

Ng, J.C., & Rury, J. (2006, July 10). Poverty and education: A critical analysis of the Ruby Payne phenomenon. *Teachers College Record*. Retrieved from www.tcrecord.org on November 15, 2006.

Patrick, S.R. (2004). Schooling in Babylon, Babylon in school: When racial profiling and zero tolerance converge. Retrieved from www.eric.ed.gov

Payne, R. (1996). *A framework for understanding poverty*. Highlands, TX: aha! Process.

Reed, A. (1992). The underclass as myth and symbol: The poverty of discourse about poverty. *Radical America, 24*(1), 21–40.

Ryan, W. (1971). *Blaming the victim*. New York: Random House.

Shihadeh, E., & Flynn, N. (1996, June). Segregation and crime: The effect of black social isolation on the rates of black urban violence. *Social Forces, 74*(4), 1325–1352.

Takaki, R. (1993). *A different mirror: A history of multicultural America.* New York, NY: Little, Brown, and Co.

Tootell, G. (1993). Defaults, denials, and discrimination in mortgage lending. *New England Economics Review,* (September/October), 45–51.

Vertner, R., & Chang, J. (2000). The war on youth. *Color Lines.* Retrieved from www.arc.org

Wilson, A. (1990). *Black-on-black violence: The psychodynamics of black self-annihilation in service of white domination.* New York: Afrikan World InfoSystems.

Wise, T. (2005). Excuses, excuses: How the right rationalizes racial inequality in America. Retrieved from www.blackcommentator.com

· 1 0 ·

Undoing Ruby Payne and Other Deficit Views of English Language Learners

Theresa Montaño & Rosalinda Quintanar-Sarellana

The view proposed by Payne to explain educational inequality and economic disparity promotes an "individualistic" deficit view of how one overcomes poverty. She puts forth simplistic explanations for challenging classism, racism and linguicism, implying that one need to only to adopt middle class values to succeed in school. Furthermore, Payne's framework reduces the complexity of group identity, language and culture and lumps all poor people of different ethnic and linguistic backgrounds into one group: the poor. The struggle of immigrant children to learn English is dismissed as merely as a consequence of language deficiencies that need to be remediated. The cultural and linguistic knowledge of the immigrant student and his/her ability to negotiate the unfriendly terrain of schooling and society are completely ignored. These views are harmful to immigrant students and fail to prepare teachers to understand that all linguistic forms of language are multifaceted systems used by speakers of a specific language community and that language is "negotiated between people in and through communicative social interaction" (Gee, 2005, p. 67). Payne's failure to acknowledge the complexities of language learning also allows teachers to easily chalk up the social discourse of Chicana/o-Latino/a and African American students as an inferior language form. Payne's depiction of English Learners is one of bilingual children who have a limited vocabulary and no knowledge of the "formal register" (Payne, 2009, 1). Payne completely ignores the students' primary language and the possibility of using it as a resource and a vehicle for learning.

Language deficit theories, such as Payne's, do not acknowledge that poverty, socioeconomic difference and economic disparity are part and parcel of a society where "discourse is directly related to the distribution of social power and hierarchy in society" (Shannon, 2001, 2). The market economy in this nation is what drives instruction and that instruction is intended to reproduce class stratification. Accepting frameworks like Payne's framework reproduces inequality and explains discrepancies in achievement by pointing to "deficient" features in groups of people. In the case of Latino/a immigrant students, the majority of whom are English language learners, this is done by explaining difficulties in language acquisition as language deficits and by drawing on already socially established views about immigrants and English learners as "slow to learn English." Payne's simplistic explanations also ignore the social and political contexts these students and their families negotiate on a daily basis. Payne's framework fails to connect race, class, language or immigrant status to the reproduction of monolingual educational policies, xenophobic legislation and poverty. The poor are depicted as deficient in the cognitive, emotional and linguistic resources needed to escape poverty and move into the middle class (Dudley-Marling, 2008). The framework implies that poverty persists because people in poverty don't know the rules of the middle class (hidden rules) and those who are poor must learn the hidden rules of poverty in order to transcend the circumstances of poverty. The framework's answer for closing the educational achievement gap contends that if those who are poor learn the hidden rules, they will transcend the circumstances of poverty. In the case of English Learners, we believe that Ruby Payne's *Framework for Understanding Poverty* has objectively promoted a deficit view of Chicana/o-Latino/a students and has contributed to school districts mandating scripted programs that purportedly accelerate the acquisition of English (quick fix" English development models that dehumanize language instruction).

There are an increasing number of urban and rural school districts throughout this nation utilizing Payne's framework for professional development directed at teachers of English Learners. The short list of states and nations with school districts currently utilizing the *Framework for Understanding Poverty* in the professional development of teachers of English Learners includes Hawaii, California, Texas and Australia. The use of Payne's framework in the professional development of teachers of English Learners is what motivates us to write a critique of Ruby Payne's views of language learning.

The Latino/a Socioeconomic and Sociopolitical Context

When speaking of those living in poverty, Payne's discourse objectively points to Latino/as living in the United States. California's Latina/o population is a significant factor in the rise of poverty in this state (Reed, 2006). According to the U.S census (2010) 36.6 percent of the population in California was Chicana/Latino and Chicanas, whereas the Latinos comprised only 15.4 percent of the total U.S. population. In California, 54 percent of poor children are Latino and African American and 26 percent are immigrant (National Center for Children in Poverty, 2008). As the economy worsened, the unemployment rate for Latino/as "was just slightly above the overall national unemployment rate" climbing to 13.1 percent from a 4.9 percent in 2006, "3 percentage points higher than the overall U.S. unemployment rate." According to the *Los Angeles Times* (May, 2010) Latinos account for about one-seventh of the U.S. labor force but comprise nearly one-fifth of the unemployed. Moreover, Latino/as have the highest rate of poverty in Los Angeles, Long Beach and Fresno (Latino Issues Forum, 2003). It is interesting to note that the majority student population in the three urban centers identified above is over 60 percent Latino. The student population of the Los Angeles Unified School District is 73.2 percent Latino/a and Los Angeles County has a student population of over 62.5 percent Latino/a (Ed-data, 2010). The poverty rate among Hispanics in 2007 was 21.5 percent, and 32.1 percent of Chicanas-Latinos lacked health insurance in 2007. A quick review of the data will also reveal that Latino/a children attending school in California are likely to be poor, speak a home language other than English and attend public school. For these reasons, we would argue those who advance deficit views of language and theories like the *Framework for Understanding Poverty* by Ruby Payne do so with Chicana/o-Latino/a (and African American) children in mind. If truth be told, the aha press website (Ruby Payne's official website) features a handout on the percentage of those living in poverty in the U.S. and prominently featured are the percentages of Latino/as and African Americans who are poor (Ahaprocess.com).

Theoretical Lenses

Deslenguadas. Somos los del español deficiente. We are your linguistic nightmare, your linguistic aberration, your linguistic *mestisaje*, the subject of your *burla*. Because we speak with tongues of fire we are culturally crucified. Racially, culturally, and linguistically *somos huerfanos*—we speak an orphan tongue. (Gloria Anzaldúa, 1999, p. 80)

Latino/a-Chicana/o students, as English Language Learners, have successfully navigated the tortuous waters of unsupportive educational institutions, have experienced the subtractive deculturalization of the public school curriculum and have survived in a xenophobic country that reaps the benefits of their parents' labor while outlawing their very existence. We write this paper for these students, who do not recognize the beauty and complexity of their language, who often feel insecure about their linguistic abilities, yet can negotiate both the dominant language (English) and the primary language (Spanish). It is not unusual to hear our K-16 students say: "My Spanish is not good enough for the BCLAD program (California's bilingual teacher preparation program)," "I have kitchen Spanish," or "My English is funny." We use this opportunity to not only critique the Framework for Understanding Poverty but to validate their language variety.

In offering an alternative to the language deficit views of Payne's framework, we will provide a definition of "language deficit" and argue that Payne's simplistic explanations on language learning promote deficit views of language learning and culture. Furthermore, we find Payne's inappropriate use of linguistic theories fundamentally flawed and will challenge it using sociolinguistic theories on discourse that advance a more humanistic and established view of language differences. Finally, we contend that instead of designing professional development models such as Payne's, school districts would be better off if they provided teachers with an opportunity to engage in a process of connecting with family, language, culture and cognitive abilities of English language learners, tap the cultural and linguistic knowledge of the students, infuse this knowledge into the curriculum and ultimately facilitate a process where students resist the policies and practices that reproduce the social inequality and perpetuate class differences.

As we engage in this critical analysis of Ruby Payne's *Framework for Understanding Poverty*, we do so as Chicana bilingual teacher educators. The recognition and affirmation of our cultural identities are important components of our research and scholarship. As activist scholars and proponents of bilingual education, we work tirelessly to insure that future teachers are both prepared to teach Chicana/o-Latino/a students and to affirm the cultural and linguistic knowledge these students bring into the classroom. The current educational reality of bilingual teachers is that they spend more time responding to misconceptions about linguistic minority students rather than tapping the cultural and linguistic knowledge of our children. Their instruction consists of reading from remedial scripts surrendered to them by district administrators compelled to raise test scores, and waging up-hill battles to protect the few bilingual education programs that remain in existence. It is in this milieu that models like the *Framework for Understanding Poverty* do nothing more than promote deficit views of language minority students, most of them from poor working class families. The professional development that evolves from these theoretical models creates the conditions where institutions of education design subtractive models of language education and where teachers are encouraged to view our children as students "who meander endlessly through a topic" (Payne, 2001, 43). Moreover, when school districts and unions promote Payne's framework, they provide an "easy way out" for the majority of teachers who are white and monolingual. This chapter is firmly established in a theoretical framework of linguistic, critical literacy and sociocultural theory that simultaneously critiques hegemonic views of language and honors the voices of linguistic minority children and youth. In this paper we engage in a critical analysis of Ruby Payne's *Framework for Understanding Poverty* by arguing that Payne's approach does little to prepare teachers to function effectively in the multiracial, multiethnic, multilingual context of today's classroom.

Deconstructing Payne

Payne claims that in generational poverty, students speak using the casual register, "much of the meaning comes not from word choices, but from non-verbal assists" (28). Casual registers as defined by Payne (1996) is language between friends characterized by a limited vocabulary of 400–800 words, word choice is not specific and general and sentence syntax is often incomplete (42). In addition, using the casual register compels poor students to "beat around the bush, circle around the mulberry bush, begin with the end first and focus on emotional characterization" (Payne, 1996, Chapter 2). Students who are able to speak from a discourse of the generational poor lack sequence, order, cause and effect and a conclusion in their conversation. According to Payne the linguistic discourse pattern for children of poverty goes something like this:

Part of an Episode

Audience Participation

Language for those who are poor, according to Payne (1996) is about "survival," but for the middle class it is about "negotiation." We would argue that the descriptors above are simplistic and stereotypic explanations of language. First of all, just as there is no "culture of poverty," there is no language of poverty. Individuals who live in poverty represent several cultural and linguistic communities. These students are Latino/a, Chicana/o, Asian and Pacific Islanders, American Indian, European American, and African American, consequently they speak several languages, several vernaculars and several language varieties. James Gee (2005) explains that language has a "magical property." It is a tool used to send messages in a specific language community, to connect members of identity groups to another one, it is a person's "most distinctive and significant type of behavior" (Crawford, 1992, p. 400). It is an extremely complex system and all people negotiate language. The poor in the Latino/a community are not an exception to this: they speak Chicana/o English, Spanglish, Spanish and yes, even English! In fact, there are several different forms of language within the Latino/a cultural world. For example, in rural areas some of words, such as *ansina* and *truje* date back to the "old Spanish" and *Don Quijote*, one of the most outstanding literary works in Spanish, The old terms that have remained in some rural areas are called *archaisms*. People who are not familiar with the history of languages label this language variety, *"hillbilly Spanish,"* when it is simply a different discourse model or a variation of the dominant or primary language. In fact, this is like the English Shakespeare used in his literary works.

There is not a single language in the world with only one variety. In fact, (Brice-Heath, 1983; Labov, 1972; Purcell-Gates, 1995; Zentella, 1997) have conducted several studies on the language varieties in ethnic communities, and they have substantiated that language differences, use and discourse are caused by geography, age, and socioeconomic status. We do not argue that language variety is somewhat dependent on social class. We take umbrage with the depiction of language variety as lacking rudimentary features like sequence and order or a structured discourse pattern. Language varieties of ethnic minority people, like Chicana/os, African Americans and other linguistic minorities may differ from the standard discourse of American English but not significantly. While it is true that not all languages are linear, contrary to what Payne purports, all languages have structure and discourse patterns that contain sequence, express cause and effect and have extensive vocabularies. All languages have some components that might appear very difficult and other components that may seem easy.

All languages also contain formal and casual registers. In fact, in the linguistic community of those who speak Spanish, every child learns the familiar form for you; *tú* is used for acquaintances and the formal *usted* reserved for those who warrant respect. The ability to tap a variety of discourse models is a measure of cognitive flexibility, not a cognitive deficiency. As language minority students acquire a new language, they develop an incredible ability to use "different varieties of language in different social situations" (Stubbs, 2003, 79). The desire for a language minority child to speak her own language provides a strong bond with his/her family and community. The ability to speak a variety of languages is a vital form of communication that enables individuals to maintain strong ties with their communities and to negotiate the dominant language, in this case the English language. It is a misconception to believe that one form of social discourse is inferior to another form of discourse.

We are also offended by the depiction of dialect as an inferior form of English purportedly used by those who are poor. Payne implies that those who are poor use words and phrases like *"messin' with me, nothin', lookin'"* (Payne, 2005, 1). We maintain that many Americans, rich or poor, use the terms listed above. It is common knowledge that the informal use of language transcends race or class. Actually, many white rappers and singers have appropriated the use of African American vernacular as means of gaining access to a broader listening audience and for financial profit. Former President George Bush, a "generationally wealthy" individual, is known to some as a speaker of "plain English." In fact, David Letterman would often poke fun at the former president's misuse of English in a segment entitled "famous presidential speeches." In addressing an audience of reporters on the war in Iraq, George Bush once declared "This is been tough weeks in that country." On the other end of linguistic spectrum, when addressing Spanish-speaking listeners in Latin America, his attempt at code switching was quite amusing. George Bush said *"Sin dula, we are going to achieve, what we want to achieve, because ester pais es-es-es-es un gran pais."* We believe he meant *sin duda* (without a doubt); *sin dula* means without a midwife. Surely, President Bush's linguistic errors are not due to living in generational poverty.

Payne also asserts that children from poverty are more likely to be familiar with the terms "deportation, green card, dissed, roach, gray tape" (Payne, 1996, 85–87). While it may be true that Latino/a immigrants may be more familiar with this terminology, it is not due only to class, race, immigration status, and politics. All languages or discourse models are formed in social communities; all language is socially constructed and culturally embedded, for

Latino/as living and breathing in a xenophobic country is a way of life. This is why Latino/as are familiar with the language; it is the "politics, significance and social relations" (Gee, 2005) that require Latino/as to familiarize themselves with linguistic forms of xenophobic immigration policies; a reality that Payne has yet to acknowledge.

Linguists do not consider dialects as caused by the failure of their speakers to master Standard English nor do they believe that the speech of working-class people is merely a form of emotional expression and that poor people are incapable of relating logical thought, as implied by Payne. In reality, language variety is a constant in the United States, and the emergence of new dialects is a process that arises when a people's language undergoes gradual change. Language varieties (dialects, lingo, patois, pidgin) go through the same process that changes Latin in French, French in Creole or Quebecois. Standard dialects are deemed dialects according to "geopolitical accident" or a "sociological determination" not according to anything inherent in the dialect itself. (McWhorter, 2000). Language varieties develop alongside standard dialects, not from them. Linguistic forms that arise in this nation are as multifaceted and nuanced as the "standard" ones.

Crawford (1992) eloquently states "Every language, dialect, patois, or lingo is a structurally complete framework into which can be poured any subtlety or emotion or thought that its users are capable of experiencing. Whatever it lacks at any given time or place in the way of vocabulary and syntax can be supplied in a very short order by borrowing and imitation from other languages."(408) Language varieties reflect the linguistic and cultural capital of a community and are a vital form of communications. Students who are metacognitively aware of their language dialect understand how other dialects and languages are structured. Furthermore, knowledge of how dialects function helps students to acknowledge why their social or spoken language differs from what appears in academic textbooks (Quintanar-Sarellana, Huebner & Jensen, 2003). Language and dialects of a particular speech community are examples of resilience in spite of centuries of linguistic suppression; such as the Latino/a-Chicana/o community has experienced with English-only movement.

Challenging Deficit Views with Critical Literacy

According to Solórzano & Yasso (2001) the cultural deficit model is used to blame the low educational achievement of students of color, especially those who are black and brown, on the "internal social structure of families of color" (5).

Solórzano and Yasso (2001) maintain, "Cultural deficiency models argue that since parents of color fail to assimilate and embrace the educational values of the dominant group, and continue to transmit or socialize their children with values that inhibit educational mobility, then they are to blame if the low educational attainment continues into succeeding generations." (6) We believe that Payne's insinuations about language and language learning promote these negative ideas and consequently inform educational policies which lead to reductionist models for language teaching. For example, 1) Payne advocates that since casual registers are the primary discourse models used by poor students, formal discourse patterns need to be taught directly to students who do not have access to these registers at home, and 2) when students use the inappropriate model in class, the teacher should use this time for teaching the appropriate register. Payne asserts that because poor students do not have cognitive structures that enable them to plan, quoting Rueven Feuerstein, Payne (2003) uses the following passage to depict the cognitive skills of poor students:

- Individuals who cannot plan, cannot predict
- If they cannot predict, they cannot identify cause and effect
- If they cannot identify cause and effect, they cannot identify consequence
- If they cannot identify consequence, they cannot control impulsivity
- If they cannot control impulsivity, they have an inclination to criminal behavior. (2)

Following the above logic, one might conclude Payne implies that poor children have a greater inclination towards crime. Further, she promotes the idea that language issues "cause many students from generational poverty to be 'unmediated,' and therefore, the cognitive structures needed inside the mind to learn at the levels required by the state tests have not been fully developed" (1). A critical perspective would look at the fact that standardized exams do not adequately measure the knowledge or learning of poor children and would consider the test flawed. Instead Payne promotes is the idea that the student must be changed in order to pass the test. Therefore, teachers must intervene, *mediate* and provide structure to an otherwise chaotic life style where parents "do not have time and energy to both mediate the children and put food on the table." (Payne, 2003, p. 3) Payne's discussion of what mediation means is contrary to the perspective of sociocultural theory. In sociocultural language theory mediation is created via a reciprocal relationship where social interaction between the individual and society, between the culture of the home and school, and between the teacher and the student facilitates the development of a solid cultural and linguistic foundation. The cultural, linguistic and intellectual capital found in Latino/a-Chicana/o homes includes *confianza, consejos, carino* and *amor (trust, advice, affection and love—although advice does not capture the depth of consejos)*. Payne overlooks the positive qualities found in the homes of poor children and describes impoverished homes as bastions where the "relationship is valued over achievement," "too much education is feared," "you don't have words to negotiate a resolution," the "noise level is higher and non-verbal information is more important than verbal," and so on and so forth. So that for these students to succeed they must be taught the hidden rules of the middle class, arguing the best instruction is direct instruction because "the undeveloped and under-developed parts of the learning structure" must be built in poor children who do not have access to such at home. These ideas objectively lead to the development of educational models where children are subjected to banking models of education. These deficit views of children might also lead to the implementation of instructional models in language arts such as scripted programs and teaching the tests.

We do not disagree that language minority children and poor children must learn academic English. As educators, we understand the need for our children to become proficiently biliterate, and we encourage our students to maintain their specific language variety. Students can have the best of both worlds when they can choose which language variety is more appropriate to the situation they are facing. The outstanding linguist Robert Politzer wrote: "I believe that it is the business of schools to teach languages and speech variations and not extinguish or make people forget anything—and this involves first dialects and non-standards dialects as well as languages" (Politzer, 1993). We agree with Politzer and others who maintain that language minority students must acquire full proficiency in English and continue their acquisition of the primary language. But as critical educators, we also recognize the attributes contained in the language varieties of those who grow up in working-class and poor communities. Labov (1972) powerfully describes the functionality of working class sociolinguistic discourse, when he observed how "working class speakers are more effective narrators, reasoners and debaters than many middle-class speakers, who temporize, qualify, and lose their argument in a mass of irrelevant detail." (142)

It is in this context that teachers must engage in a struggle for cultural and linguistic democracy, where language education must include the acknowledgment and affirmation of languages in the home and where teacher educators must question the sociopolitical and ideological underpinnings of Payne's *Framework for Understanding Poverty*. We must recognize the sociopolitical realities, which inform the educational practices and policies experienced by Latino/a-Chicana/o children that develop as a direct result of models such as Payne. Quiroz (2001) intimated that "no Latino, assimilated or bicultural, escapes the quandaries and paradoxes of prejudice, paternalism or personal dissonance and their effects on identity" (335). It is for this reason that we question the motives and ideologies contained in theoretical models that when accepted instinctively perpetuate a subordinate view of a person's linguistic and cultural knowledge. We maintain that Payne's discussion of the language of poor people promotes a deficit view of language varieties and ultimately leads to the belief that primary language(s) and language variety evolves from the discourses of those who are poor and therefore, are inferior. We believe that although she has said that her model is an "additive model," the model inevitably leads to a monolingual or "subtractive" approach to language instruction, a non-responsive, destructive view of non-dominant languages.

Further, we argue that deficit views do not account for the complex institutional and structural inequities reproduced within this society. These structural inequalities lead to the development of two educational systems, one for the wealthy and one for the poor, Schools respond to corporate interests who lament the "failure" of schools to teach poor children the basics of the English language by creating a school environment that denigrates minority languages and language variety and establishing instructional programs that consider the student the cause of poor educational achievement.

A critical perspective to language and language education

> If you believe that children's language can be deficient then you might be tempted to try and improve their language in some way. If you believe on the contrary that the concept of language deficit does not make much sense, and that there is nothing wrong with the language of any normal child, then you probably believe that schooling should not interfere with children's dialect. And if you believe that linguistic disadvantage arise largely from peoples' intolerance and prejudice toward language differences then you probably try to change people's attitudes to language (Stubbs, 2003, p. 79).

We have argued that language is political, that deficit views of language lead to reductionist models of language instruction and negative perceptions of language difference. We maintain that ideological clarity is necessary when accepting instructional models and argue that teachers must critically reflect and evaluate the pedagogical consequences of models like *Framework for Understanding Poverty*. It is our hope that teachers acknowledge that teaching is political and that in the sociopolitical arena of the United States language and knowledge have been and are created in historical context where schooling is not neutral. For over four hundred years, the schooling of Chicana/os has included silencing and debilingualization and curriculum models that ultimately lead to historical amnesia and deculturalization.

Moreover, we believe in pedagogical models founded upon critical views of education. A critical worldview requires teachers to develop an understanding of the relationships between ideology, culture, hegemony and power and to become transformative educators committed to radically changing the "traditional" curriculum, to transforming society. Critical educators also strive to develop student voice, even if this voice challenges the perspective of the educator. The key process in critical pedagogy includes dialogue, reflection and social action. (Darder, 1998). As critical educators, teachers recognize that inequality and poverty are not "relative" (as argued by Payne), but "reinforced" and "reproduced" by social and political forces intent on maintaining the status quo. Critical educators realize that changes in inequitable conditions will only happen through political action, not through the reinforcement of deficit views. Children are not changed to fit into society, but society changes to meet the realities of the student. In critical pedagogy, knowledge and meaning are dialogical and constructed collaboratively (teacher and students, students and teacher, teacher and community, home and school, etc.).

As Freire said, "students read to learn, not simply learn to read." In critical literacy, the emphasis is on critical and creative thought, the students' prior knowledge is used as the starting point and students are encouraged to question. Students understand and interpret the content of a given subject area—beginning with what they already know and move towards what they can change. Reading strategies not only focus on understanding the material, more importantly they incorporate critical thinking skills. The given subject area and/or content area is transformed into a socially relevant, comprehensible, and meaningful topic. Literacy that is grounded in the students' sociocultural-sociolinguistic communities facilitates personal and cultural identity formation, aids comprehension and the generation of new knowledge, and the student's primary language and form of discourse are respected, tapped and affirmed.

The teacher's role in critical pedagogy is to embrace the idea that language is political; as such it is a tool that may be used to develop in our students the capacity to resist, not to conform. In turn, teachers create a space for "alternative cultural production and alternative epistemology or different ways of thinking and knowledge that are crucial to creating a counterhegemonic world-view and move students beyond the limitations of Standard English." (hooks, 2003). A teacher's role is to raise the consciousness of the students' surroundings from a resistance perspective, to facilitate reflection and create opportunities for our students to reflect on their positionality and what they can do about it. Teachers and students create a new more equitable, democratic cultural climate. They enter the "historical process critically" (Darder, 1998). In other words, teachers and students learn to reflect upon the injustices, name them, and create an opportunity to engage in critical dialogue in order to understand the world and to change it. They honor the equality of languages and support an environment that respects, not devalues the "serpent tongue" (Anzaldúa, 1999) of our people.

References

Anzaldúa, G. E. (1999). *Borderlands/La Frontera-The new Mestiza* (2nd ed.). San Francisco: Aunt Lute.

Bomer, R., Dworin, J., May, L., & Semington, P. (2008). *Miseducating teachers about the poor: A critical analysis of Ruby Payne's claims about poverty*. Retrieved from *Teachers College Record* http://www.tcrecord.org/PrintContent.asp?ContentID=14591

Brice-Heath, S. (1983). *Ways with words: Language, life, and work in communities and classrooms*. New York: McGraw-Hill; Oxford University Press

Crawford, J. (1992). *Language loyalties: A sourcebook on the official English controversy*. Chicago, IL: University of Chicago Press.

Darder, A. (1998). *Teaching as an act of love: Reflections on Paulo Freire's contribution to our lives and our work*. Occasional Paper Series. Los Angeles, CA: California Association of Bilingual Education.

Delpit, L. (1997). *Other people's children: Cultural conflict in the classroom*. New York: New Press.

Dudley-Marling, C. (2008). Return of the deficit. Retrieved from the *Journal of Educational Controversy*. Retrieved from http://www.wce.wwu.edu/Resources/CEP/eJournal/v002 n0001/a004.shtml

Ed-data. (2010). *Students by ethnicity: Los Angeles Unified School District,2008–09*. Retrieved from http://www.ed-data.k12.ca.us/Navigation/fsTwoPanel.asp?bottom=%2Fprofile %2Easp%3Flevel%3D06%26reportNumber%3D16

Freire, P., & Macedo, D. (1987). *Literacy: Reading the word and the world*. Westport, CT: Bergin & Garvey.

Gee, J. P. (2005). *Introduction to discourse analysis: Theory and method*. New York: Routledge.

Gorski, P. (2006). *Savage unrealities*. Retrieved from *Rethinking Schools*. http://rethinking schools.org/archive/21_02/sava212.shtml

hooks, b. (2003). *Teaching to transgress: Pedagogy of hope*. New York: Routledge.

Labov, W. (1972). Academic ignorance and black intelligence. *Atlantic Monthly*, June 1972.

Ladson-Billings, G. (1994). *The dreamkeepers: Successful teachers of African American children*. San Francisco, CA: Jossey Bass.

Latino Issues Forum. (2003, May). *Latinos and Poverty*. Retrieved from www.lif.org

McWhorter, J. (2000). *Spreading the word: Language and dialect in America*. Portsmouth, NH: Heinemann.

Moll, L. (1992). Funds of knowledge for teaching: Using a qualitative approach to connect homes and classrooms. *Theory into Practice*. *31*(2, Spring). 131–140.

National Center for Children in Poverty. (2008, October). *Who are America's Poor Children*. Retrieved from http://www.nccp.org/publications/pub_843.html

Ng, J. C., & Rury, J. L. (2006). *Poverty and education: A critical analysis of the Ruby Payne phenomenon*. Retrieved from Teachers College Record http://www.tcrecord.org/Print Content.asp?ContentID=12596

Payne, R. K. (1996/2001/2005). *A framework for understanding poverty*. Highlands, TX: aha! Process.

Payne, R. K. (2003). No Child Left Behind: What's really behind it all?—part I. *Instructional Leader*, *16*(2), 1–3.

Payne, R. K. (2009). *Ten dynamics of poverty that undermine school success—and what schools can do about those barriers*. Retrieved from www.ahaprocess.com

Politzer, R. (1993). A researcher's reflections on bridging dialect and second language learning: Discussion of problems and solutions. In B. Merino, H. Trueba, & F. Samaniego (Eds.). *Language & culture in learning: Teaching Spanish to Native Speakers of Spanish*. Washington, DC: Falmer.

Purcell-Gates, V. (1995). *Other people's words: The cycle of low literacy*. Cambridge, MA: Harvard University Press.

Quintanar-Sarellana, R., Huebner, T., & Jensen, A. (2003). Tapping a natural resource: Language minority students as foreign language teaching. In B. Merino, H. Trueba, & F. Samaniego (Eds.). *Language & culture in learning: Teaching Spanish to Native Speakers of Spanish*. Washington, DC: Falmer.

Quiroz, A. P. (2001). The silencing of Latino student "Voice": Puerto Rican and Mexican narratives in eighth grade and high school. *Anthropology and Education Quarterly*, *32*(3) 326–349.

Reed, D. (2006, May). *Poverty in California*. San Francisco, CA: Public Policy Institute of California.

Shannon, P. (2001) *Political, too. New readings and writings on the politics of literacy instruction*. Portsmouth, NH: Heinemann.

Smith, L. T. (1999) *Decolonizing methodologies: Research and indigenous peoples*. New York: Zed.

Solórzano, D., & Yasso, T. J. (2001, Fall). From racial stereotyping toward a critical race theory in teacher education. *Multicultural Education*, *9*(1), 2–8.

Stubbs, M. (2003). Some basic sociolinguistic concepts. In L. Delpit, & J. Kilgour-Dowdy (Ed.), *The skins we speak: Thoughts on language and culture in the classroom*. New York, NY: New Press.

Tan, C. (2010, May 6). *Hispanic unemployment rate soars: The recession hits hardest in industries and regions where Hispanic workers are disproportionately represented, a congressional report shows*.

Retrieved from http://articles.latimes.com/2010/may/06/business/la-fi-latino-jobless-20100506

U.S. Census Bureau. (2010). Quickfacts. [U.S. Census Bureau: State and County QuickFacts. Data derived from Population Estimates, Census of Population and Housing, Small Area Income and Poverty Estimates, State and County Housing Unit Estimates, County Business Patterns, Nonemployer Statistics, Economic Census, Survey of Business Owners, Building Permits, Consolidated Federal Funds] Report. Retrieved from http://quickfacts.census.gov/qfd/states/06000.html

Zentella, A. C. (1997). *Growing up bilingual: Puerto Rican children in New York.* Oxford: Blackwell.

· 1 1 ·

What's Class Got to Do with It?

A Pedagogical Response to a Deficit Perspective

JULIE KEOWN-BOMAR & DEBORAH PATTEE

WHETHER IN A SCHOOL, WORKPLACE, OR COMMUNITY, SOCIAL CLASS DISPARITIES exist and they divide us. The social class continuum in the United States not only reflects disparate income categories, but it also sheds light on a much more complicated and problematic issue: the unequal distribution of opportunities and social problems. Class divides us in terms of health care, access to quality education, job security, safe neighborhoods, and political influence. In many settings, including the classroom, disparities correlate with social class but are interconnected with race, ethnicity, physical or mental disability, sexual orientation, and gender. The disparities are great and are only likely to grow worse as our economy struggles. Quality education is an expeditious and demonstrated solution to poverty. The authors believe that most educators truly want to understand how they can help children of poverty and low income succeed but they may not have adequate knowledge or the appropriate tools. Worse yet, because of their exposure to a particular framework, they may be profoundly misinformed about the causes and effects of poverty.

Need

No Child Left Behind seeks to hold schools accountable for improving the performance of all students. It requires that schools show progress to the public, and the data must be disaggregated by race, gender, English language proficiency, disability, and socio-economic status. No Child Left Behind gives new impetus for students in poverty to be viewed as a unique population. In this charged climate of educational accountability, it is not surprising that school district administrators across the nation pursue professional development that promises to educate teachers in how to work with students in poverty and help them succeed.

Aha! Process Inc., founded by Ruby Payne, offers resources and workshops for schools and communities interested in learning more about how poverty impacts learning as well as guidance in overcoming barriers and helping students in poverty succeed. In these workshops, Payne introduces her interpretation of poverty as culture. In her construct of social class culture, she defines the poor as a homogeneous group that shares similar attitudes and behaviors. According to Payne, people in poverty and with low incomes use similar language, are relationship oriented, and adopt common strategies to survive in their environments. These are defined as the "hidden rules" of poverty, but she also asserts the other two classes she addresses, middle and wealthy, have their own rules.

The appeal of these workshops rests on Payne's ability to tap a vein of rich, reticent sentiment about class differences in the United States. Using colorfully constructed case studies and personal narratives, she and her cadre of trainers affirm deeply held ideas about what sets us apart on the social class continuum. Payne has taken class differences to an elevated level, far beyond wealth, dialect, education, occupation, or other markers of social class. Using data mined from her own "anthropological research," she exhumes and validates a long contested culture of poverty model and delivers it in new form: a professional, cultural competence package relevant to what educational practitioners feel they need under the policies of No Child Left Behind.

Many participants fresh out of a Payne workshop are impressed, leaving motivated with the belief that they can help students learn skills they need in order to assimilate to a middle class culture and, therefore, move out of poverty. Some feel they had more cross-class compassion, an enlightened understanding of people different from themselves, and an increased desire to help.

Understanding poverty by culture is not a new concept (Banfield, 1970; Lewis, 1959, 1961, 1966; Moynihan, 1965), and every time this theory resurfaces its empirical validity is discredited by scholars (Gmelch & Zenner, 1996; Leacock, 1971; Zinn, 1980). What is new is the unparalleled degree to which Payne's particular interpretation of the culture of poverty has infused the K-12 educational world and produced a burgeoning multimillion-dollar professional development industry, Aha! Process Inc. Payne's framework is, for all practical purposes, hegemonic. Payne said that she speaks to about 40,000 educators a year and that she has sold more than 1 million copies of her self-published book. She estimates that she and others with her company have worked with staff from 70 to 80 percent of the nation's school districts over the past decade (Shapira, 2007).

Across the nation, it is likely that a majority of K-12 educators have been exposed to a flawed belief that children coming from poverty share a set of behaviors and values and that they constitute a unique learning group. Payne's workshops objectify poor children as people in need of fixing (Osei-Kofi, 2005). Payne's research claims are questionable (Bomer, Dworin, May, & Semingson, 2008), the prominence of the cultural deficit model and conservative underpinnings of her work are problematic (Gorski, 2006b), and the impact of her work has been called "downright dangerous" because of the misinformation that teachers walk away with (Bohn, 2006). Viewing students and their families from a deficit perspective limits teacher's understanding of the whole student. Consider how the expectations of a teacher may change if she believes Payne and her colleagues' (Payne, De Vol, & Smith, 2001) assertions that students in poverty cannot plan (153), have little room for the abstract (69), or believe the future does not exist except as a word (70). Because of the magnitude of Payne's influence, the self-fulfilling prophecy (Rosenthal & Jacobson, 1968) propagated by a single teacher or principal may take on a collective nature and afflict an entire generation of students. If teachers believe that an entire group of students is prone to deviant behaviors, lacks cognitive strategies, and is hypersexual, can we expect the prophecy of those traits and abilities to cause its own fulfillment?

As educators, the authors are concerned that curriculum may be weakened because learners' needs are not sufficiently understood but are instead simply assumed. Exaggerating the uniformity within any one group makes seeing distinctions between groups easier, but it also prevents teachers from having to differentiate between individuals in their classrooms and examine their own identity. This is not quality education.

One example of misinformation and overgeneralizing is found in Payne's claims about gender. Teachers across the nation who learned about the culture of poverty at a Payne workshop may now believe that people in poverty ascribe to rigid and exaggerated gender roles (they are hypersexual, prone to violence, etc.). Payne uses an unorthodox reference style in her book called "research notes," which makes authenticating her research claims frustrating and challenging. After going to original sources, the authors found her claims unreliable and misconstrued as have other critics (Bomer et al., 2008). One of Payne's main sources for poverty and gender roles is a 1962 book by Harrington. She paraphrases a description of men in poverty: "In generational poverty, the primary role of a real man is to physically work hard, to be a fighter, and to be a lover" (Payne, DeVol, & Smith, 2001, p. 79). Upon looking at Harrington's original work, readers can see he was quoting an earlier report written by Swados, but Harrington does not fully reference his sources so this observation is ambiguous at best. Swados, as cited in Harrington (1962), appears to have been documenting the turbulence of changing gender roles in one Pennsylvanian coal mining community: "It is truly ironic that a substantial portion of these men, who pride themselves on their ability to live with danger, work hard, to fight hard, drink hard, love hard, are now learning housework and taking over the women's role in the family" (Harrington, 1962, p. 29). Aside from the inaccuracy of using a 47-year-old description of gender roles in one working class community to typecast millions of men across the United States, the authors also take issue with Payne cherry picking phrases from a study or document to draw sweeping conclusions about gender and social class.

The fallacy of anecdotal evidence makes Payne's research highly questionable, but Payne's gender stereotypes are also classist and sexist: "The mating dance is about using the body in a sexual way and verbally and subverbally complimenting body parts. She also states that if you have few financial resources, the way you sexually attract someone is with your body (Payne, De Vol, & Smith, 2001, p. 70)." "And one of the rules in generational poverty for women is this: you may need to use your body for survival. After all, that is all that is truly yours. Sex will bring in money and favors. Values are important, but they don't put food on the table—or bring relief from intense "pressure" (Payne, Devol & Smith, 2001, p. 38)."

Many of these flawed and stereotypical assertions are negative in nature, while middle and upper classes are depicted as more desirable. The authors contend that viewing any child from this distorted lens, whether as a troublemaker in need of remediation, a victim who just doesn't know any better, or a trust fund baby in designer clothes, is unethical and ineffective. Stereotypes and constructed case studies perpetuate preconceived and oversimplified ideas of a person's most basic identity—his or her values and behavior. Given these scholarly and ethical shortcomings, how did Payne become mainstream?

Timing is part of the answer. By the time academics' peer-reviewed critiques of Payne's deficit model were disseminated through on-line and traditional education journals, Payne was ubiquitous. The academic critique lagged behind the educational staff development industry. Now that many professionals in education are aware that Payne has critics, why do they continue to spend their professional development funds on a consultant who has misconstrued research, failed to provide data, advanced stereotypical caricatures, advanced unsubstantiated "hidden rules" of class as fact, was inattentive to race and gender oppression, and ignored structural explanations of poverty (Bohn, 2006; Bomer et al., 2008; Gorski, 2006b; Ng & Rury, 2006; Osei-Kofi, 2005; Sato & Lensmire, 2009)?

Based on the authors' experience working with curriculum specialists and educational practitioners, the following explanations are offered:

- First, few if any professional development workshops or curricula exist for teachers that focus on the interface of poverty, social class and education. Payne gains authority because she is perceived as a leader in her field. The lesson for academics: when a gap exists, respond promptly with quality resources.

- Second, people want to talk about social class. For many participants, a Payne workshop is their first opportunity to talk about an important, but shadowy topic of American life with others in their profession. Little public space exists to have meaningful conversations about social class and Payne opened this door. Most teachers are genuinely concerned about children in poverty, and they want to learn effective techniques which may help them reach all children in the classroom. Because the workshops were refreshing and engaging and basically in a category unto themselves, many participants did not critically analyze what was presented. This is not to fault the participants but is helpful in understanding why more questioning does not take place.

- Third, Payne's approach is accessible to adult learners from multiple educational backgrounds. Gorski (2006a) faults administrators and teachers for choosing Payne's workshops for their entertainment value rather than their message, but the authors contend that her workshops meet the pedagogical needs of many adult learners and there are few, if any, competing messages in the professional development trade. Human stories, reflective exercises, and statistics are interwoven in the aha! curricula and participants feel engaged. For many, their experiences relating to social class, however biased, are voiced. As educators, the authors seek to find pedagogical tools that can construct knowledge from experience and, at the same time, critically challenge teachers to see how their own assumptions and biases affect their daily practice and limit their capacity to help all students in their classrooms.

- Passive learning, or the "banking" concept of education (Freire, 1970), is still the norm. Learners are accustomed to receiving, filing and storing the deposits poured into them by those in power. School districts endorse the workshops and many teachers are mandated to go. Payne was legitimated as the authority on poverty and education. Hence, most teachers in Payne workshops, because of their relations within systems of power, uncritically accept her work.

- Lastly, most people don't read the critiques from academic journals. To reach practitioners, materials need to be accessible. K-12 teachers typically do not have easy access to scholarly journals nor do they feel that these articles are intended for them. A disconnect exists between academia and the K-12 world, and it is here that Payne has found her niche.

Those critical of Payne must realize she was responding to a gap between research about poverty and what people can do to bring about change. Academics have responded with torrid critiques of Payne but have been slow to provide professional development alternatives that practitioners desire and students desperately need. If academics want practitioners to be informed about poverty, its causes and solutions, they need to develop research-based, accessible professional development opportunities and resources that educators can apply in their school systems and communities. The authors have searched widely for such products with little success.

Payne delivered what many adult learners want: a manageable framework, tools to take home and use the next day, hope, and human narratives that stick with people long after the workshop is over. However, she provided the application without substantive or accurate research. Her success underscores the noticeable disconnect between academia and K-12 professional development. As a direct result of the divide between the academic world and the K-12 world, thousands of teachers across the country are misinformed about social class and education. Pattee and Keown-Bomar seek to bridge this gap and correct some of the prevalent misconceptions already established in their communities.

Our Response

The authors' intention is to counter Payne's deficit framework of poverty and to provide tools to educators that will increase their awareness of class issues and influence their practice so that it benefits all students. They want to offer a research-based alternative for adult learners that focuses on self-analysis and intersectionality and encourages institutional reform.

The audiences are K-16 preservice and inservice teachers as well as community-based educators. Knowing adult learners value active engagement, knowledge as experience, and relevant materials (Knowles & Swanson, 2005), Keown-Bomar and Pattee developed several activities that allow participants to explore the essential question (Wiggens & McTighe, 2005) of "who am I?" This question comes before, "who are my students?" (Murphy, Rieck, Kolis, Pattee & McIntyre, 2008). Teachers must understand themselves before they can understand their students. Through interaction and reflection, the activities, *What's Class Got to Do with It?* and *The Invisibility of Class Privilege*, encourage learners to explore their life experiences through the lens of class and other categories of difference. They are able to reflect on their class roots, dialogue with other peers about their experiences, begin to understand the larger framework of class in the United States and identify institutional oppression and privilege, including the structural barriers that may or may not exist depending on one's social class.

The authors seek to provide participants with the opportunity to define and reflect on their class experience rather than defining their class culture for them. The questions in *What's Class Got To Do with It?* do not focus on culture as values or behavior, instead they focus on class experiences, hardships and opportunities. Participants dialogue about class experiences and through this process gain respect for the experiences of others. In contrast to Payne, social class is not reified. An anthropological "Other" is not constructed, but experiential similarities and differences do emerge in dialogue. By listening to others, participants can develop a deeper and more complex understanding of social class, connect with others across class lines, share what they are experiencing in their classrooms and gain ideas about how they can positively impact their school environment. In a Payne workshop, participants learn about assimilating students to a middle-class world, whereas this approach is to change one's lens from deficit-fixing to self-awareness, resiliency-building and institutional reform. Participants dialogue about life experiences, obstacles and opportunities, rather than learning a worn-out doctrine disguised as cultural knowledge that does little to break down class divisions.

Drawing from these life experiences, educators begin to see themselves as agents of change in reducing barriers and building opportunities for their students and families. By listening to the barriers faced by their own peers, such as time restraints that exist for many working families, educators are asked to implement alternative means to connect with families and their students, such as phone conferences, staggered meeting times, or off-site meetings.

In addition to experiential learning Keown-Bomar and Pattee provide research-based information in the form of a brief entitled *Social Class in the United States*. Borrowing from many scholars who study social class and poverty, they present a basic guide to social class in the United States that includes its intersection with disenfranchisement, slavery, treatment of the poor, and segregation.

Much like the issues of race and ethnicity, the issue of class encompasses both oppression and privilege. Many of the questions in the activities are designed to help individuals address these constructs and interconnect multiple categories of difference, including race, ethnicity, physical or mental ability, immigration status, religion, sexual orientation, gender, and age. For example, the authors ask teachers how race and ethnicity may intersect with their class experiences, followed by the question, "do we all start out on a level playing field?"

When discussing personal experiences of privilege and oppression, the potential for emotional reaction and tension can be high. Critical reflection can bring to light other dimensions of diversity including race, age and gender. In each facilitator's guide, the authors offer suggestions for helping learners to appreciate and hear more than one perspective, avoid generalizing and to deal with differences constructively.

Payne's curriculum does not address intersectionality except in her manufactured case studies and descriptions of gender roles. In her case studies, six of the nine caricatures are people of color, often in stereotypical situations (single moms, substance abusers, immigrants facing deportation, women offering sex for support). Her representation of poverty is racialized and genderized even though she insists class should be isolated from race and gender.

People may harbor unconscious class antagonisms that come to light in these activities. Some people from both ends of the class continuum feel stigmatized by their class roots. Addressing social class may open the door for participants to experience many emotions, but people (educators and students alike) are resilient. Being challenged in a structured, safe learning space offers enormous potential for moving participants toward a place of hope and change.

Process

Drawing heavily from their respective backgrounds in multicultural education, applied anthropology and critical pedagogy, authors Keown-Bomar and Pattee were compelled to move beyond critique to resource development. As a new faculty member, Keown-Bomar found herself in the awkward position of confronting colleagues who were strong advocates of Payne's framework and many of whom had been certified as *Bridges out of Poverty* trainers. Based on Keown-Bomar's and other colleagues's strong objections as well as the publication of peer-reviewed critiques questioning Payne's research-base, her institution severed their relationship with aha! Process, Inc. and developed a new curriculum, *Poverty Awareness for Community Engagement (P.A.C.E.)*. Keown-Bomar and Pattee contributed several of the activities described here to the *P.A.C.E.* curriculum.

After being trained by Payne in 2002, Pattee implemented the aha! framework into her teacher education diversity courses but was always troubled by the simplicity of the three-class model. Eventually Payne's framework became central in her pedagogy as an exercise in critical analysis. Pattee and Keown-Bomar's mutual interest in providing practical, interactive resources to adult practitioners led them to develop a research-based alternative to Payne.

Over a period of three years, the authors developed numerous activities and resources and piloted them through various workshops, in-services and conferences. A social class brief was developed as a basic introduction to social stratification as well as two interactive exercises, *What's Class Got to Do with It?* and *The Invisibility of Class Privilege*, that utilize the bodily/kinesthetic intelligence (Gardner,1983/2003). The brief and activities were piloted to a variety of audiences, including teachers, social service professionals, volunteer groups, and college students from various socio-economic backgrounds. Several activity questions were revised and new ones created based on feedback from the participants, who suggested addressing generational differences, technological advances, immigrants' experiences, and class mobility. The authors sought peer review from University of Wisconsin faculty and specialists who provided critique and feedback.

What's Class Got to Do with It?—Activity One

What's Class Got to Do with It? is an activity that focuses on viewing self in relation to others. It incorporates memory, reflection and dialogue to explore the intricacies of class opportunity, inequities, assets and mobility. The following goals guided the creation of this activity:

- Participants will be able to explain how socio-economic status and social class standing can impact life opportunities.
- Participants will gain awareness of class differences and experiences.
- Participants will engage in building positive relationships with people across class lines.
- Participants will develop plans to implement change in their interpersonal lives or community.

People are personally affiliated with one or more social classes during their lifetime and they have much to share from those experiences. Even though Americans tend not to discuss class affiliation, belonging to a social class presents real challenges and opportunities. Class differences and inequities also generate divisions between people that create barriers to connecting and forming relationships across class lines. As income gaps widen, now more than ever before, it is important to talk about how class matters and to understand how this plays out for children.

What's Class Got to Do with It? is not about individual effort or culture; it is about opportunities, setbacks, and the concept of a level playing field. Using questions by Holtzman (2000), as a starting point, the authors designed an interactive group exercise that allows participants to reflect and analyze their socio-economic background and some of the variables that correlate with class including education, occupation, and access to health care. Below are several sample questions from the activity:

- If you experienced a family crisis (divorce, medical issue, incarceration, death in the family) that set your family back financially, move two spaces toward the red zone.
- If you had a separate telephone line or a cell phone as a teenager, move one space toward the green zone.
- If you had to work to help your family pay the bills, move two spaces toward the red zone.
- If your parents helped pay the majority of your college or technical college costs, move two spaces toward the green zone.
- If your family had many children's books, move one space toward the green zone.

- If you ever regularly depended on public transportation or had to walk to get around, move one space toward the red zone.
- If your family had health insurance and access to quality health care for most of your childhood, move two spaces toward the green zone.
- If you lived in a high crime neighborhood, move two spaces toward the red zone.

After each break-out group completes the questionnaire, the larger group constructs a social class portrait of their learning community. The facilitator then helps the participants analyze critical experiences and events that propel families in different directions along a social class continuum. For example, several participants have underscored the importance of extended family during times of economic hardship. Others have noted how important education or hard work was to their family's well-being. Across all classes, participants note variations, assets, traits of resiliency, and commonalities. Some important facilitation questions include:

- Do we all start out on a level playing field?
- Where should we draw the lines delineating the different social classes?
- What are the strengths that accompany the working class and/or those families that experienced economic hardship?
- What were some of the critical events or issues that divided people in terms of socio-economic class?
- Did poor choices affect some people more than others?
- Do you see intersections between class/race/ethnicity, class/gender, class/sexual orientation, class/national origin, or other categories of difference?

The next step is to lead the participants into action planning based on what they determine are opportunities to eliminate barriers for students and families and build relationships across class lines. For example, one participant planned on returning to her school and working with the parent-teacher organization to eliminate the $50 "joining fee" required by the group. Others planned to get to know the parents of their children better, find out more about community resources that were available to families of low income, or help families in their community find avenues to get job training or go back to school.

Social Class in the United States

One of the ways the authors chose to disassociate class from Payne's definition of the culture of poverty was to write a brief called *Social Class in the United States*. It helps explain the history of social stratification in the United States, intersectionality, how social classes are defined, and introduces structural oppression and privilege. The brief is research-based, objective and reader friendly.

The authors wanted participants to understand that whether in a school, workplace, governing board, or community, social class inequities have and continue to exist. "Classes are historical and their effects are intertwined with their historicity (Aronowitz, 2003, p. 38)." Studying the underlying political, social and economic realities and histories of social class helps participants better understand how class operates in our everyday lives. For example, the brief on social class explains how segregation and Jim Crow laws helped to maintain wealth in the hands of a few while keeping African Americans in a lower class with narrow opportunities for advancement. The historical treatment of those in poverty is described in sections on indentured servitude, debtors' prisons, and poorhouses. Wisconsin citizens identify with this history because these same institutions, converted into health care centers, training centers, or nursing homes, still exist in their home communities.

People studying class issues need to realize that there are numerous definitions and categories of class, an important fact that Payne minimizes. A person's class is dependant on nine variables: "occupation, income, wealth, personal prestige, association, socialization, power, class consciousness and mobility" (Gilbert and Kahl, 1982). Payne chooses to focus only on three classes: upper, middle class and poor. She lumps working class, working poor and the underclass in one broad class of poverty. She draws her own distinctions between subclasses of people in poverty, those in generational poverty and those in situational poverty. Considerably more class complexity exists in the United States than can be represented by the Payne model. Class isn't a matter of fitting people into neat categories, and no definition of class is fully independent of other social categories such as race and gender. A critical analysis of class can illuminate differences, commonalities and affiliations between groups of people, but the Payne model reifies class. A complex, relative, and arguably abstract concept is presented as reality. Poor people clearly emerge as the anthropological "Other," an exotic culture that teachers can't relate to because of their own ethnocentrism. It is possible to work with others and come to an understanding of social class that does not dehumanize or objectify. Many multicultural educators do this quite well.

A template is helpful to move from understanding social class history and theory to application in a short workshop. A continuum is far more representative and reflective of actual social class stratification than a list of cultural rules.

- The *Poor/Underclass* group represents about 3 percent to 5 percent of the U.S. population, experiences chronic problems maintaining an income to cover their basic needs, such as health care, housing, and food (Seccombe, 2007). Some, but not all, receive assistance from government welfare programs because of their extremely low income, mental illness, disability or age. Many face difficult employment prospects and their circumstances are bleak. Payne offers inconsistent definitions of poverty (Bomer et al., 2008), and lumps this group, as well as one or more of the following groups, in a category she names generational poverty.
- The *Working Poor* comprise about 10 percent of the population and are employed in the lowest paid, dead-end jobs (laborers, retail or service workers, and migrant seasonal work) with little opportunity for advancement or benefits. Their income is around or only slightly above the poverty line, up to about $20,000 per year for a family of four, and some may turn to assistance programs for help as a safety net when they lose or quit jobs or illness, divorce or other hard luck strikes (Gilbert & Kahl, 1982; Seccombe, 2007). They cannot depend on steady incomes and also have a difficult time meeting basic needs and getting ahead. The working poor live month-to-month and unemployment is common (Seccombe, 2007). It is a group that has been identified more recently in the literature as invisible, vulnerable and growing (Ehrenreich, 2001; Shipler, 2004).
- The *Working Class* includes people who have little or no higher education and are employed in lower-paying positions. They earn between $20,000–$40,000 per year, and account for approximately 25% of the U.S. population (Seccombe, 2007). Their assets minus their debts create a negative or low net worth. Usually they rent rather than own their housing. Their jobs often involve physical work and/or little control within their occupation, such as sales clerks, factory jobs, cus-

todial positions, and semi-skilled labor (Seccombe, 2007).

- The *Middle Class* is the class with which most Americans identify and seems to be the hardest to define. People in the middle class may work as low-level managers, semi-professionals, small business owners, skilled blue-collar workers, and clerical workers (Gilbert and Kahl, 1982). With incomes roughly between $40,000 and $100,000 a year, 35 percent of the U.S. population can be thought of as middle class (Seccombe, 2007).

- The *Upper Middle Class/White Collar Professionals* refer to mostly college-educated, salaried professionals and upper managers, and medium-sized business owners. These people tend to be homeowners, have relative control over their own working hours, and have more economic security than those in the lower rungs of the class structure. Approximately 20 percent of the U.S. population is upper middle class, and their household income is typically in the $100,000 to $200,000 range (Seccombe, 2007) although it can be even higher in two-earner households.

- The *Upper Class/Owning Class/Corporate Elite* are defined as people with considerable financial fortunes. Investors, heirs, and corporate executives are in this tier. High incomes and wealth generation from investments and capital gains characterize this group, which is only about 5 percent of the total population. Although relatively few in number, members of this group have great influence on the economy and the rest of society (Seccombe, 2007).

In this brief, the authors describe the history of social class in the United States and how it intersects with other categories of difference including race and gender. It can be used in conjunction with *What's Class Got to Do with It*, or it can stand alone as a research-based guide to understanding social class in the United States.

The Invisibility of Class Privilege— Activity Two

Class correlates with power and privilege. The authors wanted an interactive, reflective activity that engaged adult learners in the analysis of hierarchy. The following goals were formulated for this activity:

- Participants will be able to explain how socio-economic status can lead to unexamined assumptions, unexplored feelings, and stereotypes.
- Participants will be able to describe class hierarchies and privileges that can create obstacles to connecting across class differences.
- Participants will examine the various levels of oppression: personal, interpersonal and institutional.

In the United States, people are socialized to think of themselves as individuals even though they all have membership in social groups that are relevant and consequential. Because these social groups have been and continue to be stratified, people can experience both oppression and privilege depending on their membership in different social groups in various contexts. For example, a person may experience little discrimination based on their racial status (white) but may experience poor treatment and discrimination because of their class status (poor).

The authors developed a social class checklist, modeled after the influential white privilege list created by McIntosh (1988), to explore how society privileges individuals in the middle and upper classes and how these benefits are often completely invisible to those that reap the advantages. Members may gain unearned privileges or experience undeserved treatment from institutions, policies and laws because of their social standing in larger structural systems of hierarchy.

Many checklists have been developed based on the McIntosh model that focus on other kinds of privilege, including membership groups such as heterosexual, male, and Christian. The checklist developed by the authors is based on input from middle and upper class professionals who took it upon themselves to examine their privilege. It focuses on class, but the authors stress that class status does not mean that other forms of oppression and privilege are any less important or relevant or that it is not possible to experience multiple forms of oppression and privilege at any given time by any person.

Participants are given a list of everyday privileges that were adapted from *The Invisibility of Upper Class Privilege* by Class Actions, a program of the Women's Theological Center (2007) in Boston, MA. The following is a sampling from the checklist:

- My career and financial success will most likely be attributed to my hard work.
- I feel welcomed and "normal" in common public places (schools, hospitals, libraries, stores, etc.).

- If I spend money on toys for my children, movie tickets, junk food or alcohol, I can be quite sure that no one will think of me as financially irresponsible or tell me that I should spend my money on the necessities.
- I can hide family secrets and family problems behind the doors of my home.

Reflective work is demanding, and participants may react with guilt, anger, denial, sadness, defensiveness, deep appreciation, enlightenment, shock, or silence. Facilitators can respond effectively to these emotions. They can ask participants to be willing to be uncomfortable. Class is an uncomfortable topic for most Americans to talk about because they are taught that it is a deeply personal topic. Exploring class inequities can cause people to question historical narratives, their sense of self and their place in society. Connecting with others across lines of difference involves risk. Participants may blame, withdraw, or have trouble finding their voice. Participants are encouraged to be risk takers and to be patient as people sort through their feelings, reactions, and experiences. Lastly, facilitators can remind participants that connecting across lines of difference is a worthy goal. If obstacles such as guilt, fixation, attachment to being right, or shaming occur, these obstacles can prevent us from connecting across lines of difference.

The authors have found that entitlement or individual effort may be a common theme that emerges in discussions of class difference. "I worked hard to get to where I am," comments do surface. An effective response from the facilitator is that several different things can be true at the same time. One can be a very hard worker and benefit from structural class privilege at the same time. Participants can also be asked to consider what thinking underlies a statement. Does the statement about hard work (above) contain assumptions about the poor?

Results

Over a period of two years, the authors used the activities and brief to improve awareness and build skills for participants attending in-service events and conference workshops. Using a retrospective post- then pre-evaluation design, awareness, skill development and planning were measured. Results from social class and poverty education workshops are listed separately.

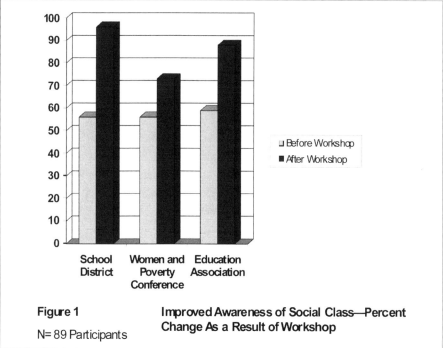

Figure 1

N= 89 Participants

Improved Awareness of Social Class—Percent Change As a Result of Workshop

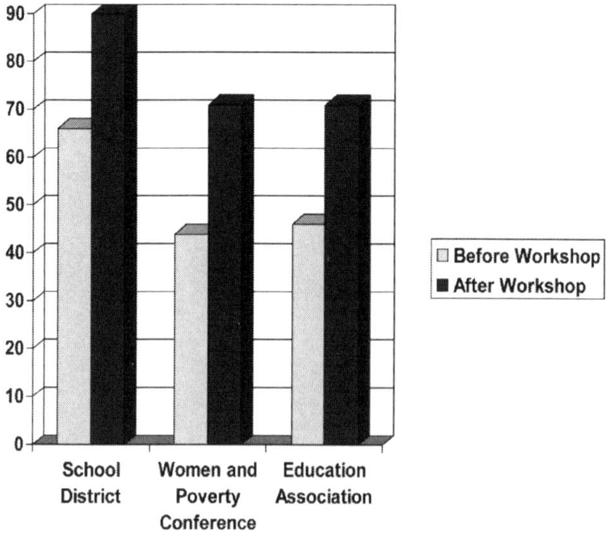

Figure 2

N= 89 Participants

Percentage of Participants That Indicate They Have Tools to Build Relationships Across Class Lines as a Result of Workshop

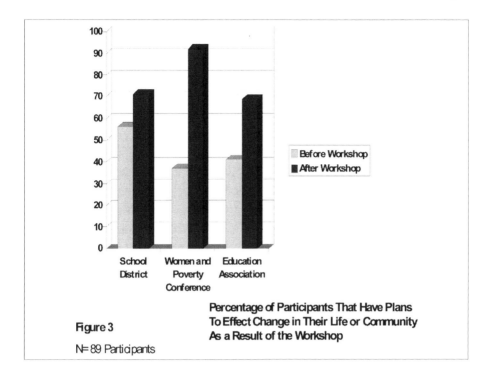

Figure 3

N= 89 Participants

Percentage of Participants That Have Plans To Effect Change in Their Life or Community As a Result of the Workshop

Social Class Awareness

The data in Figures 1 through 3 indicate that participants gained awareness, new skills and had plans to effect change as a result of attending the workshop. Teachers also noted changes in the way they viewed economically marginalized students. "The internalization of self-limitation is a dangerous habit," wrote one teacher and, "it is important for me to identify the assets of a student in poverty."

Poverty Education

Survey results from the poverty awareness workshops also indicated improved awareness, resource awareness, and planning to effect change. Other results were noted in the open-ended questions in the survey. For example, workshop discussions prompted reflection about the challenges of curricula reform for low income students in the age of No Child Left Behind. One teacher commented, "There is unfortunately an internalized stereotype that disadvantaged students can only achieve low levels of Bloom's Taxonomy, which results in curriculum that's boring, plodding, and uninspiring that winds up further disenfranchising those students from education."

Many teachers indicated that they had new motivation to effect change both in their schools and in their community. One teacher commented, "We are the key to open the door for our families. If we as educators are aware of the resources that are available [and can] 'think outside the box,' to help these families or students, it is a huge step in helping break the cycle."

At the workshop, teachers developed plans for reducing barriers in their schools. From increased social supports for teenage parents in high school, to a focused effort to increase parental involvement, participants leave each workshop with a plan for making a difference in their personal life, school or community around the issues of poverty and inequity.

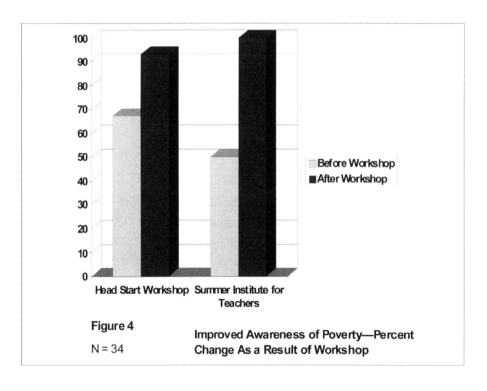

Figure 4

N = 34

Improved Awareness of Poverty—Percent Change As a Result of Workshop

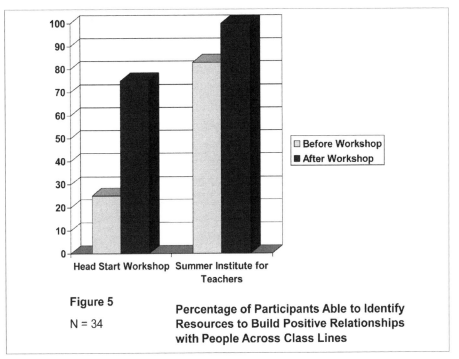

Figure 5

N = 34

Percentage of Participants Able to Identify Resources to Build Positive Relationships with People Across Class Lines

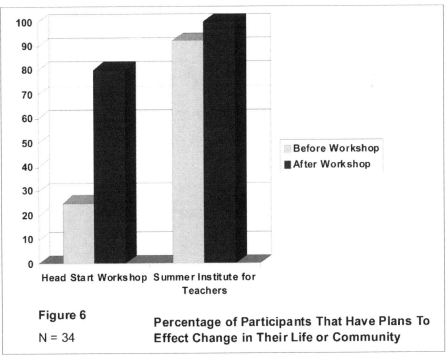

Figure 6

N = 34

Percentage of Participants That Have Plans To Effect Change in Their Life or Community

Follow-up surveys sent approximately six months after the workshop indicated those participants surveyed implemented changes in their schools. One cohort shared information about ways to reduce or mitigate the effects of rural poverty with administrators, colleagues, and students. In order to reduce barriers for low income families, one teacher now sends home positive notes to parents, writes a community newsletter, and has added contributions to the staff bulletin about poverty. Two teachers in a rural district developed a community resource directory and provided this directory to a student whose family was living in a trailer without a roof. The student was able to help his family find the community resources that allowed them to get a new roof before the winter season. Other teachers indicated that they are taking a more active approach to empowering and educating students about the importance of getting postgraduate education or training.

Conclusions

An understanding of how class operates is not sufficient to address the growing disparities in American schools, but it is a small step in a very complex system of change. Teachers do want and need an educated and critically reflective understanding of how class impacts their relationships with their students, families and communities. Towards this end, Payne's curriculum is insufficient, damaging and pervasive. The authors have demonstrated an alternative approach that is research-based and moves teachers to become agents of change, but their impact in terms of numbers of teachers reached has been nominal in comparison with the industry of professional development in our region and nationally. Unless more university educators are willing to step up and share their knowledge and skills with the K-12 world, Payne's deficit model and misinformation will continue to dominate as it does today.

References

Aronowitz, S. (2003). *How class works: Power and social movement.* New Haven, CT: Yale University Press.

Banfield, E. (1970). *The unheavenly city.* Boston, MA: Little, Brown.

Bohn, A. (2006). A framework for understanding Ruby Payne. *Rethinking Schools, 21*(2). Retrieved from http://rethinkingschools.org/archive/21_02/fram212.shtml

Bomer, R., Dworin, J. E., May, L., & Semingson, P. (2008). Miseducating teachers about the poor: A critical analysis of Ruby Payne's claims about poverty. *Teachers College Record.* Retrieved from https://www.tcrecord.org/Content.asp?ContentID=14591

Danzer, G. A., Klor de Alva, J. J., Krieger, L. S., Wilson, L. E., & Woloch, N. (2000). *The Americans*. Evanston, IL: McDougal Littell.

Ehrenreich, B. (2001). *Nickel and dimed: On (not) getting by in America*. New York: Metropolitan.

Freire, P. (1970). *Pedagogy of the oppressed*. New York: Continuum.

Gardner, H. (1983/2003). *Frames of mind. The theory of multiple intelligences*. New York: Basic.

Gilbert, D., & Kahl, J. A. (1982). *The American class structure: A new synthesis* (3rd ed.). Chicago, IL: Dorsey.

Gmelch, G., & Zenner, W. P. (1996). *Urban life: Readings in urban anthropology*. Prospect Heights, IL: Waveland.

Gorski, P. C. (2006a). Complicity with conservatism: The de-politicizing of multicultural and intercultural education. *Intercultural Education, 17*(2), 163–177.

Gorski, P. (2006b). The classist underpinnings of Ruby Payne's framework. *Teachers College Record*. Retrieved from https://www.tcrecord.org/Content.asp?ContentID=12322

Grusky, D. B. (Ed.). (2008). *Social stratification class, race, and gender in sociological perspective* (3rd ed.). Boulder, CO: Westview.

Harrington, M. (1962). *The other America*. Baltimore, MD: Penguin.

Holtzman, L. (2000). *Media messages: What film, television, and popular music teach us about race, class, gender, and sexual orientation*. Armonk, NY: M.E. Sharpe.

Katz, M. B. (1986). *In the shadow of the poorhouse: A social history of welfare in America*. New York: Basic.

Knowles, M. S., & Swanson, R. A. (2005). *The adult learner: The definitive classic in adult education and human resource development* (6th ed.). Boston, MA: Elsevier Butterworth Heinemann.

Leacock, E. B. (Ed.). (1971). *The culture of poverty: A critique*. New York: Simon & Schuster.

Lewis, O. (1959). *Five families: Mexican case studies in the culture of poverty*. New York: Basic.

Lewis, O. (1961). *Children of Sanchez*. New York: Random House.

Lewis, O. (1966). *La Vida: A Puerto Rican family in the culture of poverty*. New York: Random House.

McIntosh, P. (1988). *White privilege: Unpacking the invisible knapsack*. Retrieved from Case Western University Website: http://www.case.edu/president/action/UnpackingThe Knapsack.pdf

Moynihan, D. P. (1965). *The Negro family: The case for national action*. Washington, DC: United States Department of Labor.

Murphy, V., Rieck, A., Kolis, M. Pattee, D., & McIntyre, S. (2008). Breaking tradition: Teacher education classrooms as safe learning communities built upon PIES-M! *Wisconsin School Musician, 79*(3), 22–24.

Ng, J. C., & Rury, J. L. (2006). Poverty and education: A critical analysis of the Ruby Payne phenomenon. *Teachers College Record*. Retrieved from https://www.tcrecord.org/Content.asp?ContentID=12596

Osei-Kofi, N. (2005). Pathologizing the poor: A framework for understanding Ruby Payne's work. *Equality & Excellence in Education, 38*, 367–375.

Payne, R. K. (2003). *A framework for understanding poverty* (3rd rev. ed.). Highlands, TX: aha! Process.

Payne, R. K, De Vol, P., & Smith, T. (2001). *Bridges out of poverty: Strategies for professionals and communities*. Highlands, TX: aha! Process.

Payne, R. K., & De Vol, P. (2005). *Toward a deeper understanding of issues surrounding poverty: A response to critiques of a framework for understanding poverty*. Retrieved from Emporia Unified School District 253 Website: http://www.usd253.0rg/respect/documents/Deeper_Understanding_of_Framework_2005.pdf

Rosenthal, R., & Jacobson, L. (1968). *Pygmalion in the classroom*. New York: Holt, Rinehart & Winston.

Sato, M., & Lensmire, T. J. (2009). Poverty and Payne: Supporting teachers to work with children of poverty. *Phi Delta Kappan, 90*(5), 365–370.

Seccombe, K. (2007). *Families in poverty*. New York: Pearson Education.

Shapira, I. (2007, April). Author's poverty views disputed yet utilized. *The Washington Pos,*. p. A01.

Shipler, D. (2004). *The working poor: Invisible in America*. New York: Knopf.

Wiggins, G., & McTighe. J. (2005). *Understanding by design* (2nd ed.). Alexandria, VA: Association for Supervision and Curriculum Development.

Women's Theological Center. (2007). *The invisibility of upper class privilege* (pamphlet). Retrieved from Women's Center Publications: http://www.thewtc.org/publications.html#BP

Zinn, H. (1980). *A people's history of the United States*. New York: Harper Colophon.

Contributors

Roberta Ahlquist is professor of education in Department of Secondary Teacher Education at San Jose State University in California. She has taught critical multicultural education, educational sociology, critical issues in education, comparative education, and she supervises prospective high school teachers. She has been a visiting scholar at QUT in Brisbane, Australia, and she was a Fulbright Scholar in Turku, Finland, where she taught about anti-racist, anti-hegemonic and social justice pedagogy. Her areas of research include critical multiculturalism, social justice education, indigenous studies and post-colonialism. She is active in the teachers' unions at both the k-12 and higher education levels. She is president of a non-profit, Our Developing World, a multicultural resource center for teachers. She has been a long-time peace activist and sings with the 'Raging Grannies.'

Ann Berlak has been teaching for critical thinking, social justice and empowerment for over fifty years at the primary, college, and post-BA levels and writing about her teaching experience for almost as long. Her first published paper in 1987 was entitled "Teaching for Outrage and Empathy in the Liberal Arts." In 2001 she co-authored, "Taking It Personally: Racism in Classrooms from Kindergarten to College" with Sekani Moyenda.

Recently she has been documenting her experience with and observations of the effects of high stakes testing of credential candidates in an attempt to preserve the memory of a time when teachers and teacher educators were a great deal more respected than they are today, and preparation for critical citizenship was more highly valued.

Sue Books is a professor in the Department of Secondary Education at SUNY New Paltz, NY, where she teaches courses in the social foundations of education, comparative education, and teacher research. Her scholarship has focused primarily on issues of equity in U.S. schooling, especially school funding and poverty as an educational issue. She is the editor of *Invisible Children in the Society and Its Schools*, 3rd edition (Erlbaum, 2007) and the author of *Poverty and Schooling in the U.S.: Contexts and Consequences* (Erlbaum, 2004). In recent years she has enjoyed conducting research and teaching in South Africa as a visiting scholar and in Iceland as a Fulbright scholar.

Paul C. Gorski is founder of EdChange and assistant professor in Integrative Studies at George Mason University, where he teaches classes on social justice education, animal rights, and environmental justice. He's published three books and more than 35 essays on these topics in *Educational Leadership, Teachers College Record, Teaching and Teacher Education, Rethinking Schools, Teaching Tolerance, Equity & Excellence in Education, Intercultural Education*, and *Multicultural Education*. Gorski currently is serving his second term on the board of directors of the International Association for Intercultural Education. Gorski also developed several Web sites housing free resources for teachers, trainers, and activists. His first site, the Multicultural Pavilion, has received more than fifteen national awards, including NAME's annual Multicultural Media Award.

Annette Henry is Professor and Head of the Department of Language and Literacy Education, University of British Columbia, Vancouver, Canada. Her scholarship examines Black women teachers' practice in the U.S. and Canada as well as race, language, gender and culture in socio-cultural contexts of teaching and learning.

Julie Keown-Bomar earned her Ph.D. in Anthropology in 2003 with concentrations in gender studies, family diversity and applied research. She is the author of *Kinship Networks Among Hmong-American Refugees* (2004). Her current work focuses on poverty reduction and building community capacity to support and work with underserved families. She has taught a variety of classes and workshops including: Families in Poverty, Rural Poverty and Its Barriers in Education, Social Problems, and Race/Class/Gender.

Brian Lack, Ph.D., is a recent doctoral graduate from the Department of Early Childhood Education at Georgia State University. His current research interests are mathematics discourse communities, teaching for social justice, consumerism and commercialism in schools, and the politics of educational reform.

Richard D. Lakes is an associate professor in the Department of Educational Policy Studies at Georgia State University, Atlanta. He teaches in the Social Foundations of Education program and publishes on critical education policy in the areas of work and schooling.

Virginia Lea is an Associate Professor of Multicultural Education at the University of Wisconsin-Stout. She earned her doctorate in Social and Cultural Education from the University of California at Berkeley. Virginia sees her research, teaching, and social justice activism as a means of empowering students, peers and community educators to gain a deeper understanding of the complex ways in which national and global hegemonic power perpetuates inequality through socioeconomic, political, legal, educational, cultural, racial, ethnic, gender, linguistic, and ability narratives. She is committed to working in collaborations that lead to the development of sustainable, equitable, counter-hegemonic systems. Virginia is the Executive Director of the Educultural Foundation, a 501(c)3 educational organization that facilitates critical consciousness about social and cultural issues through the arts.

Lisa Martin began her teaching career in Hayward, CA where she was Activities Director of a large public high school. She taught in Abu Dhabi, United Arab Emirates and Kuala Lumpur, Malaysia, teaching across the social studies curriculum and developing community service opportunities for the expatriate student population. Her teaching background includes work with the International Baccalaureate program and Model United Nations. After a year of teaching for an online school, she returned to the UAE, where she lives with her husband and two daughters. She hopes to continue teaching in the UAE.

Paul McLennan is a retired member of Amalgamated Transit Union Local 732 and a volunteer organizer with Atlanta Jobs with Justice.

Theresa Montaño is an associate professor of Chicana and Chicano Studies at Cal State University Northridge. She teaches courses to prospective teachers in the area of Equity and Diversity in School, Chicano/a Childhood and Adolescence, and a senior seminar in research in Chicano/a education. Before coming to CSUN, Theresa was faculty advisor and instructor with UCLA's Teacher Education Program. From 2000–2002, she served as co-director of UCLA's TeachLA program, a union-district-university collaborative in Los

Angeles. Theresa's research is in the schooling of Latino/a students, teacher education and activism. Dr. Montaño is past president of the Association of Mexican-American Educators (1992) and the National Association for Multicultural Education (2005–2007). Theresa currently serves on the Board of Directors for the California Faculty Association and the National Education Association.

Deb Pattee currently teaches courses in middle level pedagogy at the University of Wisconsin—Eau Claire. She earned her Ed.D. in Critical Pedagogy in 2004 and continues a research agenda on the impact of white privilege on educational practice. Her current research projects center upon working with the Hmong, girls in the middle school, community building, culturally responsive pedagogy and giving students of all ages a voice in their own education. She has taught courses in women's studies, diversity and teacher education at Winona State University, Saint Mary's University and at the University of Wisconsin-La Crosse. She began her teaching career in urban Milwaukee, where she taught middle school for 8 years. She runs an after-school program called Ms. Adventure Girls for middle school girls in Eau Claire which centers on wellness, self-esteem, teaming, and leadership.

Rosalinda Quintanar-Sarellana has a Ph.D. from Stanford University in the area of Literacy, Language and Culture, and a Masters in the area of International Education and Development. She is a professor at San Jose State University, where she teaches First and Second Language Acquisition and Multicultural Education. She has written numerous articles on language acquisition and language development, social justice and multicultural education. She has also taught at Stanford University, UC Davis, Universidad Metropolitana in Mexico City and INACAP in Santiago, Chile.

Monique Redeaux is a full-time middle school teacher on Chicago's Westside as well as a full time doctoral student in the University of Illinois (UIC) at Chicago's Educational Policy Studies in Urban Education. Her interest in issues of social justice stems from her own experiences as a student of color in both racially segregated and integrated schools and her current work with low income youth of color. As a middle school social studies teacher, she struggles daily with adhering to the mandates of a school system that does not advance the interests of her students and their community while at the same time working with these youth in developing a critical political consciousness so that together they can actively challenge and dismantle such systems in favor of ones that are truly democratic and liberatory.

Jennifer Sauer is a public school science teacher working on her master's degree in science education at Georgia State University. She is a founding member of Metro Atlantans for Public Schools and is active in the Atlanta Workers Project.

Mary Anne Smith is a high school Latin teacher who lives and works in the Atlanta area. She is a founding member of the Metro Atlantans for Public Schools network and an active member of the Fulton Federation of Teachers.

Index

Studies in the Postmodern Theory of Education

General Editor
Shirley R. Steinberg

Counterpoints publishes the most compelling and imaginative books being written in education today. Grounded on the theoretical advances in criticalism, feminism, and postmodernism in the last two decades of the twentieth century, Counterpoints engages the meaning of these innovations in various forms of educational expression. Committed to the proposition that theoretical literature should be accessible to a variety of audiences, the series insists that its authors avoid esoteric and jargonistic languages that transform educational scholarship into an elite discourse for the initiated. Scholarly work matters only to the degree it affects consciousness and practice at multiple sites. Counterpoints' editorial policy is based on these principles and the ability of scholars to break new ground, to open new conversations, to go where educators have never gone before.

For additional information about this series or for the submission of manuscripts, please contact:

Shirley R. Steinberg
c/o Peter Lang Publishing, Inc.
29 Broadway, 18th floor
New York, New York 10006

To order other books in this series, please contact our Customer Service Department:

(800) 770-LANG (within the U.S.)
(212) 647-7706 (outside the U.S.)
(212) 647-7707 FAX

Or browse online by series:
www.peterlang.com